CANADIAN STUDIES IN CRIMINOLOGY

EDITED BY J.LL.J. EDWARDS 1970-76
AND BY G.A.B. WATSON 1976-

# Burglary: The Victim and the Public

## Irvin Waller &
## Norman Okihiro

Published in association

with the Centre of Criminology, University of Toronto, by

UNIVERSITY OF TORONTO PRESS

Toronto   Buffalo   London

©University of Toronto Press 1978
Toronto Buffalo London
Printed in Canada

**Library of Congress Cataloging in Publication Data**

Waller, Irvin.
  Burglary.

  (Canadian studies in criminology ; 4)
  Bibliography: p.
  Includes index.
  1. Burglary — Ontario—Toronto. 2. Burglary
  protection. 3. Victims of crimes — Ontario—Toronto.
  I. Okihiro, Norman, 1948-       joint author.
  II. Title.  III. Series.
  HV6665.C2W34       364·1'62     78-5720
  ISBN 0-8020-5421-8

# Foreword

Criminological research in the decade of the seventies reflects several characteristics of contemporary society at large. One of these is the growing distrust of simple explanations and single-track approaches to general problems. Another is the need to re-define the basic concepts and categories through which we view human actions and institutions. And another is the urgent attempt to read in the data of the present the state of the future.

All these characteristics are, of course, part of the mood which arises now, as it has always done in our history, out of the combination of new knowledge, disillusionment, and anxiety. Just as the earlier conventions and assurances of our modern culture, with its values and institutions, have been discredited by the revelation of some harsh realities in human nature along with persistent evidence of failure and bad judgment in one collective enterprise after another, so the earlier conventions and assurances of our modern science have been discredited by new scientific discoveries and the bitter social consequences of old ones. And always there is the pressure of time, as though, whether in international relations, national politics, ecology, economics, energy, or criminal justice, the fuse is short and fast-burning.

Much in all this is undoubtedly the painful part of the process of maturing – the consequence of replacing fancy with realism, and learning to see things in more than one dimension and through more than one perspective. This would be, for example, to recognize and take seriously the fact that just as the motives of individuals are always mixed, so also each of our social institutions serves more than one end and has more than one function at any given time, and that the configuration of these goals and functions at any one time – particularly the real, as distinct from the stated priorities which order them – varies according to a wide range of circumstances having to do with, among other things, personalities, position, perception, and politics. We have become all too well aware that, although the stated principles of our society and its formal institutions constitute a more or less rational system (just and democratic), the reality is a sprawling mosaic of conflicting interests, which appears much of the time to be hopelessly beyond our grasp both to understand and to act upon.

In the face of this, the concerned citizen struggles with feelings of frustration and impotence, and, if also a scientist, returns to his first principles and looks again.

Crime and criminal justice, and the enterprise we call criminology, are, taken together, a case in point in every respect. From the view of crime as something isolable in the person of a 'criminal' or in the 'criminal personality' to the view of crime as a diffuse and pervasive quality of human relationships and institutions (or simply of society) is a swing from one extreme which appeared to be a dead end to another extreme which has its own problems; but that is the direction of the present movement of the pendulum. To find the concepts and categories by which we can describe and account for the distillation of that quality in particular forms that trigger particular reactions is the challenge for criminologial research; and in meeting this challenge it now knows that it must attend, not only to the person accused of a crime, but to the victim as well, and to the institutions and attitudes that both define and react to 'crime' and 'justice.' In this type of approach it is possible to imagine the disappearance altogether of anything like a prototype of a criminal act, except in so general a sense that for practical purposes it would convey little of value, and to see in its place only a complex of individuals and institutions involved in a continuous process of defining and precipitating these acts, as part of a ritual of self-fulfilment.

Some would put the point a different way. If there is an essence to crime and to justice it is being obscured by the very steps we take to deal with it and dispense it, respectively, methods which in becoming institutions and in moulding attitudes, acquire a life of their own, the preservation of which becomes their first priority. Such a view still reflects the prevailing mood. Fortunately, however, we do not seem to have been reduced to a state of impotence as sometimes appears to be the case elsewhere among our contemporary social problems. On the contrary, there is great and increasing energy being devoted to the subject — almost too much, in this sense that so much willingness to look again, to look inward and to be looked at can create its own confusion unless disciplined by caution, sound method, patience, and thoroughness.

Even as the research pendulum swings, a balance must be sought in the way of careful studies of typical, even if not prototypical, phenomena which instinct seems to tell us are in a fundamental way criminal — whatever extenuating circumstances may exist in given instances. From such studies light should be shed in both directions of the swing, giving us the means of regulating the broader process of enquiry.

In the pages that follow is the report of such a study. Burglary touches basic chords which vibrate deeply in a victim and a neighbourhood. In the experience of most people it is the point of translation of the violation of law into the violation of a person, something which neither the conventions of our system nor the sophistications of the most advanced criminological theory can obliterate.

Centre of Criminology                                      G.A.B. WATSON
University of Toronto

# Acknowledgements

This monograph is based on analysis undertaken as part of a systematic study of the experience of the public with residential burglary in Toronto, Canada. It was carried out at the Centre of Criminology, University of Toronto, in collaboration with the Survey Research Centre of York University. Financial support came primarily from a grant from the Canada Council. Important supplementary financial support for various phases of the study was provided indirectly by the University of Toronto and the Solicitor-General of Canada. The interviews with convicted burglars were facilitated and partly funded by the Ministry of Correctional Services of Ontario. The book has been published with the help of grants from the Social Science Federation of Canada, using funds provided by the Canada Council, and from the University of Toronto Press.

Chief Harold Adamson of the Metropolitan Toronto Police arranged access to police records on burglary events in 1971. Staff Sgt. Bill Ferguson of the Metropolitan Toronto Police, Break and Enter Squad, acted as liaison officer with us, providing insights into police operations related to burglary as well as facilitating the task of taking the necessary data from police records and reviewing questionnaires. Leah Lambert, formerly chief of research services for the Ontario Ministry of Correctional Services, was instrumental in arranging for us to visit and interview incarcerated burglars during the exploratory part of the project.

There are many colleagues in North America, the United Kingdom, and France, who have directly or indirectly provided stimuli to the development of the ideas in this project. The exchange of views on the design and conclusions of the project with Tony Turner, then of National Criminal Justice Statistics Information Service and now the US Bureau of Census in Washington, with Tom Reppetto, author of *Residential Crime*, with Harry Scarr, author of *Patterns of Burglary*, and with Dick Sparks, formerly at the Institute of Criminology in Cambridge, now at Rutgers University, should be mentioned particularly.

The moral encouragement and intellectual stimulation that has been provided by our colleagues in Canada has been particularly important to the successful completion of the project. Hans Mohr, previously with the National Law Reform Commission and now at Osgoode Hall, in his inimitable fashion, has pushed us to reinterpret some of our data, clarify our thoughts, and above all bring to completion a study that might aid the process of making criminal justice relevant to the needs of the public and of limiting unnecessary intrusion into our daily lives. He has read two drafts of this manuscript, providing detailed comments and enthusiasm when it was most needed. Keith Jobson, originally with the Law Reform Commission, and now at the University of Victoria in British Columbia, has commented on our analysis of public attitudes and encouraged us to take the difficult step of suggesting practical implications, particularly in the area of insurance coverage. Philip Stenning, Stephen Waddams, and many others at the Centre of Criminology have debated particular issues with us. In the final stages, Tony Doob has provided systematic comments on the manuscript, forcing us to clarify our ideas and verify our conclusions. Jim Giffen provided criticisms that made us appreciate the relative importance of burglary in Canadian society. Each has provided the stimulus and encouragement to bring the manuscript to its present stage.

During the course of the project, many have facilitated its completion. We owe a particular debt to Janet Chan who has patiently collaborated with us throughout the study, ensuring that data were systematically and reliably put in a form which made possible the analysis of trends and associations. Clifford Shearing took the responsibility of supervising this project during the absence of the senior author. Rita Donelan has guided the manuscript through to the final stages. The library staff at the Centre of Criminology has aided us with the bibliography. There are several persons who have acted as secretary to this project over its duration and have typed drafts of the text. Last, but not least, it is John Edwards, director of the Centre of Criminology during the course of this project, who had confidence under difficult circumstances that this study was worthwhile and would be completed. He created a work environment and gave us the flexibility needed to complete the project.

Finally, we must express our appreciation to the 1655 households in Metropolitan Toronto who collaborated with the interviewers and staff of the Survey Research Centre; they provided their time and their experiences to make this book possible.

The sacrifices made by all those directly and indirectly affected by this research project can be justified only by courageous action, discussion, and experimentation to orient criminal justice towards the real needs of its victims and to ensure that society reacts to crime in proportion to the real harm done.

# Contents

BURGLARY: THE VICTIM AND THE PUBLIC

# 1

# Introduction

What is crime? When does it occur? What is its impact? What are its causes? What does the victim do? Can we prevent and alleviate it? What is the fear of crime? Why do we want revenge? In this book, these questions are answered by looking systematically at the realities of the experience of residential burglary in Toronto, Canada. We shall examine the implications of the answers for policy-makers, policemen, urban planners, researchers, the security industry, insurers, and those who want to understand the public's experience of crime from a systematic but human and quantitative perspective.

Residential burglary is a crime for which the maximum penalties are high, in which the fear of confrontation is widespread, and about which concern is regularly expressed. It is the source of the fear of unpredictable violence in one's personal residence and generates some of the desire for more severe punishment of crime. It is a crime which was committed by many persons in prison, and yet it is often not reported to the police; its perpetrators are rarely caught, prosecuted, or incarcerated. Broadly, residential burglary is defined as breaking into a residence with felonious intent, including the crime of 'break and enter' familiar to police and lawyers. Each year in Canada more than $40 million dollars in property and cash is stolen by burglars, with an average loss of approximately $300.

The police are the main agency of society concerned with the prevention of burglary and the repression of burglars. They come when called by victims or witnesses, investigate offences, and try to recover stolen property. In some instances, they organize programs that are supposed to prevent the crime.

Insurance companies compensate victims for losses associated with burglary. Locksmiths and burglar alarm companies manufacture equipment for residences to slow down the entry of offenders. In addition, architects, city planners, private security agencies, and many others provide their services in a manner which may influence the number of burglaries.

The public pays each of these groups directly or indirectly to provide these services and modify its way of life. Yet, few of these groups have any systematic information available to them on how burglaries occur or could be prevented. Most use police records, often from the United States, collected for a different purpose, but which record less than two out of three burglaries that occur. In short, the public and its agents appear to be directed by misleading statistics, subjective experience, and exceptional cases that receive publicity.

In this book, we shall try to understand the subjective experiences of victims and their contribution to the offence. In a systematic manner, much of the analysis tries to describe the realities of the burglary experience with a view to improving the way society reacts. We shall question the myths of the typical burglary as a vicious stranger-to-stranger crime, where rape, murder, and robbery are the eventual aims of 'professional' or 'obsessed' burglars. We shall demonstrate the importance of reassurance to a frightened householder, of insurance for property stolen, and the deterrent effect of having people nearby. Indeed, we shall suggest that these are more important to a reasonable management of crime than the panaceas of the seventies of 'defensible space' and 'diversion' and that they must be considered more carefully if we want to reduce the waste of resources in the criminal justice system and respond to the harm done to the victim or the needs of the public.

Our analysis will be based principally on detailed interviews which took place during the spring of 1974 with 1655 members of households in Metropolitan Toronto, Canada.[1] Interviews were held also with convicted residential burglars to examine how they chose particular residential targets, why they broke in, and what types of goods they sought. A complementary analysis was undertaken of more than 5000 burglary occurrences from police records and census information in Metropolitan Toronto for 1971.

Much of the previous work undertaken on a systematic basis to better inform those concerned with crime prevention has not focused on a specific type of crime such as burglary. Moreover, the problem was analysed from the perspective of the offender. In the classical approach, crime was seen as an event which an offender committed wilfully and by rational choice, and so its prevention would be carried out through deterrence — increasing the potential cost of crime to the offender. In the positivist approach, crime was seen as the result of abnormal personality attributes and so its prevention would be carried out by the correction of the personality deformities of the offender. Recently, there has been a plethora of studies which indicate that neither of these approaches has been very successful in the reduction of crime. Specific deterrence of those offenders caught apparently has only a marginal effect in terms of influencing their future involvement in crime (Waller, 1974). Doubts still remain as to the exact effect of general deterrence on potential offenders in specific situations for specific behaviour (Zimring and Hawkins, 1973). On the other hand, the overriding conclusion from study after study of the ability of correctional measures to reduce the likelihood of reconviction for those who undergo them is that those measures are either totally ineffective or, with few rare exceptions, as effective as doing nothing after conviction (Hood and Sparks, 1970; Robison and Smith, 1971; Martinson, 1974; and Waller, 1974). Further, preventive police patrols may not reduce crime or public feelings of fear (Kelling, 1974).

From these trends, it seemed that directing research to questions of crime prevention by examining the full circumstances of a specific type of event would be more effective than further examination of the offender or the criminal justice system itself. In the same way that criminologists have tried to compare offenders with non-offenders to provide an understanding of why a person is an offender, we have tried to examine how the burglary victim and non-victim differ in an attempt to understand the extent to which a victim vicariously contributes or precipitates the offence.[2] Jeffery (1971), Newman (1972), and Fooner (1971b) have emphasized the vicarious contribution of the victim to property offences, through opportunities presented by the environment and carelessness of the victim. These are but a few of the authors who have examined the role of the victim in crime in general (Silverman, 1971).

Importantly, from these studies, there also seems to be room for substantial savings in the costs of the criminal justice system by improving our understanding of what the public wants. In the United States, fear of crime has markedly affected the lives of ordinary citizens (USA President's Commission, 1967a; Rosenthal, 1969; Gallup, 1969; Furstenberg, 1971, 1971). In extreme instances, urban dwellers are described as living in barricaded fortresses, popular journals show photographs of stripped-down televisions and stereos bolted to the floor, and others talk about neighbourhoods where individual citizens live in fear of talking to other citizens. Is such fear generated by a real understanding of crime? Does the desire for more severe punishment of criminals arise from this fear, from frustration with the system, or from more fundamental beliefs in retribution and vengeance? Commentators increasingly are seeing the criminal justice system as an expensive and archaic aggregate of sub-systems that has been failing to protect the public or reduce this fear. As a result, practitioners and politicians appear to be torn between the desire to save taxpayers money by eliminating the services that appear to be ineffective and the need to respond to the public pressures to do something about crime. One cry is for prevention – but how?

Other cries are to provide more justice and reduce the cost of the criminal justice system, but politicians are reluctant to do this too fast, because an organized and vocal minority wants more police and tougher sentences. But does the general public? The questioning of the ability of the system to reduce crime had refocused researchers' attention on other objectives. Does the system reduce public fear? Is punishment consistent, humane, and efficient? Are the escalating costs of criminal justice justified? In the name of crime reduction, has the criminal justice system been managing the poor, young, and alienated, often to the extent of selectively guarding the rights of the powerful, old, rich, and involved?

Finally, the concentration on the offender and fear of crime has obscured the needs of individual victims and their conflicts with offenders. Can effective insurance or state compensation alleviate some of the desire for vengeance? If the harm done to individual victims is reduced, does society still need to use or threaten imprisonment in order to denounce certain behaviour, such as burglary.

This study focuses on three general areas of enquiry: (1) what is residential burglary, where does it occur, and what effects does it have? (2) what causes it and can it be prevented? (3) what are the victim's reactions to the crime? In the next few pages, we shall outline these themes, look at Metropolitan Toronto, and then discuss the key aspects of our methodology.

In chapter 2, we define burglary, describe how it is distributed in Toronto, and make some broad comparisons with the USA.

Chapter 3 focuses on the offence itself, to see when and where it occurs how the offender entered the residence, what goods were stolen and how much they were worth, what damage was done, and how often and what sort of confrontation occurred between victim and offender. This chapter also describes offenders.

In chapter 4, we turn to the reaction of the victim to the offence – what he felt, what effect it had on his life, whether and why he reported it to the police, to whom else he turned and how satisfied he was with their response. We also examine the reasons for being insured and how commonly insurance is used as a way of mitigating the impact of burglary.

In chapter 5, we try to identify those aspects of the victim, his property, or his immediate environment that may have predisposed him to residential burglary. We examine the relative importance of factors such as affluence, proximity to offenders, the socio-physical characteristics of the residence. We see the minor, but endemic nature of residential burglary.

Chapter 6 describes the 'real' experience of residential burglary and examines the attitudes of the public to the 'abstract' problem of crime. We examine the victims' personal experience with the police and courts, as well as their own experience as burglars.

In chapter 7, we examine the abstract fear of crime (which appears to be the principal crime problem) and review the public's views of the goals of sentencing, police efficiency, and their retributive reaction to crime.

We have tried to answer these questions in a city that appears to be of little interest to criminologists — one often referred to as 'Toronto the good,' as opposed to the well-known crime-ridden cities of the American criminologists.

Metropolitan Toronto is a rapidly expanding city, covering fourteen hundred square miles, with over two million people. It is situated on the north shore of Lake Ontario in what is known as the 'Golden Horseshoe,' which is the chief industrial belt of Ontario, and of Canada, extending from St Catharines to Oshawa. Toronto has a centralized business district, surrounded by a suburban area with rural farm land north, but not directly to the east and west, of the city.

The metropolitan area is served by one police department which contained 18 police divisions in 1971. Each division was responsible for all crimes in its area. There was a small centralized police operation specializing in breaking-and-entering offences. Some of its functions included investigating the 'big jobs,' helping with liaison between divisions in respect to burglary, and checking out pawned goods for stolen items.

It is a point of pride to many Torontonians that their city is safe and relatively crime-free compared to many other large North American cities. Despite occasional media campaigns on police brutality, systematic surveys show relationships with the police to be good (Courtis, 1970; *Toronto Star*, 1 January 1973). Over 85 per cent of Torontonians worry little or not at all about their house or apartment being broken into and robbed. In the conclusion to his study, Courtis writes, 'it seems that the crime problem in Toronto was not regarded as an overwhelmingly serious one' (1970:14). Indeed, it is a common occurrence for visitors from the United States to comment on the safety of Toronto streets as compared to their own city's streets. These are feelings and perceptions rather than crime rates themselves, but these feelings are probably as crucial as the rates.

Toronto does not have a large central core area of deteriorated housing units, populated predominately by poverty-stricken minority groups, as do many high-crime cities in the United States. Metropolitan Toronto does have, however, over 200,000 persons of Italian ancestry, 100,000 of German descent, and areas that are largely Chinese, Greek, Jewish, Portuguese, and West Indian in its cosmopolitan make-up. The population of the city grew by 11 per cent from 1966 to 1971. It is surrounded by rapidly expanding areas and attracts persons both from abroad and Canada. Many of these people come to Toronto seeking better jobs and better lives. More than one-third of the residents were born outside Canada, and one in five do not hold Canadian citizenship (Canada, Census 1971). Thus, nearly half a million Torontonians did not hold Canadian citizenship in 1971 and half of their number had immigrated to Canada since 1966.

At one time, Toronto contained downtown a region which has been characterized as the largest Anglo-Saxon slum in North America. By 1971, however, much of this region (dubbed 'Cabbagetown' because many of the residents grew cabbage in their front yards during the Depression) had been razed in favour of public housing, and also infiltrated by a transient student and bohemian population. Recently many of the houses have been bought and renovated by members of the affluent middle class who are leaving the suburbs to live downtown.

To know what burglary involves, where it occurs, or what its effects are, we needed to collect systematic information in an objective way for a representative sample of burglaries. We have used both a systematic sample of police records and a random sample of households, drawn so as to enable us to make reliable and valid conclusions about Metropolitan Toronto.

We have used police information for the location of victims who report to the police, the time these offences occurred, as well as the details of means of entry or approximate value of property stolen or damaged. We will also use these data to estimate how often an event recorded by the police is cleared by charge.

Our police data consisted of a random sample of 5428 records of burglary events (occurrence reports) which took place in 1971 in the Metropolitan Toronto police district. Burglary was defined as robbery, break and enter, theft under and over $50,[3] or malicious damage that occurred in a dwelling house. These data were combined with 1971 census data from Statistics Canada.

Police records do not include, on a systematic basis, information we will show to be crucial to determining whether burglary was likely to occur. To overcome this problem and the potential distortion in reporting the facts of the offence to the police, other researchers have used a technique called 'reverse record checks.'[4] Using police records to obtain the names and addresses of persons who had reported burglary victimization, an independent interviewer goes back to the household. A major advantage in the reverse record check procedure over the victim survey is the reduction in the expense of locating victims of crime. This would have been particularly important for our project in those areas where the burglary rates were extremely low. Using this method, additional information could have been obtained on the victim and the victim's household. The major disadvantage of the procedure is that the sizeable group of victims not known to the police – the 'dark figure' – would not be contacted.

Even though reverse record checks have been carried out as standard practice in the United States and in a major survey in the United Kingdom

(Sparks, 1977) the police in Metropolitan Toronto decided that a victim called the police in confidence and that a further interview might raise feelings of harrassment. They were concerned that their relations with the public would deteriorate if it became widely known that researchers were using that information to go back to the persons who were victims. Fortunately for our purposes, there were more useful alternatives. However, for other offences, the advantages of the reverse record check method in understanding the impact and etiology of crime will have to be explained more fully to law enforcement agencies if progress is to be made in prevention and reduction of crime.

As more than one out of three events fulfilling the legal definition of a burglary are not reported to the police, we needed to obtain the information from a sample of victims that included these events. In addition, we needed information on the effects of burglary, the fear and retributive reaction to crime, and factors associated with these that could only be answered by contacting the public in general.

The history of large-scale surveys of the public on these issues dates back only to the work of the US President's Crime Commissions in 1966 and 1967. Being a victim of a serious crime is a relatively rare event in the USA and therefore a general survey which will yield sufficient victims for any useful analysis has to be very large and expensive. These US surveys handled this problem partly by paying the large bills and partly by dealing with crime in general.[5] Neither option was available to us. Instead we used a systematic technique designed to increase the likelihood of finding enough victims of residential burglary to do a meaningful analysis. We also developed a multiphase questionnaire, which via a screening question made it possible for six out of seven of our interviews with non-victims to be abandoned after only a few minutes.

The unit of analysis chosen by us was the household, which was represented by an adult member over 18 chosen at random from a list.[6] Households were selected for interview on the basis of a systematic 'disproportionate stratified sampling' technique.[7] Briefly, small areas of Metropolitan Toronto (enumeration areas) were grouped into strata which were relatively homogeneous with respect to police-recorded burglary rates; pro-rata more households were interviewed in the enumeration areas with higher burglary rates. However, within each stratum, a random sample of households was drawn. Using this technique, a reliable estimate of the real burglary rate, for instance for Toronto, can be computed using a system of weights.[8]

An interviewer approached 2483 households and was successful in completing a screening interview with 1665 or 67 per cent of the cases.[9] Six per cent of the 2483 were not completed due to language problems between interviewer and interviewee.[10] The absence of the respondent accounted for a loss of 15 per cent. Eleven per cent of the persons screened refused to participate in the survey.[11] The refusal rate was generally lower in strata where the police-recorded burglary rates were highest. Of those who were eligible for an intensive interview after the screening, 3 per cent were lost in the general process of attrition, which includes those who refused to answer the full questionnaire, language problems, further absence, and so on. This left 65 per cent of the original 2483, which is a rate that is normal for this type of research.[12]

In analysing and extrapolating our data to the whole of Metropolitan Toronto (or to any large modern city) two points must be kept in mind. Our sample heavily oversampled the high police-recorded burglary rate areas, and therefore we had to weight our cases appropriately. Secondly, our techniques for extrapolating to Metropolitan Toronto incorporated only those households for which interviews were completed.

In order to investigate the size and direction of the bias introduced by weighting and non-response, we compared the characteristics of the sample with the same characteristics of the population using census information.[13] In terms of household and structural variables, the sample closely resembled the population: approximately four out of five interviewed had a male head (using the census definition); two out of five of the households lived in single detached dwellings, compared to one in seven in attached and slightly more than two out of five in apartment-type structures. Four out of five households consisted of a single family. Our weighted sample of respondents was 52 per cent female, slightly more than in the general population. Of the sample, one in four were aged between 25 and 35 and another one in four were between 35 and 45. Forty-four per cent were over 45. We undersampled respondents in the 18 to 24 age range, especially men, by about 7 per cent, probably because they are frequently away from home. Fortunately this factor was not found to be related to the burglary rate.[14] The median educational level of the sample was a completed secondary school education. However, less than 1 per cent had had no formal education and 7 per cent had some form of post-graduate university education. The median household income was in the range of $11,000 to $15,000, with the average income close to $13,500. Six per cent of the households had incomes of less than $3000, while 3 per cent exceeded $40,000.

The final interview schedule is included as Appendix A. It was designed to accomplish three main tasks. The first was to allow us to screen out residential burglary victims from non-victims in a short interview time. By applying the detailed and time-consuming sections of the questionnaire only to victims and a systematic proportion of non-victims, a great saving in field work costs was achieved. Secondly, the questionnaire was designed to pinpoint details of residential burglary experiences accurately enough to enable us to establish a burglary profile for Toronto. Thirdly, it was designed to enable us to examine public attitudes generally, as well as to compare, for a sample of victims and non-victims, characteristics we felt were salient either to residential victimization, or to burglary-related attitudes to the criminal justice system.

Before drawing the sample of households to be interviewed, an analysis was undertaken of the data obtained from police records and from interviews with a small sample of convicted residential burglars. This, together with several unstructured interviews with known victims, and discussions with police experts and researchers, formed the major development process for the questionnaire schedule.[15] In some cases we also adapted items which have been used successfully in other victim surveys (for example, the question on reasons for not reporting to the police are generally taken from Ennis' pioneering victimization survey in 1967).

We specifically encouraged comments from the police on items we had overlooked, on mundane matters we had misunderstood, and generally to ensure that, where appropriate, our specific questions were also relevant to their concerns.

The screening part of the document consists of the background household and respondent data, a few general questions, and the items pertaining to burglary. In developing these latter items, careful attention was paid to both the phrasing and the administration of the questions. Each of the questions is specific. Each question was asked in sequence to elicit all incidents which may have befallen the victim before any relevant details about any incident were asked. The questions were also worded so that the people (victims) were not thinking in terms of legal categories such as unlawfully in a dwelling place or 'break and enter.' Instead they were phrased in common, everyday language with which respondents would be familiar and used to describe the ways in which they remember such events. The questions were designed to elicit a 'yes' or 'no' response not only for simple cases of breaking in, but also for any attempts to break in, including cases where, say, a door was jimmied or a window broken.

In this type of interview, burglary is one of the best reported traditional crimes in the USA. In the San José Methods Study (1972) over 90 per cent of the police-recorded incidents of burglary in a one-year period were related to an interviewer. It was further found that asking questions did not affect the rate of reporting to a survey covering a 12-month period rather than a shorter span, although it did affect accuracy of recall of the specific date. Because burglary is remembered so well, we decided to extend the recall period to about 16 months, from 1 January 1973 to the time of interview, but tried to have the respondent identify special events such as snow storms or major news stories to determine the date as accurately as possible.

Once the screening section had identified the victims who were eligible, answers were recorded to a section of detailed questions pertaining to the incident itself and to the later parts of the questionnaire which were also applicable to non-victims. If the respondent was not an eligible victim, a further sampling procedure was used. In areas defined as having medium or high burglary rates, 195 households, forming a random sample of 1 in 7 non-victims, were questioned regarding aspects salient to the probability of being victimized.[16] In areas defined as having low burglary rates, 1 in 14 non-victims was interviewed. This procedure obtained for us 116 victims and 309 non-victims who had been intensively interviewed for comparison purposes. The non-victims who were not intensively interviewed were asked a few questions and the interview was terminated. This intensive sample of 425 households was asked the questions concerning fear of crime, retributive reaction, and experience of criminal justice, as well as about their involvement with burglary as offenders.

NOTES TO CHAPTER 1

1   These households were represented by an adult chosen at random from each dwelling. The households were drawn in a disproportionately stratified design, which concentrated the bulk of interviews in those census tracts where the police-recorded burglary rate in 1971 was above the median for Metropolitan Toronto. However, 'weighting techniques' were used to allow the data to be representative of the metropolitan area as a whole.

2   The term 'non-victim' is used here to indicate someone who was not burglarized during the period of the study. Scarr (1973:23) suggests there is no such thing as a non-victim. Rather, there is at best simply someone who has not yet been victimized.

3   Since 15 July 1972 revisions to the Criminal Code have changed the offence to theft under and over $200.

4   Reverse record checks have been used in Washington, Baltimore, and later in San Jose by the US government (San José Methods Test, 1972). They have been used to control or avoid the two major methodological deficiencies of 'recall' and 'telescoping' identified in the victim surveys by authors such as Biderman (1967b), Ennis (1967) and Reiss (1967b). Telescoping occurs when a respondent inadvertently moves up or back the date of victimization so that it improperly falls into the period of study. The conclusions from those tests show major differences in recall and telescoping for different offences. For burglary there is extremely high recall to a census bureau interviewer and even over 12 months later a fair amount of accuracy in placing the event in or near the month recorded by the police (for other offences this was not necessarily so).

5   Recently, some studies have been designed to collect data on a number of related offences to which groups of victims are prone. For example, Aromaa (1973, 1974) deals with all crimes of violence against individuals, and *Crimes Against Small Businesses* (USA Congress, 1969) deals with business losses through burglary, robbery, vandalism, and shoplifting, though Reppetto (1974) looked at residential burglary itself.

   Other victimization surveys on public attitudes rode 'piggy-back' on enquiries with other goals. This enabled large samples and therefore more victims to be approached with lower over-all costs. Two examples of this are the *Census Bureau Surveys* (Argana, 1973:4) and the *Black Buyer Surveys* (Crosby and Snyder, 1970). Once again, there is little or no opportunity for intensive examination of any issue.

6   Police records typically would have been obtained from the householder or the member of the household most affected by the event. It was suggested to us by Biderman in a personal communication that in terms of the impact of a burglary on the household the best respondent would be the homemaker — that is, the person who spent the longest number of hours in the home or in other ways had 'egotized'

the home more than others. This person would usually be the housewife. Unfortunately in other parts of the questionnaire not concerned directly with the impact of the burglary this would have led to biases in responses due to a disproportionate number of female respondents, particularly in the age groups 20 through 40. The National Crime Panel surveys suggest that this age group is more likely to be victimized than the older age group, particularly males in assaults and offences generally involving personal violence or personal violence and theft. Thus we would have over-represented those with a special experience of the criminal justice system. Also, we particularly wanted to ensure that the sample would not be biased by sex or age on the large number of questions concerned with attitudes and knowledge of the criminal justice system itself.

It has been the practice of the US National Criminal Justice Information and Statistics Service to use a household respondent over age 14 as the informant, usually a parent. Indeed, Argana (1973: 14) and others describe plans by the NCJISS to use a random adult over age 12 in a study that was planned for early 1974 in San Francisco. However, we felt that the unproven reliability of responses in using such young respondents, combined with ethical problems regarding parental consent for minors and the longer period of recall we used, were sufficient reason for restricting ourselves to adults aged 18 and over. The Advance Report of the National Crime Panel, entitled *Crime in the Nations Five Largest Cities*, April 1974, in fact has used 12- and 13-year-old household reporters.

7    A detailed technical report on the sample design of the household survey, prepared by the Survey Research Centre of York University, may be consulted at the Centre of Criminology, University of Toronto. This contains a map of Metropolitan Toronto showing census tracts in which interviews were carried out and the 1971 police recorded burglary rate. Data tapes are also available at the Survey Research Centre, York University.

8    While a disproportionate stratified sampling is a relatively efficient way of obtaining victims, it has the disadvantage of tending to increase the error or variance when an attempt is made to generalize to the total population. This was exacerbated by the sampling ratios (or the number of persons whom each respondent in a stratum is designated to represent) which varied considerably. Wherever this problem is seen as affecting our results in this study the reader's attention is drawn to it.

9    Because the stratification procedure resulted in a heavy concentration of interviewing in downtown areas which in some cases were being demolished for new buildings, there was a reduction in the number of eligible addresses. We started with 2618 addresses, however only 2483 were located. This was unfortunate since in many cases houses that were demolished were generally more vulnerable physically to burglary than newer houses, particularly with respect to locks, flimsy doors, etc. They may also have been areas with low social cohesion, another important factor thought to be related to burglary.

10    There were interviewers fluent in all of the major languages spoken in the Toronto area and attempts were made to follow-up original attrition due to language by re-interviewing using an interviewer fluent in the appropriate language.

11    In those instances where the respondent was present in the residence, but refused to be interviewed, details of sex, language ability, and other socio-economic data were estimated. There was no tendency for language ability to be related to refusal. However, there was a slight tendency for more females and older persons to refuse. As our technique for selecting respondents should have provided an equal sample of males and females and of different age groups, it can be inferred that males and younger persons are frequently absent. The reasons given for refusal in over half the cases were 'too busy' or not interested.

12    Compared to the National Crime Panel which reports completion rates of over 90 per cent, our completion rate of 65 per cent is very low. In fairness, though, the National Crime Panel involves a series of interviews with the same household every six months and might expect a higher degree of cooperation as the respondents recognize and accept the *bona fide* nature of that panel study. Discussions with the

staff at the Survey Research Centre of York University suggested that, while 75 per cent is a realistic completion rate goal for a one-time survey with up to four call-backs budgeted for, the lower figure of 65 per cent is at least partially explained by the high number of apartment dwellers in the sample. Furthermore, it was felt that the completion rates in Toronto were dropping off, probably as a result of the growing skepticism of respondents concerning the identity of persons calling themselves 'researchers.' In many cases, these persons turn out to be door-to-door salesmen.

Other victim surveys in the United States had similar completion rates. In Ennis' study, 73 per cent of the Eligible screening interviews were completed (1967: Field Surveys II, iii), while Hawkins (1973: 442) in Seattle, Washington, reports refusal rates of 25 per cent in his study not including inaccessible respondents, which would have brought his completion rate down below 70 per cent. Using a different technique, Kauko Aromaa (1973, 1974) in Finland estimated a completion rate of 75 per cent. In London, England, Sparks (pre-publication draft) showed an over-all response rate of 40.9 per cent, but the author suggests that this rate was not abnormal in view of the short period of fieldwork and the nature of the area in which the survey was carried out. In addition, Sparks's study involved the use of names rather than addresses of households in screening his sample, a technique which he believed caused the exclusion of about 12 per cent more than if addresses had been used regardless of the occupant's name (as Sparks's study included a reverse record check input, this procedure was necessary).

13  A detailed comparison of the sample and the eligible population is available through the Centre of Criminology, University of Toronto.

14  The one burglary-related variable in which markedly different results seemed to be obtained was the percentage of households with lodgers. In our sample, only 1 per cent of the households were recorded as having lodgers, while the population statistic was 9 per cent. However, as the only way we could determine this was by checking over the list of household members and their relation to the head of the household, it is likely that lodgers were either omitted from the list completely, or labelled otherwise. Hence, we do not feel that much importance should be attached to this particular sample-population difference.

15  Two formal pretests of the questionnaire were administered where about 35 victims (not all of whom were victimized recently) and 80 non-victims were interviewed.

16  The sample design involved five strata – extra high, high, medium, low, and special low – with recorded police victim mean per 1000 households of 72, 48, 27, 15 and 14 respectively. There were 535, 515, 530, 69, and 61 completed interviews in each of these strata respectively.

# 2

# Burglary Rates in Toronto and Other Areas

Every year, headlines appear in the national press stating that 'crime' has increased. Such statements are usually based on the number of crimes recorded by the police, and the figures may be very misleading if they are taken to mean that more criminal harm is occurring or that an individual citizen is more likely to be the victim of harm. Criminologists, realizing this, have made attempts to develop other measures which would reflect the varying degrees of seriousness of individual crimes. Studies using police records to determine the amount of harm resulting from a crime have been undertaken in the United States by Sellin and Wolfgang (1964) and in Canada by Akman and Normandeau (1966). Studies by McClintock et al. (1968) have examined other ways to measure crime in England and Wales. For particular types of crime, researchers have emphasized the need to relate the number of crimes to the amount of opportunity: thus, the number of cars stolen must be related to the number of cars on the road. For residential crime, the number of burglaries must be related to the number of residences.

In this chapter, our data are used to examine the rate at which residences in Metropolitan Toronto are the victims of burglary. First, we shall compare the distribution of police-recorded burglary in Toronto with other police jurisdictions or geographical areas, using the standard, though inappropriate, Uniform Crime Rate (UCR) measure of burglary per 100,000 persons. Then we shall look at the figures for Toronto, based on our household survey, and compare these with data from other surveys using residences as the denominator.

Comparing crime rates between jurisdictions raises many definitional problems. Throughout this study, as in common legal usage, we shall use Webster's definition of burglary, as the act of breaking into a building at any time, especially with intent to steal (Webster's, 1976).

There is no legal category of burglary in Canada. The section of the Criminal Code that comes closest to our use of the term is commonly referred to as breaking and entering, which includes the intent to or the committal of an indictable offence, such as theft (Criminal Code, 1974: S 306-8). In relation to a dwelling house, a convicted offender is liable to a maximum penalty of imprisonment for life. If a person is simply found in a place without lawful excuse (the proof of which lies upon him), the only possible charge is being unlawfully in a dwelling house, which carries a maximum penalty of ten years. In practice, there is some confusion between the two crimes. To distinguish the two, it has been suggested that if an offender just walks in a door without opening it, he is unlawfully in a dwelling, whereas if he pushes the door ajar a little more, he has broken in.[1]

### The Distribution of Police-recorded Burglary

In order to examine the distribution of burglary-like incidents which were reported to the police in Toronto, we took 5428 occurrence reports drawn at random from all the occurrences recorded for 1971 which were classed as either break and enter, theft, robbery, or wilful damage to a *residence* (or an attempt at such). Each occurrence was linked to the census tract in which the residence was located. Using 342 of Metropolitan Toronto's 351 census tracts (which account for 99 per cent of the official 1971 population) as units of analysis, we found that the distribution throughout Toronto of those cases labelled 'break and enter' was similar to our omnibus label of 'burglary.'

When we compared apartment burglaries per 1000 apartments and house burglaries per 1000 houses, the correlation was only .05, indicating that the distribution of apartment burglaries was different from the distribution of house burglaries within Metropolitan Toronto. However, burglaries occurring in the evening showed the same pattern of distribution in Metropolitan Toronto as did those after midnight ($r = .59$); and those during the day ($r = .33$); those netting less than \$1000 of property stolen tended to be in the same area as those netting over \$1000 ($r = .65$); burglaries perpetrated on weekdays tended to be in similar places to those at weekends ($r = .66$).

Appendix B contains a map of Toronto showing the location of census tracts, shaded according to three levels of residential 'burglary' rates: low, medium, and high. With the exception of a few suburban pockets, the pattern seems to fit the gradient hypothesis that crime rates get lower as one goes away from the centre of the city. The area bounded by the Don River to the east, the CPR tracks to the north, Bathurst Street to the west, and Lake

Ontario on the southern extreme, seems to delineate the central city high-burglary area. This region embraces the Cabbagetown area mentioned earlier. The Scarborough area seemed to be the suburban region with generally the lowest rates of residential burglary. Affluent pockets of suburban North York and Etobicoke had higher rates and so were anomalous to the pattern of high residential burglary restricted to the city centre. One of these exceptions is known in Toronto as the Post Road or Bridle Path district, and it is one of the wealthiest areas of the city. It contains mostly large, landscaped lots, with some of the city's most elegant houses. Certainly, as a high burglary area, this census tract does not fit in with the urban core area of crowded, deteriorated housing that is often associated with a higher likelihood of crime. However, besides attracting crime through affluence, these houses are single-family, detached dwellings designed to give maximum privacy to their occupants, characteristics that we will suggest make them highly vulnerable to burglary.

Most census tracts have a low rate of residential burglary. More than half the census tracts have an estimated rate of police-recorded burglary of less than 24 per 1000 dwellings. It appears that a relatively few census tracts account for a disproportionately large number of residential burglaries. In fact, the 34 census tracts which formed the 'high' (the top 10 per cent) burglary rate areas accounted for 18 per cent of the 5428 burglaries in our sample, but only 6 per cent of the population of Metropolitan Toronto. This pattern was even more pronounced when we consider only break and enter cases.

American police statistics suggest a dramatic increase in residential burglary rates (per 100,000) in recent years. From 1960 to 1970, night-time burglary of dwellings increased 120 per cent and daytime burglary 337 per cent. The over-all increase for both residential and non-residential burglary (per 100,000) persons was 113 per cent (USA FBI, 1971: 19, 20).

From 1962 to 1970, the absolute number of incidents of breaking and entering in Toronto (residential and non-residential) more than doubled to over 14,000 following the American pattern. However, their total number *decreased* by 11 per cent from 1972 to 1973 and 4 per cent from 1971 to 1972, while there was a marginal increase of 1 per cent recorded from 1970 to 1971 (Metropolitan Toronto Police Department, 1973: 72, 71).

Using the American official national statistics (USA FBI, 1971), the work of Scarr in the contiguous area of Washington, DC, and surrounding counties (Scarr, 1973), as well as the work of Chimbos on a northern city in Ontario, (Chimbos, 1973), we compared the rates of police-recorded burglary (and breaking and entering) per 100,000 population for various places in Canada and the United States. This is the standard UCR form for presenting crime rates.

The burglary figure for Toronto was 840 per 100,000 population. However, this figure includes cases of theft, robbery, and wilful damage in residences, while the burglary figure for the United States did not include cases involving confrontation that are classed as robbery. The UCR burglary rates for the west, northeast, south, and north central regions in the USA were 894, 618, 557, and 570 respectively. In downtown Washington, the affluent suburb of Fairfax county, and the semi-urban region of Prince George County, the rates were 406, 463, and 707 respectively. Using the Canadian legal category of break and enter, the rate for a small northern city in Ontario was 237, whereas for Toronto the rate was 386.

In general, given the disparity of sources and reporting differences of these varied police departments, it appears that Toronto has police-recorded residential burglary rates similar to other large urban sections of the United States. However, since burglary rates are known to diminish as one goes outward from central city cores to rural areas,[2] Toronto appears to have a marginally lower rate than expected. In comparison to Washington, DC, Toronto appears to have a much lower rate of residential burglary. However, the Washington area is not strictly comparable to Metropolitan Toronto, since it includes the downtown area only and would thus be expected to have higher burglary rates.

## Victimization Survey Statistics on Burglary Rates

The previous discussion was based on police statistics, which are filtered in a variety of ways, as they are shunted from the dispatcher's desk through to the central registries of Statistics Canada. For this, and for many other reasons (some of which are mentioned in the previous chapter) the United States government has invested millions of dollars in contacting the public directly to get their view on whether a crime occurred. These surveys can be systematic and use sophisticated sampling techniques similar to our own for Toronto. Although it is not the main interest of our survey or of the United States' surveys, it is possible to provide estimates of the incidence of residential burglary that can then be compared to the police statistics. In the questionnaire we used with households, we identified all recent incidents of breaking and entering or illegal entry or any attempt to enter the actual living quarters of the householders.[3] This definition was chosen as similar to the one used by the FBI of 'an unlawful entry of a structure to commit a felony or theft, even though no force was used to gain entrance' (USA FBI, 1970: 18), so that comparisons could be made with jurisdictions in the United States.

The typical reasons given by respondents in the United States for not reporting a crime to the police, but reporting it to the research interviewer were that nothing could be done, usually because of lack of proof, and that the event was not important enough. There are thus good reasons to suppose that reported crime will be different from crime not reported (or at least not recorded) by police. We will examine these differences later.

In a 12-month period, it is expected that an estimated 26.4 dwellings per 1000 or approximately 3 dwellings in 100 will be burglarized in Toronto.[4] Of these events, it may be expected that 62 per cent will be reported to the police. This rate excludes cases which did not occur in Metropolitan Toronto, although the respondent was a resident of Toronto when interviewed. Thus, if the resident of the dwelling victimized was abroad or at an out-of-town cottage the case was excluded from consideration in Metro's burglary rate.[5]

In Table 2.1, our estimates of burglary rates are compared with those from studies in the United States using similar methods and criteria.[6] Precise comparisons should be viewed cautiously as the US cities' estimates were confined to the central city, whereas our estimates also covered suburban areas in Toronto. However, incidents involving confrontation between victim and offender were included as burglary in our study, but not for the US cities surveys. Even so, Metropolitan Toronto's burglary rate is only 40 per cent of that of the lowest of the American cities – New York – and 15 per cent of that of Detroit. In fact, the burglary rates in Metropolitan Toronto are only marginally higher than the rates found in *non-metropolitan* areas of the United States and substantially below that of the United States as a whole.

The reasons for Toronto's apparently lower burglary rates are not clear, nor entirely within the scope of this study. Indeed, regional disparities in the distribution of crime have been long noted (see Harries, 1973). Nevertheless, several plausible conjectures can be made. Scarr has suggested that for Washington, DC, a higher rate of burglary is associated with the presence of a higher proportion of the relatively more disadvantaged portion of the population (Scarr, 1973a: 40). Toronto is fortunate in this respect, in that the central core of the city has no really distinguishable ghetto-like area, although there are enclaves of lower socio-economic ethnic groups such as the Italians, Portuguese, Chinese, and Jews. The Cabbagetown area referred to before has been characterized as North America's largest Anglo-Saxon slum (see Garner, 1968), although, as suggested before, its nature as a lower class area is rapidly changing.

It is possible that the different culture that has accompanied the growth of Canadian society relative to that of the United States may be a contributing factor in the lower Toronto burglary rates. Pierre Berton (1972: xi-xx) has described the relatively orderly development and ethos which pervaded the settlement of Canada's west compared to the frontier justice that characterized the settlement of America. We tentatively suggest that a residue of this respect for law and order – perhaps a respect for order imposed from the outside – may still remain in Canadian society, possibly to the extent that the transmission of values relatively unfavourable to the development of criminals operates here. This notion might be a subject for further research.

TABLE 2.1

Burglary rates in Toronto and selected central city areas in the USA from household surveys

| Source | Location | Rate per 1000 dwellings |
|---|---|---|
| Waller and Okihiro, 1974 | Metropolitan Toronto | 26.4 |
| (a)  National Crime Panel (central cities) | Chicago | 118 ⎫ |
|  | Detroit | 174 ⎪ |
|  | Los Angeles | 148 ⎬ 125 |
|  | New York | 68 ⎪ |
|  | Philadelphia | 109 ⎭ |
| (b)  High impact Anti-crime Program (central cities) | Atlanta | 161 ⎫ |
|  | Baltimore | 116 ⎪ |
|  | Cleveland | 124 ⎪ |
|  | Dallas | 147 ⎬ 138 |
|  | Denver | 158 ⎪ |
|  | Newark | 123 ⎪ |
|  | Portland | 151 ⎭ |
|  | St Louis | 125 |

## Rates of Reporting to the Police

The decision to initiate formal sanctioning procedures – in this case to call the police – has become a major issue in criminology, both because of its effect on officially recorded crime rates and because it reflects to some extent people's attitudes to criminal justice, particularly their role in directing the offender away from the system. The discretion exercised by the citizen is only one way of perceiving the issue. Probably, like the court room or parole situation, it would be more appropriate to use a phenomenological approach in examining decisions arising out of police-citizen encounters. In chapter 3 we examine more closely the situation and reasons for calling the police. In the following paragraphs, we confine ourselves simply to rates of reporting to the police as established through household surveys.

The surveys done by Biderman and Reiss (1967) for the President's Commission on Law Enforcement and Administration of Justice were among the first to explore the nature and extent of unreported crime. However, the authors themselves have already suggested that any set of crime statistics, including those of survey research, involve some evaluative, institutional processing of people's reports. Thus, when one phones the police one sets into motion a process which may result in the production of an 'official' crime statistic. Nevertheless, the operating assumption of most victimization survey research is that provided one's methodology is sound, every possible event for which one might call the police is recorded. Thus, for example,

TABLE 2.2

Rates of reporting residential burglary or related crimes to the police

| Author of report | Year of publication | Year of survey | General location of study | Type of crime involved | No. of victims in sample | Police reporting rate (%) |
|---|---|---|---|---|---|---|
| Waller and Okihiro | 76 | 73-4 | Toronto, Ontario | Residential burglary | 116 | 62 |
| Ennis | 67 | 66 | Continental USA | Burglary | 313 | 41.6 |
| Reynolds et al. | 73 | 71 | Central City Area, Twin Cities | Burglary | 95 | 41.6 |
| | 73 | 72 | Suburb of Twin Cities, Minnesota | Burglary | 16 | 56 |
| Hawkins | 73 | 68 | Seattle | Burglary | not known | 58 |
| National Crime Panel | 74 | 73 | Chicago, Detroit, Los Angeles, New York, Philadelphia | Household burglary | not known | 53<br>57<br>53<br>52<br>55 |
| High impact Anti-crime cities | 74 | 73 | Atlanta, Baltimore, Cleveland, Dallas, Denver, Newark, Portland, St Louis | Household burglary | not known | 55<br>57<br>53<br>50<br>57<br>51<br>50<br>56 |
| Beran and Allen | 73 | 70, 71 | 'Lincoln' (small midwest town in USA) | Household crime | not stated | 47 |
| Sparks | 77 | 72, 73 | Brixton, Hackney, Kensington (London, England) | Burglary and theft from dwelling | based on estimates | 48<br>55<br>60 |

Hawkins talks about 'actual' and official rates of criminal behaviour (1973: 428).

Since 1965, there have been many studies which have compared the crime rate from information obtained directly from victims with the amount of crime recorded by the police. The first large-scale surveys were those by Biderman (1967a) and Ennis (1967) for the president's crime commissions. In Table 2.2, we show for residential burglary, or closely related crimes, that the rate of reporting to the police in Toronto is marginally higher than in other studies. This finding is consistent with the image of Toronto 'the good' with a commitment to upholding morality and closer relationships between the public and the police. However, these figures for Metropolitan Toronto do reveal that less than two-thirds of all residential burglary is reported to the police.

The reporting rate is sometimes used to infer the quality of the relationship between police and public. However, the rate is affected by other considerations, such as how the crime is defined and the seriousness of the offence. The following chapters will examine some of these considerations.

NOTES TO CHAPTER 2

1   Phillip Stenning, in a personal communication, has noted that in the new English *Theft Act*, this problem has been overcome by requiring 'entry' not 'breaking.'
2   For a summary of studies of urban-rural differences in crime patterns, see Wilks (1967: 141).
3   For the specific questions asked, see Appendix A, questions 9a-15.
4   Utilizing our weighted estimates for Metropolitan Toronto, 22,100 or 3 per cent of the households in Metropolitan Toronto were victims of at least one residential burglary since 1 January 1973. Of these, 13,700 (62 per cent) reported to the police. Since the study covered the period from 1 January 1973 to the date of interview, this figure was pro-rated to obtain an estimate for 12 months. Full details of the calculations used to arrive at confidence intervals for this estimate of the burglary rate are available at the Centre of Criminology, University of Toronto.
5   One hundred and two (or 88 per cent) of the raw or actual total of households victimized since 1 January 1971 fell into the 'within Metro' category. In estimating the burglary rate, we made the assumption that the burglary was committed at the address of the interview, though this was not always so. In nine cases, a person had moved within Metropolitan Toronto and was victimized at his last address. We expect that the effect of this is relatively low, as the moves probably tend to cancel one another out in arriving at the final burglary rate. In addition, we probably underestimated the number of burglary incidents, since we did not reach persons who might have been victimized in Toronto and had since moved away.
6   Table 2.1 represents only those studies which seem to have similar criteria for defining a burglary as our own. However, other victim survey studies (e.g. Reynolds et al. (1973) and Sparks (pre-ublication draft) have been done which tend to show very different rates for burglary largely due to different victimization-probe methodologies. Perhaps what is needed is a standardized screening technique if one wishes meaningfully to compare area crime rates.

# 3

# A Profile of Residential Burglary in Toronto

In the earlier chapters, burglary was defined but the varieties of burglary were not described. Discussion had not moved to what goods are taken or at what time it occurs. Is burglary more frequent in summer, during the day, in apartments? How common is confrontation? In this chapter, answers to some of these questions will be provided.

Scarr has already suggested, for the Washington, DC area, that burglary (including residential burglary) is profitable, requires relatively little skill, and has a low clearance rate. If caught, consequences to the offender are relatively light (Scarr, 1973: 73).

The characteristics of persons arrested by police in the USA for burglary are homogeneous on a number of dimensions and match those of the 'average' criminal. Federal Bureau of Investigation statistics show that persons arrested for burglary are almost all males under 25. Juveniles referred to juvenile court jurisdiction accounted for over half of all persons processed for burglary in 1970 (USA FBI, 1970: 21). Our own interviews with incarcerated burglars in Canada indicated that burglars who broke into houses were even younger than those who entered non-residential buildings and were possibly on the first rung of a potential criminal career.

In this chapter, our focus is on the offence of burglary. The analysis is based on all of the 116 burglary cases[1] reported to us, occurring between 1 January 1973 and 31 March 1974.[2] This includes 19 (16 per cent) cases of attempted burglary and 11 (10 per cent) cases which appeared to fit into the category of unlawfully in a dwelling. Wherever possible, we have compared our household survey results with information gleaned from police records, both from other studies and from our own analysis of Metropolitan Toronto police records.[3]

**Temporal Patterns**

Several studies in Canada and the United States using police-recorded data suggest that residential burglary rates in different areas are higher at certain times of the day, on certain days of the week, or during certain times of the year. However, there does not seem to be any real consensus on what those times are. Part of the reason for this may lie in differences in definitions used by particular police forces and researchers. For example, in Toronto, the police record only the earliest possible hour of the day of the week that the burglary could have occurred. Conklin and Bittner, criminologists (1973: 213), used the midpoint of the police-recorded time interval in which a burglary could have taken place as a reasonable guess of the time of occurrence.

In addition to these definitional problems, the victim himself is rarely sure of the exact time of occurrence, since most residential burglary is committed without the victim's knowledge, often because he is absent from the house.

In arriving at a time of day in our survey, we asked the victim to give us a time range within which he felt the event had occurred. Most of the victims were able to give such time limits. Fifty per cent were able to recall the hour within a two-hour range, and 70 per cent within a four-hour range. As shown in Table 3.1, we divided the time of these occurrences into three five-hour periods, morning, afternoon, and evening, and a nine-hour period at night, and then compared the time of day of victimization for our respondents with our 1971 police-recorded data.[4]

If burglaries were evenly distributed throughout the 24-hour day, 38 per cent would be in the night category, and 21 per cent in each of the morning, afternoon, and evening categories. Our victim survey reveals that burglaries occur less frequently in the morning. These survey results differ from the conclusions of police data in both our analysis and that of Scarr (1972) in Prince George's County, which suggested that burglary was primarily a daytime operation.

The analysis of the police records for Toronto and our household survey found that only marginally more occurrences happened on Saturday or Sunday than other days of the week. Other studies have come to differing conclusions as to whether residential burglary would occur more often on weekends than weekdays. Scarr suggests from his analysis of police-recorded data of one of the three counties in the Washington, DC, area that residential burglary is a weekday phenomenon (1973: 32). On the other hand, both

TABLE 3.1

Time of day of victimization

| Period | Percentage of day | Victim survey | | 1971 police records | |
|---|---|---|---|---|---|
| | | *N* | Percentage | *N* | Percentage |
| Morning 7:00 AM to 11:59 AM | 21 | 8 | 7 | 1230 | 24.3 |
| Afternoon 12 noon to 4:59 PM | 21 | 32 | 28 | 1223 | 24.1 |
| Evening 5:00 PM to 9:59 PM | 21 | 27 | 23 | 1419 | 28.0 |
| Night 10:00 PM to 6:59 AM | 38 | 49 | 42 | 1193 | 23.6 |
| | 101 | 116 | 100 | 5065 | 100.0 |

Chimbos (1973: 323) and Conklin and Bittner (1973: 215) found that more of the residential break-ins known to the police in a small town in Northern Ontario and their New England city were committed on Saturday or Sunday.

Crime is thought to be influenced by seasonal variation and by social factors related to the seasons. This should be more apparent where the seasonal variation is more marked (e.g. in Toronto as opposed say to San Diego). Von Mayr (in Falk, 1952) suggested as early as 1917 that changes in the length of days and in temperature affect crime rates, principally through effects on the offender. Theft, for instance, occurs more frequently in winter when it is more difficult to make a living (in Falk, 1952-3: 206).

For both data sets in Toronto, we noted a marginally higher concentration of residential burglary in the summer months. However, seasonal variation is certainly not great.

Although Conklin and Bittner (1973: 215) specifically suggest a victim-related variable – occupancy of the home – as being related to seasonal variation in burglary rates in a suburb, they found little seasonal variation in their police-recorded data. Similarly, Scarr (1973: 30) did not find any significant difference in residential burglary rates when he divided the year into cold, mild, and hot weather months. However, Chimbos (1973: 322) showed that breaking and entering would increase in the summer months in Northern City, Ontario; that is, when more families are vacationing and mild weather permits more outdoor activity.

**Means of Entry**

The US Federal Bureau of Investigation *Law Enforcement Bulletin* (1966) as well as novels of the James Bond type, the Watergate affair, and television programs propagate notions that most thieves are masters in skills such as picking locks and bypassing alarms. However, recent systematic research has shown that more mundane methods of getting inside a dwelling are generally used by burglars. In his interviews with 97 adjudicated burglars, Reppetto (1974: 7) states that over 80 per cent of the entry methods could be classed as 'semi-skilled.' Interviewees in all categories were more likely to simply pry the door or break a window than to use more sophisticated techniques such as picking locks and cutting glass. Scarr (1973: 138) found that between one-half and three-quarters of the burglary occurrences in two counties were committed either by breaking glass or forcing a lock. Even Shover, looking at professionals, found only 10 burglars he considered to be 'good' from a total of 135 convicted and 9 'free' men in his sample. These men had, among other criteria, either entered a place at some time by cutting a hole in a roof or wall, or opened a safe by burning or drilling. Shover goes on to state that: 'the skills and techniques necessary to successfully commit such acts (more lucrative burglaries) are not widely diffused in the social structure. Instead, this knowledge has remained rather esoteric and limited in its distribution to select groups, chiefly the security-protection industry and good burglars' (1972: 542). The notion that residential burglars employ relatively unskilled types of *modus operandi* is consistent with the youth and inexperience of most persons committing burglary.[5]

Information available from Toronto police records does not add much substantial knowledge of burglars' techniques of entry: 51 per cent of the entries were classified as by a door and another 41 per cent as by a window, with the remaining through a coal or milk chute (6 per cent), combination of door and milk chutes (3 per cent), and only 5.2 per cent by cutting through a roof or wall. However, for Toronto, the household survey results show burglaries were typically unskilled or semi-skilled. As expected from other studies (Reppetto, 1974: 7), most burglaries in Toronto were committed either through the door or the window. There were no recorded entries made either through the roof or through a wall. In 17 per cent of the 116 households, the entry attempt reported to the interviewer was a failure. In 5 cases the respondent was not sure of the place of entry.

Doors were the overwhelming choice of place of entry (77 per cent), and the almost exclusive way for apartments. Of those whose houses were entered through the door, half of the attached houses and one-third of the single houses were entered through the front or main door. Fifteen per cent of the respondents, mostly those who lived in attached houses, told the interviewer that they had left the door either partly open or wide open, and another 25 per cent had shut but not locked the door. Only one in four of the door entries were accomplished by forcing or breaking the door open. Techniques requiring higher levels of skill or planning included slipping the lock (13 per cent), using a duplicate key (12 per cent), and picking the lock in 3 of the 74 door entries.

Of the 18 cases where the window was the point of entry, it was shut in 17 and locked in 10 cases. Back windows were selected in 3 out of 5 of the cases, and it was always either a first floor window or a basement window, with first floor windows being the more usual choice. Three out of 5 of the window entries involved breaking or otherwise forcing the window open.

The proportion of persons reporting entry through a door is significantly higher for our victim survey (three-quarters) than for police records (one half) or for Scarr's police records (two-thirds) in the Washington, DC, area (Scarr, 1972b: 45).[6] Probably, where the offender simply walks in an unlocked door, takes something, and then vanishes, the victim is less likely to report the case to the police, because he would feel the police would not be able to do anything about the offence due to lack of evidence. In addition insurance claims are one of the important reasons for reporting an offence to the police and it is often believed that policies require signs of break and enter before giving compensation for loss through theft. We will examine the factors affecting reporting of incidents to the police in greater detail in the next chapter.

**Type and Value of Property Stolen**

Taken together, residential burglaries committed in the United States constitute a large proportion of the national loss to individuals from serious property crimes. In 1965, this figure was set at approximately $150 million (USA President's Commission, 1967b: 47). In 1970, this figure was estimated at $400 million, excluding unreported burglaries (USA FBI, 1970: Table 19). This increase exceeds the spiral inflation effect. Yet the average loss to any particular residence is likely to be low. In his pioneering victimization survey, Ennis estimated this to be about $190, a relatively modest sum for a crime considered to be serious (1967: 75). Estimates based on police records are usually higher. The average value of property stolen in Toronto in 1971, using our police-recorded data, was estimated at $285,[7] just lower than an estimated $322 for the average loss in police-recorded residential burglary in the United States in 1970 (USA FBI, 1970).

The mean value of property stolen from our household sample in 1973 was $345, which is marginally higher than the mean value for police-recorded burglaries in Toronto. However, much of this is due to the large jewelry theft (involving items worth $8000) in our relatively small sample of the 57 burglaries resulting in something stolen. Eliminating this case results in an average value of property stolen of $210, which is much closer to Ennis' figures.[8]

TABLE 3.2

Items most frequently stolen showing average and median values

| Item | Frequency | Percentage mentioning item | Median value |
|---|---|---|---|
| Cash | 29 | 51 | $ 33 |
| Jewellery | 13 | 23 | 96 |
| Television | 7 | 12 | 150 |
| Radio | 7 | 12 | 65 |
| Alcohol | 6 | 11 | 15 |
| *N* = 57 | | | |

Of the 97 persons who reported that entry of their houses by burglars had been successful, 41 per cent reported that *nothing* was taken. For the 57 victims who had something taken, Table 3.2 shows the number of respondents reporting particular items stolen, and the median values of each category of items. The most frequently stolen item was cash, which was taken in half the cases involving theft. As Scarr and Reppetto and others have pointed out, taking cash has none of the disadvantages associated with other 'goods' which usually require location of a fence or other buyer as well as increasing the dangers of being caught through subsequent identification of property. Cash is the most compact and negotiable item one can take. Electronic equipment and jewellery were also popular items. Jewellery was taken in 13 burglaries. Other than cash and alcohol (which is probably used for personal consumption) the major types of goods taken are those which are portable and probably easily fenced, sold, or given to friends if not enjoyed personally. This is consistent with our research on residential burglars' own desires.

Most household surveys involving property crimes arrive at an estimate of total value of goods stolen which is usually reported an an average value per offence.

Unfortunately, it is not always clear on what the estimate for each offence is based. In order to get a reliable and valid estimate of the replacement value of stolen property from our survey we followed the steps indicated below. First, we ascertained whether there was an insurance evaluation. If there was, we took the estimate that was *accepted* by the insurance company, on the premise that this would give us a reasonably fair and objective evaluation of the *replacement* value of items and cash taken. Secondly, if there was no insurance evaluation, we took the police estimate, if any. We felt that the police probably had more experience than the householder in setting values of goods stolen, and also had no systematic reason to distort estimated lósses. (We recognize, that in many cases the police may simply echo the informant's estimate.) Finally, if no police

TABLE 3.3

Average and median values of property stolen by source of estimate

|  | Insurance estimate | Police estimate | Personal estimate | Over-all |
|---|---|---|---|---|
| Average | $884 | $215 | $131 | $345 |
| Median | $278 | $155 | $ 42 | – |
| $N$ | 15 | 8 | 33 | 56 |

Number of missing cases = 1

estimate was available, we asked for the personal estimate made by the householder of the replacement value of the goods taken. The same procedure was used for individual estimates of the value of items. In Table 3.3 the medians of the values of property stolen for each of the three sources of information are compared.

The estimates based on insurance acceptances were higher than those based on police estimates which in turn were higher than the personal estimates. This gives further support for the hypothesis that people are reluctant to call police for relatively trivial losses. Insurance estimates are higher than police estimates over-all probably because one insures goods only if they are valuable enough to warrant paying at least the minimum insurance premiums. These data also would suggest that the minimum value of possessions leading one to purchase insurance is usually higher than the minimum value of possessions stolen which would lead one to phone the police.

We compared the proportions of events in which the value of property stolen was less than $100, $1000, and $5000 for our household survey, the police-recorded data, and police-recorded data for Prince George County in 1969 from Scarr's study. The distribution for Prince George County in 1969 is almost identical to that of Fairfax County in 1969.

In both our survey and police-recorded data, Toronto had proportionally more under-$100 incidents reported than Prince George County, suggesting that property is more sacrosanct in Toronto, that there is a greater belief in police efficiency, or that the moral duty to report is higher in Toronto than Washington.

In Toronto, we also found that there are more thefts under $50 recorded by the police than reported by our household victims, but the reverse was true for those in the $50 to $99 range. In 1971, there was a distinct legal category of thefts under $50. On the margin, the police might have been expected to 'push' offences under the bar of $50, so that there would be fewer serious offences not cleared. The public, on the other hand, would not generally be aware of the significance of $50.

### Damage and Disarrangement

With increasing public concern about crime, especially in large urban cities, the home is more and more being regarded as a sanctuary from crime. Indeed, many writers (e.g., Conklin and Bittner, 1973) have reiterated the proverb that one's home is one's castle. In a way, the law has long recognized the importance of the home to people in distinguishing between public and private space, such as in the higher maximum penalty for break and enter of a dwelling as opposed to a commercial building. Newman, in *Defensible Space* (1972), has tried to extend the idea of private space – people taking a territorial and proprietorial attitude to their home territory – to a corporate (or semi-private) turf with ramifications for preventing residential burglary.

During the pretest interviews, one or two victims of residential burglary voiced quite strong emotional reactions to the damage and disarrangement of articles and contents of their house. One woman felt that her house had been 'raped' by the offender(s) as they had disarranged everything, even though there was relatively trivial damage or property loss.

Thirty-five per cent of the respondents of victimized households reported that some damage was done to the dwelling during the burglary incident. The vast majority related that the damage done consisted of damage to the place of entry. Typical comments referred to doors damaged and window panes broken. About half mentioned damage was done to the contents of the dwelling. These were minor things like having a bottle of liquor dropped on the rug by the offenders.

There were only three incidents where we had evidence of intentional destruction of property by burglars. This has been labelled 'trashing' by West (1974: 116) who suggested it is usually performed by younger, 'irrational' thieves, especially if they are disappointed in what they find. In one, the respondent stated that the offender scarred the linoleum in the living room with a knife or razor blade, and also slit the chesterfield cushions. Another victim had pillows ripped, ornaments broken, furniture thrown around, and so on.

An indication of the generally low extent of damage done is given by the cost of repairing the damage done as estimated by the respondent. In over one-third of the cases, the repair costs were estimated at around $10 or less. Half of the repairs were estimated as less than $20, and four-fifths as less than $50. The highest estimate for damage was $700, which was one of only 5 cases out of 116 where the repairs were estimated as $100 or more.

It is sometimes suggested that burglars thoroughly comb a target, looking for valuables, and that no niche or cache is a safe spot from this indiscriminate rifling. While this may sometimes occur, our data suggests that it is only in a minority of cases where this happens. Of the 116 victims in our survey, 15 reported that their possessions were extensively disarranged and scattered everywhere, while another 21 had a few things scattered about. In general then, residential burglary in Toronto seems to involve little major damage or disarrangement of property.

## Confrontation

From the point of view of the offender, burglary is generally thought to be a relatively peaceful crime. Burglars try to avoid confrontation and violence. Both from our interviews with incarcerated burglars and from similar work by Reppetto (1973) in the northeastern United States, we have concluded that burglars are primarily concerned with ascertaining whether or not a building is occupied before they decide to enter a target residence. In 92 per cent of the 1910 police reported cases studied by Repetto, the premises were unoccupied when the burglary occurred. Nevertheless, several studies indicate that burglary is a major factor for the general climate of fear of crime that pervades some larger North American cities (Conklin and Bittner, 1973; USA President's Commission, 1967a; Reppetto, 1973). Indeed it is particularly significant that the Law Enforcement Assistance Administration included burglary with stranger-to-stranger crime in its expensive High Impact Anti-Crime program. Their aims were to reduce those crimes most clearly associated with 'fear of crime' in the US by 5 per cent within two years and 20 per cent within five years.

Our findings indicate that the fear of confrontation has more basis in reality than would be expected if one believed that unoccupied houses were burglars' primary targets. When we asked the respondent of a victimized household whether anyone was at home at the time of the incident, a surprisingly large proportion, 44 per cent, responded affirmatively. Of these, just under half indicated that there was a confrontation between offender and person in the household. In other words, 21 per cent of the victims in our sample were involved in some sort of confrontation with the offender(s) and another 23 per cent felt that they had been burglarized while someone was home.[9]

We probed for the nature of the confrontation by asking the respondent the details of what happened. Three of the 25 respondents said that they left the scene before an actual confrontation with the burglar took place. Over half of those who confronted the burglar said that the most serious thing that happened was a verbal exchange with the burglar. Even though the victims had not given any verbal or tacit consent for the offender to enter the dwelling, most of the offenders tried to legitimize or rationalize their entry within the dwelling. Typical responses of victims who were confronted were:

> 'He said he wanted to sell books. Said he thought he heard me say come in. I spoke to him and asked him who he was and what he was doing here.'

'I still thought he was a friend of a friend and suggested coffee after about five minutes. We asked him did he know our friends? He said "no" and then he started talking really strange and said he was Jesus Christ.'

'He said he was a rug cleaner but we didn't believe him, he said he would clean the rugs with detergent and walked all over the apartment — our rugs were new and we felt he was just fooling around.'

'Two people engaged me in conversation while the third wandered around admiring artifacts — took some valuable pieces of amber. Well I didn't know anything was going on until they left.'

One person was threatened by the burglar ('He said if I ever talked to anyone about this, he'd choke me'), and in two cases the offender actually physically attacked the householder. The most serious confrontation involved a woman who reported that a man had entered her dwelling and tried to rape her.

In 21 of the 25 cases involving confrontation, there was only one offender, while two respondents mentioned two offenders and the remaining two respondents mentioned three taking part. This contrasts strikingly with adjudicated burglars were almost half are charged with accomplices. One possible explanation of this apparent difference is that accomplices who are often lookouts (Reppetto, 1974: 6) were used in a large number of incidents not resulting in confrontation (since the job of lookout is to avoid just that), and also, it is unlikely that an accomplice acting as a lookout would be 'caught' at the scene.

In keeping with the typical peaceful profile of burglary portrayed by police records, only 3 of those confronted reported that the burglars were armed, two with knives, while 18 said they were unarmed and 4 did not know. No offender was seen with a firearm. Reppetto reported that one-quarter of his sample admitted to carrying a weapon (knife, gun, mace). Two persons reported that someone in the household received minor bruises or injuries, while one respondent reported an injury occurred to a member of the household which required hospitalization and days off work. However, even to this respondent, the estimated total cost of the injury, including wages lost, was $50.

## Known Offenders: A Profile

In the 25 cases in which the offender or offenders were seen by the victim, we asked for a description of the offender, if alone, or whoever the respondent felt was the leader if a group was involved. For simplicity, we shall call this person the principal offender. The twenty-five cases correspond to those answering affirmatively to our confrontation question. Since the number of confrontations is relatively small, caution should be used in extrapolating the results of this part of the analysis to the population of burglars in Metropolitan Toronto or any other large area.

In 21 of the 25 cases, the principal offender was a male. Over half of the respondents categorized the principal offender as more than 25, which is old for residential burglars, when compared to police data which puts the median age of adjudicated burglars at 18 (Reppetto, 1974: 14).

Eight respondents said they thought that the principal offender lived within a half mile of the victimized residence, and an equal number thought not. In almost half the cases, the incident involved a stranger, while in the other half the victim had some knowledge of the offender, though there was no indication from our data which was the best description of the relationship – friend, relative, neighbour, acquaintance, employee, etc.

One in three felt the principal offender was definitely under the influence of alcohol at the time, and another three felt that this was probably the case. In contrast, only three persons thought that the offender was under the influence of other drugs.[10] When asked about employment, half of the offenders were thought or known to be unemployed. No clear pattern emerged with respect to the ethnic origin of the offender.

In addition to those who actually saw the offender, we also asked victims what hunch or suspicion they had of the identity of the principal offender. Forty-one did have such hunches. In general, they were likely to feel that the offender lived within a half mile of their residence, and was under the influence of alcohol at the time. In other respects such as prior knowledge of the offender, number of offenders and so on, their responses were not significantly unlike victims who had actually seen the offender.

In conclusion, we have not found that burglary occurs at any particular time. However, we have found that burglars usually gain entry by the door; that cash and jewellery are common items stolen; but usually the total loss is less than $250. If there was a confrontation between the victim and the burglar it was typically peaceful, and often the two were acquainted, but in a couple of instances there was some violence. The crime is thus relatively amateur and typically minor. The common burglary is certainly much less alarming than the event that hits the headlines in the press. In the next chapter, we will examine the victim's reaction to these 'real' events.

NOTES TO CHAPTER 3

1   Each burglary incident was given equal weighting so that, strictly speaking, the patterns that emerge from the data in the next two chapters (where we are focusing on victims only) overrepresents the areas of Toronto which are above the median in police-recorded burglary rates. However, on the issues under discussion, there is no reason to suppose any difference between victims in high or low burglary rate areas. In view of the small numbers involved, only major or statistically significant trends will be analysed.

2    This included cases reported as occurring in dwellings other than that in which the interview took place. Of the 116 households victimized in our sample, 88 per cent (102) were victimized in Metropolitan Toronto and 80 per cent (93) were victimized at the address where the interview took place. Others took place in a previous residence elsewhere or a cottage.

3    See chapter 2.

4    As the respondent was free to use his own range, we used the midpoint of his range to decide in which category his occurrence should be coded. Those unable to give hourly time limits were categorized by their estimate as to whether the incident occurred in the morning, afternoon, evening, or night.

5    See pages 23 and 32-3.

6    When we examined differences in the place of entry for those reporting to the police, we found a higher proportion of window entries reported.

7    In making this estimate, the following offences were classified as 'burglary' if they occurred in a dwelling place: robbery, break and enter, theft under $50, wilful damage, theft over $50, and all attempts at these offences.

8    If we assume parity of the Canadian and American dollar and a yearly inflation rate of a conservative 5 per cent, Ennis' figures would be equivalent to $281 in 1973 Canadian dollars.

9    In most police jurisdictions in the USA these would be classified as robberies.

10    The relative importance of alcohol and drugs may have changed if the order of these questions in the interview schedule had been different.

# 4

---

# Reactions of Victims

---

We have now examined in some detail what appears to happen in a residential burglary and how frequently burglaries occur. However we have not yet described how the victim experiences the event, what he does about it, or how the event affects his way of life by increasing his fears, changing his attitudes to punishment, or encouraging him to take additional precautions. In this chapter we examine these questions for the 116 cases in our sample who were victimized. As in chapter 3 we are again using unweighted data so that relatively more victims come from areas with higher police-recorded burglary rates, but we feel that our data show patterns which are typical of burglary victims across Toronto.

What is it like to have your home broken into? Surprisingly there has been little systematic research to provide an answer to this question. The results of surveys of public attitudes in the United States (USA President's Commission, 1967a; Rosenthal, 1969) suggest that concern for crime including residential burglary is widespread and acute. Furstenberg (1971: 608) has also shown that people have a relatively accurate notion of the amount of crime in their neighbourhoods. Apparently this knowledge is attained through accounts given by friends and neighbours, and it may be hypothesized that, if these accounts also communicate the negative feelings of fear or anger felt by victims, concern for crime would grow throughout a neighbourhood into a very serious social problem.[1]

Alternatively, particular ways of reporting crime in newspapers (Quinney, 1970) can influence public perception of crime levels even though the crime level itself has not varied. A similar mechanism may apply to concern for crime. There are sensational accounts of burglary victimization that make 'news'. For example, in *Today's Health*, Arthur Henley relates several dramatic accounts of psychological scars left after burglary.

> One evening last summer, a Boston widow returned home from visiting friends and discovered she had been burglarized. Startled, but not dismayed, she telephoned the police. When they arrived, she told them calmly what had happened. An hour later, the widow experienced a delayed reaction to the frightening incident and suffered a heart attack (Henley, 1971: 39).

> ... The burglar can leave his unseen victims equally demoralized by fear. And it is a contagious fear, with the victim's neighbours likely to worry that they may be next. Poetess Marianne Moore resided for many years in a once-fashionable area in downtown Brooklyn but became so terrified of intruders that she moved. ... 'The neighbourhood changed. It just wasn't safe any more,' she explains. 'One of my neighbours, a lovely girl, was robbed three times ... It's a terrible thing to be beset by fear. It wears on you a great deal' (Henley, 1971: 40).

> Upon advice from police, the family changed the lock, but were terrified for months to enter their home 'The anxiety is terrible,' confesses the mother. 'I had to take my daughter to a psychiatrist because she became so nervous ... And I've become an awfully protective mother, always warning my daughter to be careful of this and careful of that' (Henley, 1971: 71).

How often do these psychological traumas take place? Are they caused by the event itself or by perceptions of burglary, which distort the significance of a relatively harmless event? Is it just the weak or maladjusted that experience these traumas? As reactions to confrontation appear to be the root of fears, we examine these first.

## Reaction of Those Confronted

Neighbours or relatives entering a home without consent were excluded from our definition of burglary. Yet it is important to realize that many of the events involving confrontation were only marginally different. In one extreme case the respondent was 'mad that people don't bother to ring our doorbell and just walk in.' In contrast, if the offender was known to the respondent (rather than a stranger) the victim was more likely to remember having been afraid.

Forty-four per cent of the victims were at home when the event took place, although only half of these actually confronted the offender. The feeling most frequently ($N = 10$) recalled during confrontation was described as 'generally upset.' However, fear ($N=8$) and anger ($N=6$) were mentioned almost as often. Two persons mentioned being surprised and three characterized their feelings during confrontation as calm.

Almost half of the 17 female respondents who were victims of confrontation reported fear, in contrast to none of the 8 males. Not surprisingly, in all four cases where the offender-victim interaction was more 'serious' than a verbal interchange, as for example when the victim was threatened or actually harmed, fear was reported, whereas only in one-fifth of the confrontations where nothing more than a few sentences were exchanged (without threats) was fear mentioned as a feeling during confrontation. Feelings of anger and upset were reported about equally by persons of both sexes (though there were only eight men confronted). There was a tendency for feelings of anger to be more prevalent when the offender(s) was known to the victim than when he was a stranger.

## Emotional Reactions

The majority of victims were not confronted during the offence. We asked all of the victims to recall their reactions immediately after discovery if they were not confronted, or after the event was over for those confronted.

The most often mentioned emotion was limited to surprise, which 1 in 3 of the victims mentioned. Fear and anger directed at the offender were each mentioned by about 1 in 5 of the victims and a more general upset feeling by 1 in 4. Only a few persons mentioned feeling relaxed or calm.

It was found that males were less likely to report fear as an immediate reaction to burglary,[2] although there was no difference for surprise or anger.

If the territory that is invaded is more private, then some writers such as Ardrey (1966) or Lorenz (1966), would suggest that the reaction of the householder would be stronger.[3] It was therefore hypothesized that there would be a stronger retributive reaction from victims who placed a higher emotional value on their homes. We used two variables to provide indirect measures of the value of the home to the respondent. One was how long the respondent planned to live there. While many other factors affect this response, it seemed reasonable to suppose that people who plan to live in a house for a long time are more likely to be attached to it than those planning only a short stay. Similarly, we felt that those who had made major alterations to the residence would value their home more than those who had not. However, neither of these variables showed a significant association with fear.

The desire to see the offender imprisoned was a common reaction and was systematically associated with the educational level of the victim and the of damage done to the dwelling. Table 4.1 shows that only 22 per cent of the victims with some university education felt that the offenders should be imprisoned, compared to 45 per cent of those with less than secondary education and 50 per cent of those who completed high school but did not attend university. Thus, having a university education was associated with less likelihood of immediate retributive reactions reported by victims. Income level of household, however, was not associated with the percentage reporting a desire to see imprisonment for the offender at the time of the incident. This suggests that the relationship between educational attainment and retributive reaction amongst our small number of victims is not so much associated with general socio-economic status as attendance at university in particular. This in turn suggests that lack of retributive reactions towards offenders is an element of the liberalization of attitudes associated with university attendance.

Table 4.1 also shows that the degree to which possessions were disarranged or otherwise disturbed during the incident was significantly related to desire for imprisonment. Most respondents reporting extensive disarrangement felt a desire for offender imprisonment, compared to few reporting little or no damage. It was found, however, that other measures of the seriousness of the incident, in particular the value of goods stolen and damage to the dwelling or its contents were not related to desire for imprisonment. This indicates that retributive reactions are affected not so much by how much was taken as by the way the offender treated the possessions of the victims once inside. 'Trashing' behaviour within the dwelling, with its connotations of irrational and potentially violent motivations on the part of the offender, usually resulted in retributive reactions.

It was surprising to note that reported feelings of anger, fear, upset, or surprise were not associated with the desire to see imprisonment of the offender. Similarly, retributive reactions were not significantly related to whether confrontation occurred.

Up to now, most household surveys of victims have concentrated on fixing a dollar value or a measure of the seriousness of the crime. These often include medical expenses or treatment in hospitals as well as the value of goods taken and damage done. The effect of a crime on a victim, however, cannot always be measured by dollar costs or scales that attempt to measure the seriousness of the offence from limited data collected shortly after its occurrence. In this subsection we attempt to delve more deeply into aspects of the emotional effect of burglary on victims – aspects which may last long after the incident occurs.

We have seen that residential burglary, even involving confrontation, is generally non-violent, and at the time of the incident generates feelings of general upset or anger more often than fear. However, victims also reported some long-term consequences of victimization. In over half the cases, the respondents mentioned that the event had generally increased their suspicion or distrust. As shown in Table 4.2, women were more likely than men to

TABLE 4.1

Percentage desiring imprisonment of offender at the time of the offence, by education, disarrangement of dwelling, and mention of fear

|  | Desiring imprisonment | $N$ | $X^2$ |
|---|---|---|---|
| *Educational level* |  |  |  |
| Did not complete secondary school | 44.8 | 29 | |
| Secondary school, but not university | 50.0 | 24 | |
| Some university or more | 21.6 | 37 | |
|  |  | 90* | $p < .05$ |
| *Disarrangement of contents of dwelling during incident* |  |  |  |
| Extensive | 69.2 | 13 | |
| A little | 12.5 | 16 | |
| None | 37.3 | 59 | |
|  |  | 88* | $p < .01$ |

\* Does *not* include cases where respondent was unable to recall his reaction at the time of the incident.

TABLE 4.2

Percentage of victims suffering long-term effects from the incident by sex (multiple response)

|  | Male | Female | $X^2$ |
|---|---|---|---|
| Fear of being alone (self) | 1.9 | 41.9 | $p < .01$ |
| Fear of entering your residence or rooms within your residence (self) | 7.7 | 30.6 | $p < .01$ |
| $N =$ | 52 | 62 | |

report as an aftermath of burglary fear of being alone, and fear of entering the residence or rooms within the residence.

In summary, official punishment is desired by about a quarter of the victims.[4] 'Trashing' behaviour by the offender results in retributive feelings by the victim, but the magnitude of loss or damage done during the crime does not. Persons with university education tend to be less retributive than others, but there is no relationship between the degree to which a person values his home and feelings of retribution. The emotional reactions experienced by a person immediately after victimization are not related to immediate retributive feelings.

TABLE 4.3

For burglary victims who reported to police, rank order of reasons*

| | Number of times item ranked in top three | Percentage of times reason given |
|---|---|---|
| 1  It was the right thing to do, it was my duty | 39 | 52.8 |
| 2  To prevent the offender from committing similar acts in the future | 34 | 32.1 |
| 3  To get the goods back | 23 | 28.8 |
| 4  It was just instinct, never thought about it | 22 | 13.2 |
| 5  It was necessary to claim insurance | 12 | 9.6 |
| 6  Nobody else to call | 7 | 1.9 |
| Other reasons mentioned | | 28.3 |

* Question 40 d and e

## Citizen Discretion in Reporting to the Police

The most important decision taken consciously or implicitly in criminal justice is that of a victim or a witness calling the police and thereby initiating and making possible the official investigations and sanctions of police, lawyers, and the courts. It is also believed that the delay between the occurrence of the offence and calling of the police (especially during the first few minutes after the crimes) is closely related to the probability of the offender being arrested.[5] And so, both the attitude to reporting to the police and the speed with which action is taken are central to the effective operations of criminal justice.

As a phone call to the police is the normal way in which prosecution, judicial hearings, and correctional services are activated,[6] the attitude of a member of the public to the police may also influence attitudes to these other components in criminal justice. In this section we will examine the reasons for reporting to the police of those victims who did so. In Table 4.3 the reasons are set out in rank order of frequency of mention.[7] Apparently, the main reason a Toronto citizen calls the police is because it is his duty. However, victims are also concerned to see the offender prevented from committing the offence again and as many as one in four persons called the police to get their goods back.

In contrast to the 51 victims who called the police, there were 65 who did not. In Table 4.4, the principal reasons for not reporting have been ranked. Lack of confidence in police effectiveness is the principal reason. It is not clear whether this can be related to the fact that the offender would not be caught, that goods would not be returned, or for some other reason. A

TABLE 4.4

For burglary victims, who did *not* report to police, rank order of reasons*

|  | | Number of times items ranked in top three | Percentage of times reason given |
|---|---|---|---|
| 1 | Police couldn't do anything about it | 30 | 31 |
| 2 | Thought it was a private, not a criminal matter | 23 | 25 |
| 3 | Police would not want to be bothered about such things | 19 | 19 |
| 4 | Did not want harm or punishment to come to the offender | 13 | 17 |
| 5 | Not sure real offenders would be caught | 10 | 12 |
| 6 | Did not want to take the time. Might mean time spent in court or loss of work | 8 | 5 |
| 7 | Afraid of reprisal | 7 | 3 |
| 8 | Fear of trouble from police | 4 | 5 |

* Question 50 a and b

second important reason for not reporting was that it was not a police matter.

Table 4.5 compares the *most important* reasons given by the respondents in several American surveys for not notifying the police with the reasons mentioned in our residential burglary-specific survey in Toronto. In these studies, victims not reporting to the police were given a similar (but not identical) list of reasons for not notifying the police. The Toronto study has a slightly more extensive list and some of the alternatives were spelled out in more detail than, for example, in Ennis' NORC study (1967). Hence, only broad categories are considered.

In these studies, the similarities are striking. The reasons for not reporting are related to police ineffectiveness and belief that the offence was not a police matter. We also asked those who reported to the police whether they were hesitant to do so. Only 5 of the 58 respondents replied affirmatively. The main reasons were once again a feeling that this was not a police matter, or the police would not be able to do anything.

**Tolerance of Residential Burglary**

Because this study focuses on a range of criminal behaviour which is relatively homogeneous compared to the broad range of behaviour which can be subsumed under the rubric of 'crime,' it is possible to specify the variation in aspects of residential burglary which are tolerated without calling the police. Other studies have shown that aspects of offences are related to reporting. For instance, in shoplifting, the decisions of victims to report to the police

TABLE 4.5

A comparison of most important reasons for notifying police in several studies
(in percentages)

| Category | Toronto 1974 | USA* 1967 | Dayton† 1974 | San José† 1974 |
|---|---|---|---|---|
| 1  Police would not be effective | 39 | 55 | 32 | 33 |
| 2  Not a police matter | 36 | 34 | 41 | 49 |
| 3  Personal refusal | 9 | 9 | 12 | 9 |
| 4  Fear of punishment | 4 | 2 | 1 | 1 |
| 5  Other | 13 | – | 13 | 8 |
|  | 101 | 100 | 99 | 100 |

* Ennis, 1967: 44, 45
† National Crime Panel, 1974a: 24

have been shown to be related among other things to the value of items stolen, what was stolen, and how it was stolen (Hindelang, 1974a).

As with the desire to see the offender imprisoned, the damage and disarrangement done are shown in Table 4.6 to have significant positive associations with rates of reporting to the police. This supports our earlier hypothesis that the greater the perceived violation of one's personal territory, the stronger the reaction by the victim. Unlike the desire for imprisonment, however, the value of the property stolen is also closely related to calling the police. This may reflect the fact that higher property losses tended to be in residences insured, where recovery and prevention were crucial.

Apparently, the victim's own assessment of the household's precipitation of the crime by carelessness is not related to a propensity to involve the police. As fear of confrontation appears to be a major element in the public's fear of burglary, it is surprising that there was no significant difference among those households where confrontation occurred, those that were occupied but where no confrontation occurred, and those that were vacant at the time of the incident. However, there were very few where confrontation occurred and the offender got away with any goods. Also, as shown in chapter 3, over four-fifths of the cases of confrontation involved a non-threatening verbal exchange as the most serious interaction. Regrettably, there were too few victims in our sample to examine the effect of violence or the threat of violence on reporting to the police. We simply observe that both cases involving actual violence were reported to the police, while the one case of attempted rape was not reported. In one of the two cases involving threat of violence, we know the police were not called. There were no significant relationships between the fear, anger, or surprise felt at the time of the incident and reporting to the police.

TABLE 4.6

Percentage of victims reporting to the police by selected characteristics of incident ($N = 116$)

|  |  | Reporting to police | $X^2$ |
|---|---|---|---|
| Value of stolen property | greater than $100.00 | 87.5 | |
| | less than $100.00 | 58.1 | |
| | no property stolen | 31.1 | $p < .01$ |
| Property damaged | yes | 68.3 | |
| | no | 40.0 | $p < .01$ |
| Disarrangement | much | 80.0 | |
| | a little | 76.2 | |
| | none | 38.5 | $p < .01$ |

TABLE 4.7

Victim related variables in police reporting

|  | Percentage reporting to the police | $N$ | $X^2$ |
|---|---|---|---|
| *Rent/Own* | | | |
| Rent | 42.4 | | |
| Own | 70.0 | 115 | $p < .05$ |
| *Type of Dwelling* | | | |
| Single house | 55.6 | | |
| Attached house | 70.4 | | |
| Apartment | 34.5 | 109 | $p < .01$ |
| *Insurance called (if something taken or damage done)* | | | |
| Yes | 100.0 | | |
| No | 54.5 | 51 | $p < .01$ |

Selected victim-related (as opposed to offence-related) variables were related to reporting to the police.[8] In Table 4.7, the significant associations are displayed. Victims who own their residence and who live in attached houses are more likely to call the police. However, no significant differences were found between victims who reported to police and those who did not in household income, in burglary-insurance coverage, or in the burglary rate of the area as known from police records.

However, it was found that all of those who had something stolen or property damage to their residence *and* who had called their insurance company had also called the police. In contrast, of those who had not called an insurance company, only half called the police. Thus, it appears that a situation which warrants calling the insurance company also warrants a police call, though the reverse is not true.

Our data suggest that the insurance companies usually advise the victim to report the incident to the police. This can also be a stipulation in the insurance policy depending on how burglary is defined. However, two-thirds of the respondents who called the insurance agent had already called the police.

We have seen, then, that the victim has a variety of reasons for calling the police but that aspects of the offence are also correlated with calling. The question remains as to what are the most important factors — especially since some of the variables (e.g., home ownership, type of house, property damage, and property disarrangement) which affect calling the police, are themselves interrelated. We used a multiple-regression technique on our nominal data in order to try to isolate the independent effects of these variables on reporting to the police. Following objective rules, the variable most closely associated with reporting to the police is selected; the computer then follows pre-established rules to find that variable which, combined in our equation, gives the most effective 'prediction' of police reporting. This goes on until the improvement in predictive power is not significant, or the increase in predictive power is very small. Table 4.8 shows the variables which added significantly to explaining police-reporting.

Value of property stolen was the most important variable related to calling the police, while disarrangement added some additional predictive power; both are independent factors related to the decision to report to the police. Table 4.8 suggests that knowledge of aspects of the victim such as home ownership or type of house, whether insured or not, does not add independently to our knowledge of police-reporting behaviour.

It is interesting to compare the conclusions on how characteristics of the offence related to victims' desire for imprisonment (Table 4.1) and their behaviour in reporting an event to the police (Table 4.6). In both cases, disarrangement is related to the more severe reaction, while value of property was important only in reporting the event to the police. This suggests that the action perceived by the victim as being without any immediate economic motive raises an additional emotional vindictive response in the victim. The victim seems threatened personally more by disarrangement of his personal territory than by the evident economic loss. The lack of simple motive implies also the possibility of personal harm.

The value of property stolen is, however, related to the 'instrumental' response of calling the police. We saw previously in Table 4.7 that all of the victims who had called the insurance company had also called the police. To test whether calling the insurance company was an independent factor not associated with the variables shown in Table 4.8 in predicting police reporting, we performed another stepwise multiple-regression analysis 'forcing' into the equation the value of property stolen, property damage, and

TABLE 4.8

Summary table of stepwise multiple regression of police reporting by victims (Dependent variable: reporting to police)

| Variable entered | $R^2$ | $\beta$ | $F$ | $p$ associated with $F$ |
|---|---|---|---|---|
| 1 Value of property stolen | 0.205 | −0.307 | 22.1 | <0.01 |
| 2 Disarrangement of contents of household | 0.273 | 0.211 | 8.0 | <0.01 |

disarrangement, and then adding insurance agent called to see if significant additional prediction resulted. Calling the insurance company was a factor that added only a small, though statistically significant, increment to our understanding of why people report to the police.[9]

In summary, then, the value of property stolen and property disarrangement are the most important factors in predicting whether the victim will report to the police. Calling the insurance company is also, however, an important factor.

## Satisfaction with the Police and Their Actions

Police actions in burglary are *reactive* in that they are initiated usually by the victim after the commission of a crime.[10] In addition, police effectiveness in burglary is limited because confrontation is not frequent in events reported to them and so direct evidence is often lacking. However, police actions are also important because they influence the victim's image of and satisfaction with the police, and eventually public support for the police.[11] In spite of this, little has been written on the victim's perceptions of police actions related to an incident. What is it that the police actually do when called to investigate? This is a crucial question in the case of residential burglary in Toronto, since it is clear that the over-all 'satisfaction with the police' found by Courtis (1970) is high, yet we found from our analysis of police records that in only 10 per cent of burglaries does the action of the police result in a charge or charges being laid. In our sample, only 3 of the 116 cases resulted in an arrest which was known to the victim.

Table 4.9 shows the number of cases in which different actions were taken by police as a percentage of those cases where it was recalled that the police successfully arrived at the victimized household. In most cases, the police asked questions and inspected the premises. Only in a small proportion, however, were fingerprints taken or other evidence collected or action taken. The case was followed up with the resident by another

TABLE 4.9

Police actions in victim households reporting to police
(multiple response)

| Action by police | Number | Percentage |
| --- | --- | --- |
| Asked questions | 48 | 94 |
| Inspected residence | 38 | 75 |
| Fingerprinting | 5 | 10 |
| Took samples and other evidence | 4 | 8 |
| Other | 4 | 8 |
| $N = 51$ | | |

\* This is the percentage of respondents who knew what action had
  been taken and who answered 'yes.' In a few cases, the respondent
  did not know or the question did not apply.

policeman in 43 per cent of the reported cases, most often by telephone as opposed to in person. There was no letter follow-up.

We do not know which of the 51 cases where the respondent called the police became part of an official police record. However, findings in the USA suggest that for crime generally an incident is more likely to be officially recorded if the legal category of the incident is more serious, if the complainant is observed to prefer police action, if the complainant and offender are strangers, if the complainant is white collar rather than blue collar, and if the complainant defers to the police (Black, 1970: 733).

In over half the cases where the police arrived, the respondents agreed that the police had filled out an occurrence report, when the interviewer showed them a blank one. Seventy per cent mentioned that the officer took notes in a notebook (with or without completing an occurrence form) which might form the basis of an occurrence report filled out later. About 20 per cent of the victims did report, however, that the police questioned whether a crime had occurred.

In 30 per cent of the cases, the victim reported that either he or someone else in the household emphasized to the police that every effort should be made to have the offender arrested. However, the victims knew of only three persons arrested, one of whom had been convicted and fined; the outcome of the other two cases were either not known to the respondent or had not been settled at the time of the interview.

Two-thirds of the respondents said that, in the end, they were satisfied with the police action. For those not satisfied, the most often mentioned reason was that the police did not follow up the case after the initial contact. In one victim's words, 'there was no evidence that the police had done anything.' The other, rather less frequently mentioned reason given, was the slow, inefficient service given by the police.

## Instrumental Reactions – Others Turned To

Besides the police, people sometimes turn to others for assistan
they find they have been burglarized. Who do they turn to and
appears that, as in the case of the police, one of the major reas    .or
turning to other persons or agencies is to recoup the losses experienced
in burglary. Eighteen persons reported the incident to the insurance
company. Of these, half received full compensation for their loss, and
another quarter received partial compensation. Three were expecting
compensation, and only one did not receive anything. Only two persons
had or expected to have their insurance premium rise because of the
incident, so that the economic impact of burglary on individuals from
increased premiums was felt to be minimal.

Of the 57 victims who had something stolen from the residence,
recovery of some of all of the items occurred in only four cases. In one
case, the value of goods recovered was a substantial $3500. Five persons
mentioned they received some form of financial compensation or restitution from the incident, but not surprisingly in view of the rarity of
violence in residential burglary no one cited the Criminal Injuries Compensation Board.[12]

When we combine those who had their goods covered by insurance,
received compensation, or had some or all of the goods recovered, they added
up to fewer than half of the cases where something was taken. Those who had
something taken or damage done to their residence, but who did not have
insurance coverage or did not receive compensation or whose goods were not
recovered, formed a group suffering financial loss, and we asked them
whether they would be prepared to settle the case out of court if the offender
returned the goods or whatever was taken and repaired any damages that
might have been done. Of the 35 victims to whom the question applied,
about two-thirds said they would be prepared to accept an out-of-court
settlement. This suggests that after the initial feelings of upset, anger, or fear
that most victims have, they put the event in perspective and are prepared to
settle with simple restitution of the goods stolen. Possibly what happens is
that retributive feelings fade and the major remaining concern in burglary is
just getting the goods back.

Many victims mentioned turning to persons other than the police and
insurance agents for assistance immediately after the incident. The most
frequently mentioned persons were the landlord or superintendent, followed
by a neighbour or friend. The landlord tended to be called in for more
technical assistance, such as to repair damages, secure the residence to make
sure the offender had left, etc., while the friend or neighbour was usually
called to help calm the victim down or to offer advice.

TABLE 4.10

First mentioned precautions taken as a result of victimization

| Category | N | Percentage |
|---|---|---|
| None | 27 | 23 |
| Lock door or window | 30 | 26 |
| More careful (hide valuables, check ID, neighbours check) | 11 | 9 |
| Hardware improvement (more locks, stronger locks, barricade, stronger doors, dog) | 25 | 2 |
| Disguise vacancy | 10 | 9 |
| Move | 3 | 3 |
| Other | 7 | 6 |
| Missing | 2 | 3 |
| Totals | 116 | 101 |

## Prevention Strategies Taken by Victims as a Result of Victimization

Changes in routine behaviour or physical structure brought about by the fact of victimization can be considered another cost of burglary to the public. This must be distinguished from routine precautions taken if a social cost is to be attributed to a particular victimization. Table 4.10 shows the first mentioned responses to the question 'What precautions do you now take as a direct result of this incident?'

Twenty-three per cent of the victims said that they took no additional precautions as a result of victimization. Another 26 per cent specifically mentioned making sure that existing doors and windows were locked, and an additional 9 per cent cited other minor precautions.

In view of the relatively low rate of victimization found in Toronto (less than 3 per cent of the dwellings per year) and the relatively petty and peaceful profile of burglary, doing nothing except perhaps being more careful by locking doors and windows seems like a sensible course of action.

Failure to take more extreme precautions is tied in with the feeling expressed by over 35 per cent of the respondents that the incident was partly or fully a result of their own carelessness and with the finding that one-quarter of the victims felt that just locking existing doors or windows could have prevented the last occurrence. In addition, the one-quarter who felt that nothing could have prevented the incident would probably not have taken more precautions.

In conclusion, the victim of residential burglary is likely to be upset by the experience more than angry. If the victim is a woman, fear is likely to be felt. Even so, as time passes concern for return of goods or compensation seems to be more important. At the time of the offence, official punishment was desired by only a quarter of the victims. Those who called the police did so out of a sense of duty more than to prevent the offender from repeating his offence (or indeed punish him) or to get goods back. Those who did not call the police felt either that the police could not be useful or that the matter was private. If the value of the property stolen was high and the victim's belongings had been disarranged, it was likely that the police had been called. If the police came, the victim was dissatisfied with police action as frequently as one time in three. Over half the victims took no additional precautions as a result of the incident. Only one in five made hardware improvements.

NOTES TO CHAPTER 4

1 The way fear of burglary is communicated throughout a neighbourhood is not examined here.
2 Contingency Table $N = 116$ $X^2 = 7.89$ $p < .01$.
3 At a different level, Robert Ardrey in *The Territorial Imperative* (1966) has put forth an argument, based on observation of animals, that the urge to protect property or space which one has come to recognize as one's own is part of a non-rational, biological drive inherent in man and animals.
4 These findings are slightly different from those of Reynolds et al. in Minnesota, who reported that in 36 per cent of the property incidents in their household survey, victims felt that the incident should be handled by the police or some other public agency, while 31 per cent suggested it was a private matter. Reynolds' data were based on ratings on a nine-point private-public handling scale (Reynolds, 1973: vi-5).
5 Conklin notes that the most common means of clearing a robbery in 1968 was an arrest at or near the scene of the crime (1972: 138).
6 Hawkins (1973) found 82 per cent of most 'serious' crimes recorded by the police were reported by citizens, 76 per cent by telephone.
7 Our pre-test experience showed that many persons are surprised at being asked why they called the police. Many felt that no justification was needed for reporting to the police. Calling the police was just a natural response to a crime. Therefore, we phrased our question on reporting reasons: 'Was there any *special* reason you had in mind when you reported the incident to the police?'
8 Because we were concerned primarily with comparing *households* reporting victimization with those not reporting, we did not include a comparison of age and sex of respondents, since the respondent is not always the one who decides whether to call the police, and may have delegated that task to someone else even if he did make that decision. We found that the respondents placed the call in 62 per cent of the cases, another member of the household in 22 per cent, and someone else in the remainder.
9 Stepwise multiple regression data for the variable 'insurance called' entering into the equation was: $F = 5.002$ with $4,109$ $d.f.$, sig. at .01. The change in $R^2$ was .032.
10 A main duty of the break-and-enter squad of the Metropolitan Toronto Police in fact seems to be the monitoring of pawn shops in hopes of locating an offender after he tries to exchange identifiable goods for cash.
11 Block has shown a negative relationship between victimization, resulting in experience with the police and support for the police (1971: 96).
12 The Criminal Injuries Compensation Board is a provincially funded and federally subsidized agency which compensates victims of crime. Injured people apply showing evidence of injury, loss of pay, expenses, etc.

# 5

# Factors Associated with Residential Burglary

In this chapter, we examine differences between victims and non-victims with a view to identifying factors by which residential burglary may be understood and controlled. Much of the analysis is concerned with placing the theory of defensible space in the perspective of its relative importance to other factors associated with burglary and, above all, testing its key concepts systematically against empirical facts.

Our interest focuses on three interlinked concepts of burglary causation. In the first, 'crime *as* opportunity' (Mayhew et al., 1976), the key factors are those relating to socio-physical characteristics of the residence. We shall examine the extent to which the dwelling is left unattended and special precautions are taken to 'fortify' it. We shall examine the ease of entry, and also the 'defensible space' notions of demarked territory, of surveillance, and of social cohesion between neighbours deterring penetration into dwellings. These factors all affect the extent to which an offender, who wants to burglarize a dwelling, can do it.

In the second concept of burglary causation, 'crime *and* opportunity' (Cloward and Ohlin, 1960), the key factors are those relating to the presence of potential offenders. We will examine in the area near the residence the extent to which there are young single males, a loosely knit social environment, unemployment, rich people living near poor, and concentrations of deprived and alienated persons.

In the third concept, 'crime *of* opportunity', the key factors are those relating to availability of goods to be stolen or dwellings to be entered and the affluence of neighbourhoods.

## Socio-demographic Characteristics and the Police-recorded
## Burglary Rate of Census Tracts

We turn first to the socio-demographic characteristics of census tracts and our study of police-recorded burglaries, where we can examine the importance of factors likely to be associated with the presence of potential offenders and begin to identify the importance of factors associated with the victimization of both dwellings and householders. The analysis is concentrated on identifying the socio-demographic characteristics of census tracts with high burglary rates. Correlation coefficients were calculated between the rate of police-recorded burglaries and the socio-demographic characteristics of the census tracts. The nearer the coefficient comes to one, the more closely the two variables are linked.

As shown in Table 5.1, the most important predictor of a high burglary rate is a high percentage of the male population 15 years of age and over who were single. The percentage of households with lodgers was important, and not unsurprisingly these two measures correlated at .76. The percentage of unemployed in the tract was also important. The fewer owner-occupied and single detached dwellings, the higher was the burglary rate.

These variables probably indicate a higher proportion of persons who are relatively disadvantaged and unattached and so confirm Scarr's findings for Washington, DC (1973). They suggest an environment that has more potential offenders in it. However, the high proportion of single males could also be an indicator of low 'social cohesion.' This could be associated with more offenders, but could also create more opportunity for burglary. Jacobs (1961) and later Wood (1967) and Newman (1972) have all suggested that the prevention of crime is in large part the result of social cohesion between neighbours, who safeguard not only their own particular dwelling, but also nearby dwellings and the area around them. They recognize strangers and will act on behalf of the community to determine what a stranger is doing in this area and whether he is acting suspiciously. Although detached houses are physically easier to break into than apartments, the association between lower burglary rates and a higher proportion of owner-occupied and detached houses suggests that crime is less likely to occur in neighbourhoods that are socially cohesive and stable, as such areas produce few offenders.

We found that the more families in the household, the more two-parent families, and the more persons in the family, the lower the burglary rate. These findings are consistent with the conclusion from our interviews with incarcerated burglars and studies in the US (Scarr, 1973; Blackburn and Repetto, 1973) that where someone is home most of the time, the house is much less likely to become a target for burglars, as they like to avoid confrontation. However, these findings also confirm the importance of family ties in reducing the number of potential offenders and of neighbourhood cohesion in reducing opportunities by deterring offenders.

TABLE 5.1

Correlations between socio-demographic factors and police-recorded 'burglary' rates in Metropolitan Toronto in 1971*

| | 'Burglaries' per 1000 Dwellings (more) | Apt. 'Burglaries' per 1000 Apts. (more) | House 'Burglaries' per 1000 Houses (more) |
|---|---|---|---|
| 1 Percentage of single males over 15 (higher) | .61 | .21 | .29 |
| 2 Percentage of households with lodgers (higher) | .46 | .15† | .20 |
| 3 Avg. number of families per household (less) | .46 | | .39 |
| 4 Percentage of families with both parents (lower) | .40 | | .20 |
| 5 Percentage unemployed (higher) | .39 | .22 | .15† |
| 6 Percentage of single detached dwellings (lower) | .36 | .15† | .32 |
| 7 Percentage of owned dwellings (lower) | .35 | | .41 |
| 8 Percentage of 2-person families (higher) | .33 | | .37 |
| 9 Percentage of apartments (higher) | .24 | | .40 |
| 10 Avg. number of persons per family (less) | .24 | | .33 |
| 11 Avg. number of rooms per dwelling (less) | 16† | | .30 |

* The table shows only those correlations that were statistically significant ($p < .01$).
  The factors are ranked by size of correlation with the burglary rate.
† Significant only with $p < .05$.

All these variables are much more important to house than to apartment burglaries. This is probably because there is much less variability in the physical opportunity for burglary in apartments. To some extent, the correlations for apartment burglaries may indicate the importance of environments associated with creating potential offenders rather than opportunities which attract them. The relative importance of the availability of potential offenders and the opportunities for burglary will be examined systematically below using our household survey data.

We also divided Toronto's census tracts into those in the city and those in suburban areas. As shown in Table 5.2, the variables that were highly associated with burglary over-all remain highly correlated for the core area of Toronto but show a much lower degree of association in the suburbs.

TABLE 5.2

Comparison of city and suburbs: correlations between selected variables and 'burglary' rates

|  | Overall | City | Suburbs |
|---|---|---|---|
| Percentage of single males over 15 (higher) | .61 | .63 | .23 |
| Percentage of households with lodgers (higher) | .46 | .35 | .18 |
| Average number of families per household (less) | .46 | .45 |  |
| Percentage unemployed (higher) | .39 | .33 |  |
| Percentage of single detached dwellings (lower) | .36 | .38 | .17 |
| Managers/workers ratio (more managers) |  |  | .34 |
| Numbers of census tracts | 342 | 156 | 181 |

Although most burglary rates are low in the suburbs, they were relatively higher where there was a preponderance of managers. This variable was constructed by dividing the number of persons in the top census occupational categories by the number of persons in the bottom two categories. Although this variable was designed to indicate relative deprivation of poor near rich, it appears to be a measure of affluence: a score indicating relatively more managers was correlated with more employed, more rooms per dwelling, and more owner-occupied houses. Once again, we see that attractiveness of opportunity is more important than the factors which generate offenders.

In order to assess the relative importance of each of these variables and also produce an equation to predict the burglary rate in a census tract, we have used a stepwise multiple-regression technique.[1] We have shown the conclusions from this analysis in Table 5.3 together with the interpretations we gave to these variables earlier. The availability of potential offenders and the affluence of the area are independently important to the burglary rate. We will be able to interpret the importance of occupancy or social cohesion after we have examined the household survey.

In a separate analysis, we examined differences in these relationships between the city and suburban areas. The over-all results remained roughly the same, though in the suburban areas, the measure of affluence — the ratio of heads of household defined as managers as opposed to workers — was the most important predictor.

Stepwise multiple regression is a predictive technique that capitalizes on chance; if these exact weights were applied to a new sample, it is likely that less of the variance would be explained. Although stringent stopping rules were used in the equations to ensure reliability, the reader should look to

TABLE 5.3

Summary of stepwise regression analyses on police record data from socio-demographic data for census tracts

*Burglaries per 1,000 Dwellings* (more)

| Variable Entered | $R^2$ | $\beta$ | Interpretation |
|---|---|---|---|
| Percentage of single males over 15 (higher) | .409 | .738 | availability of potential offenders |
| Percentage of families with both parents (lower) | .439 | −.139 | social cohesion to protect victim better *or* house more often occupied *or* fewer offenders |
| Percentage of households with lodgers (fewer) | .457 | .416 | less affluence |
| Percentage of single detached dwellings (lower) | .474 | −.252 | social cohesion to protect victim better *or* less offenders |
| Constant 37.58 | | | |

other studies before he uses these equations for prediction and tries to draw implications for policy-making. However, these equations do enable us to examine the problem of covariation and have provided us with empirical evidence of important relationships between the variables examined. As yet, the implications of these findings are not clear for urban planners or others concerned with the problems of burglary in residential areas. In our household survey we will try to clarify further what these associations mean and what could be done that would control burglary.

## Defensible Space, Other Socio-physical Concepts, and Burglary Victimization

We know now that the presence of potential offenders is linked importantly to burglary. We do not know how the socio-physical characteristics and the affluence of dwellings affect the likelihood of burglary. In this next section, we will first clarify what we mean by the various concepts underlying the socio-physical characteristics and then examine how our three broad factors come together. To do this we will go back to our household survey.

What is defensible space? The concept of defensible space is a relatively new one in the area of crime prevention. In the words of its most ardent exponent, Oscar Newman (1972; 1973a; 1973b; and several other publications), it connotes a residential environment which 'enables residents to become the critical force in providing their own security' (Newman, 1975: 4). Freed from the fear for their own safety, they can live more enhanced and fulfiling lives. 'The effect is an environment that is intensively utilised and continually monitored by its inhabitants. Residents and non-residents alike should feel that they will be recognised easily by other residents and that their presence can be questioned' (Newman, 1975: 4).

Much of the work on the concept has been concerned with ways to create defensible space by evolving physical mechanisms, such as by grouping dwelling units in particular ways, by delineating paths of movement, by defining areas of activity, or by providing for visual surveillance. These should give inhabitants and strangers a clear understanding of the function of a space and its intended uses. Properly designed areas are said to lead residents to adopt potent territorial attitudes and self-policing measures. These mechanisms are not better hardware with which one can physically bar the entry of potential criminals or intruders. While such static barriers may have some impact, they could create isolated castles where one is safe inside but in danger outside, and so could increase the problems of residential crime.

The concepts subsumed under defensible space are not yet well defined, but having become popular recently, they may be better considered as an approach, a way of looking at things, rather than a systematic theory. If the applications of this approach are successful, it may be due to the artful implementation of its practitioners. What may be effective in promoting a safe apartment building or neighbourhood may not always be a solution that can be transposed to another area.

Unfortunately, there have been few attempts to test the extent to which these design notions really do reduce residential crime. Newman (1972) illustrated his ideas on apartment buildings in public housing projects. Attempts in the US to test these notions in new housing projects will take several years at huge cost to complete, as the new buildings had to be created and a way of life developed within them. In Toronto, there were buildings that to some extent had characteristics of defensible space, which could be used to test the validity and importance of the concept.

However, this required us to articulate the concepts more clearly than Newman, so that they could be measured for a specific building. We discuss below how we measured social cohesion and surveillability, which are the two most important.[2] There are other aspects of the socio-physical environment of the household that may also be important: the extent to which a structure is left unattended (occupancy); the amount of security hardware and techniques used in a dwelling (fortification); carelessness; and a number of other factors. Each of these will be developed and related individually to victimization.

For technical reasons, our analysis is restricted to persons interviewed in dwellings of those census tracts which were either above the median for police-recorded burglary rates, or based on our prediction equation were areas of high burglary rates, once unreported burglaries were included.[3] As shown in the previous section, these census tracts relative to Toronto as a whole tend to have more males over 15 who are single, fewer two-parent families, fewer households with lodgers, more apartments, and fewer single detached dwellings.[4]

SOCIAL COHESION

The first scale developed measured social cohesion. One of the main assumptions of defensible space is that it can be enhanced through facilitating the recognition and repulsion of strangers and intruders. Buildings are designed so that residents will share feelings of mutual ownership over the area surrounding their dwellings. This concept has been termed 'social cohesion,' and is reflected in permanency of residency, trust of neighbours, and feelings that they would act on behalf of the respondent. Our measure of social cohesion is the sum of favourable responses to a series of questions, which included: the length of time the respondent planned to live in the dwelling, whether his closest friend was a neighbour, knowledge of the names of next door neighbours, frequency of talking to immediate neighbours, number of persons to whom the respondent could arrange to have a parcel delivered, and likelihood of neighbours noticing and approaching strangers.

Social cohesion alone was found to differentiate victimized from non-victimized houses at only a marginal level of significance. For houses, 62 per cent of victims and 45 per cent of non-victims reported low social cohesion. Although not significant for apartments, the opposite trend seems apparent. One contributing factor to the different patterns between houses and apartments is the different level of social cohesion found in the dwelling types. Our data confirm public beliefs that, relative to houses, apartment residents are more isolated. The life styles are very different. Thus houses have social cohesion levels high enough that they can begin to affect stronger recognition and hence crime prevention.

SURVEILLABILITY

Another major component of defensible space is surveillability. If a particular dwelling cannot be watched adequately by neighbours or if potential offenders can loiter about a residence unnoticed by persons in the vicinity, that building is more likely to be burglarized.

We attempted to measure the surveillability of houses (apartments were not included in this part of the analysis) by having interviewers assess for *each side* of the house where access was possible: (1) for the front, the distance from the street of the front of the dwelling and the presence and magnitude of obstruction to a clear view of the front of the house from the street; (2) for the sides and back, the distance to the next residence, since this resident is the primary agent of surveillance for each side and the back of the house; (3) the presence of surveillance points from which that neighbour might survey the respondent's house; (4) the presence of obstructions to a clear view of that side of the house from the neighbouring house, and the magnitude of the obstruction, e.g., wall which was a fairly large obstruction, hedges, landscap-ing, etc.

The criterion we used for magnitude of an obstruction was whether a potential intruder would be camouflaged by the obstruction. Interviewers gathered the relevant information by inspection usually accompanied by the respondent.

For each face of the building, the interviewer was asked to assess the surveillability, by completing the items listed above. Scores of 1 through 4 were given to responses, ranging from a score of 1 for no residence next door or total obstruction of view, to a score of 4 for excellent, unobstructed view. As some types of houses are attached to their immediate neighbours (e.g. townhouses), and as some detached houses may not have windows or doors on one side, a surveillability score was taken from the average surveillability of the sides of the house to which 'surveillability' applied.

Fifty-nine per cent of victims were found to be in houses coded as difficult to supervise (a score of less than 2.5) compared to only 36 per cent of non-victims. This confirmed at a statistically significant level that victimized houses are less surveillable than non-victimized houses. As a result of further analysis, we found that surveillability became important only for dwellings which had surveillance scores above a threshhold level of 2 on our scale.

OCCUPANCY

The extent to which a dwelling is left vacant has been suggested in several studies, including our own analysis, as a major determinant of residential burglary (Reppetto, 1974; Scarr, 1973). Indeed burglars themselves empha-size their concern to avoid houses where somebody is at home.

As an indicator of occupancy, we used the sum of the number of hours which the respondent indicated that the household was vacant for the week previous to the interview. The previous week was used as it would be easily remembered by the respondent. We felt that it would be sufficiently typical as most people do not take holidays in the spring, when our field work was done. Also, when asked to compare the week for which we obtained data (the 'test' week) with the over-all pattern in the spring, 79 per cent of house dwellers and 59 per cent of apartment dwellers said the residence was occupied about the same amount of time. Only 2 per cent of houses and 9 per cent of apartments were occupied either *much* more or *much* less. Similar results were found when respondents were asked to compare the number of hours the dwelling was occupied in the test week with the pattern in other seasons. The exception was summer, when over half the respondents in both types of dwelling said that their dwelling was unoccupied more often. However, victims were not different from non-victims in this regard. Although the previous week is a good indicator, one would need to adjust the absolute number of hours of vacancy upwards in the summer.

For apartments, 69 per cent of victims compared to 42 per cent of non-victims reported their residence unoccupied for more than 47 hours – the equivalent of the minimum time a typical working person might be away from home. This finding is significant, but is strengthened by the fact that the interview was held after the victimization, when victims might have been expected to spend more time at home. For houses, 30 per cent of victims compared to 16 per cent of non-victims reported their residence unoccupied for more than 47 hours. A marginally significant and less important difference than for apartments.

### FORTIFICATION, SPECIAL PRECAUTIONS

Much of the current literature about preventing crime has concentrated on the security hardware and techniques that residents can use for 'hardening' their homes against burglars. Residences differ in their ease of entry not only because of the *special* devices mentioned in this section, but also because of factors not easily measurable, such as type of window or number of entry points. Nevertheless, from a list, the respondent was asked to identify precautions taken that were 'special,' that is, considered to be over and above the locks on the residence at the time of the interview. We then treated the number of special precautions which the respondent acknowledged as a score. Unfortunately, we were unable to examine the precise importance of such precautions, as a few victims added such items after the event.[5] The list included: burglar alarms; special door locks such as chain locks or dead bolt locks; bars over doors or windows; special lighting equipment; key locks on windows; volunteers patrolling area; security guards, private police, community guards; watchdogs.

In houses, many of the respondents took no special precautions. In apartments, special locks were more common and as a result, approximately half took at least one special precaution.

The taking of special precautions only marginally distinguished victims from non-victims. For instance, for apartments, 83 per cent of non-victims compared to 94 per cent of victims took three or fewer precautions. Given that some victims initiated special precautions after being burglarized, these figures indicate that the number of precautions taken could have been marginally more important than we were able to show.

### CARELESSNESS

Several indications in our survey suggest that offenders tend to take advantage of the carelessness of householders. For instance, in a large number of cases in our study, the offender simply opened an unlocked door, and in several cases the door was widen open. Fooner (1971a, 1972) suggests that the victim's carelessness is a major factor in some types of theft, and that campaigns to educate the victim to take better care of possessions and cash can effectively eliminate some crime. Thus, we expected that victims are more prone to be (and to have been) careless in their security-related habits than non-victims.

We attempted to measure the level of carelessness through the construction of a scale based on responses to a number of questions. Respondents were asked whether they took the precautions listed usually, sometimes, or never, and scores of 1, 2, and 3 were given for each response respectively. The total or summary score formed the scale. Forty-eight per cent of victims, compared to 28 per cent of non-victims in apartment buildings had above average scores on carelessness. There was no difference between victims and non-victims in houses.

OTHER VICTIM–NON VICTIM DIFFERENCES FOR HOUSES

In addition to our five scales, we examined other factors which differentiate victimized from non-victimized residences, first for houses and then in the next section for apartments.

*Socio-physical*
Our data suggest that few other physical or structural aspects of houses were important. For instance whether the house was on a corner lot did not seem relevant to victimization. In our pilot interviews, it appeared that 'public' land bordering on a house was likely to increase the likelihood of victimization, but once again the presence of a laneway, park, ravine, school, or factory did not occur more frequently among victims. The number of rooms was not important, nor was the composition of the block in terms of the presence of commercial structures (stores, shops, etc.), industrial structures (factories, plants), parks, schools, or churches.

The average number of persons in a household was not related to victimization although it was to police-recorded burglary rates at the census tract level, and to fear levels among adults.

*Potential Offenders*
We have already seen the importance of a high concentration of single males. Nearness to subsidized public housing, was importantly related to victimization. A residence was categorized as near public subsidized housing if the respondent indicated that the residence was either within a few blocks of a housing project, or was itself a publicly subsidized dwelling. Over one-half of the victims were near subsidized dwellings, as compared to 12 per cent of the non-victims. Nearness to public housing appears to be an offender-related variable, since most arrested offenders are seen as coming from lower socio-economic environments. However, it is important to note that presence of nearby public housing projects is not necessarily identifying public housing itself as the cause, as such housing is usually found in areas that are low in socio-economic status and have other factors which have been shown to be related to general crime rates (see Scarr, 1973).

*Affluence*

The other important factor which was found to differentiate victims from non-victims in houses was household income. Sixty per cent of victims compared to 36 per cent of non-victims came from households with incomes over $15,000. This suggests that a house is more attractive to an offender if items inside are more valuable.

OTHER VICTIM–NON VICTIM DIFFERENCES FOR APARTMENTS

*Socio-physical*

A key notion in defensible space is that of control over territory by residents. Structures should be built so that resident and intruder alike will clearly understand what areas are the responsibility of the resident, who in turn will be able to control these areas. Surveillability and social cohesion are two parts of this control. However, their levels are so low in apartments that they do not appear to be important in preventing victimization. One concept of control over territory was measured by examining when the area or corridor on which an apartment was located was used for play by the residents' children, for informal meetings, for drying boots, and as an extension by leaving the door open. Newman (1973b: 51) has suggested that this sort of use of hallways provides a natural mechanism for asserting proprietorship as well as supervising an area and screening strangers. With our data we were unable to demonstrate any relationship. Nor were we able to demonstrate any association between likelihood of victimization and whether the apartment was placed next to or opposite a stairway, on one or two sides of the corridor, or with few as opposed to several other apartments on the floor. While these notions are difficult to measure, our findings seriously question the importance of defensible space to the prevention of burglary in apartments.

The defensible space literature also suggests that blocks with industrial structures would not have well identified territory and that stores and offices in apartment buildings would decrease the chances of controlled territory. These activities increase the number of people and so decrease the ability to recognize strangers. Jacobs (1961) has suggested that this mixed use increases the number of 'eyes' and so protection. As shown in Table 5.4, our findings appear to reject the hypotheses of defensible space and accept those of Jacobs. A mixed block was less likely to have a victim on it. However, we will suggest below that neither theory is important and that this finding results from a spurious association that apartments on mixed blocks tend to be tall and have doormen – variables that appear to be more fundamental.

Another notion following from defensible space is to design low-rise apartment complexes to reduce crime (National Institute of Law Enforcement and Criminal Justice, 1973a and b; Newman, 1973: 14) as these would tend to encourage social cohesion. Our findings show that the higher the

TABLE 5.4

Other factors differentiating victims from non-victims in apartments

| | Non-Victims (in percentages) | Victims (in percentages) | $N$ | Corrected $X^2$ | $p <$ |
|---|---|---|---|---|---|
| SOCIO-PHYSICAL CHARACTERISTICS | | | | | |
| *Presence of industrial structures on block:* | | | | | |
| Yes | 24.8 | 0 | | | |
| No | 75.2 | 100.0 | 187 | 10.75 | .01 |
| *Presence of church on block:* | | | | | |
| Yes | 28.1 | 6.1 | | | |
| No | 71.9 | 93.9 | 190 | 7.76 | .01 |
| *Floor level of dwelling:* | | | | | |
| Less than 7 | 39.9 | 76.3 | | | |
| 7 or higher | 60.1 | 23.7 | 193 | 16.90 | .01 |
| *Doorman:* | | | | | |
| Yes | 15.9 | 0 | | | |
| No | 84.1 | 100.0 | 193 | 6.76 | .01 |
| *Persons in household:* | | | | | |
| One | 38.2 | 20.9 | | | |
| More than one | 41.8 | 79.1 | 193 | 3.86 | .05 |
| POTENTIAL OFFENDERS | | | | | |
| *Presence of potential offenders:* | | | | | |
| Yes | 90.9 | 73.8 | | | |
| No | 9.1 | 26.2 | 193 | 7.43 | .01 |
| AFFLUENCE | | | | | |
| *Income* (dichotomized at median): | | | | | |
| Below $11,000 | 54.3 | 36.6 | | | |
| $11,000 or more | 45.7 | 63.4 | 182 | 3.56 | NS |
| *Rooms in apartment:* | | | | | |
| Less than 4 | 55.0 | 33.9 | | | |
| 4 or more | 45.0 | 66.1 | 193 | 5.32 | .05 |

apartment the less likely it is to be a victim. This finding is reinforced by noting that higher apartments also tend to be rented by more affluent persons.

Although our sample is different from the publicly subsidized housing projects in New York or St Louis that appear to have inspired Newman, some of the differences between the defensible space hypotheses and our findings reflect serious questions that urban planners and researchers must address. If residents are to be protected as a result of these theories, it is going to take a huge amount of new construction over a number of years. We will see below that there are other more practical factors that are related to burglary and at more important levels.

One of the more important findings has to do with the deterrent effect of personal confrontation. None of the victimized apartment buildings employed a doorman. When we compared the proportions of victimized apartments having working intercom systems with non-victimized apartments, a slight and statistically insignificant effect was noticed. Victims were marginally less likely to have working intercom systems. This suggests that these systems function to screen visitors but not as efficiently as doormen. This screening is closely linked to the affluence of the apartments.

Despite the importance of absence from the dwelling, there was a smaller proportion of one-person households among the victimized apartments. The low rate of burglary in single-person apartments may be due partly to a large number of older persons living alone, who can be expected to be home for most of the day. However, this is not clear from our data. An alternative explanation is that the income of two-or-more-person apartments is higher. As we will see later, income is importantly related to victimization in apartments.

*Potential Offenders*
Residents of victimized apartments were much more likely to say that there were persons or groups of persons in their area that they felt contributed to the likelihood of their residence being broken into. However, because the presence of potential offenders was ascertained after the fact of victimization, part or all of this difference may be due to the heightened salience of such information to victims as a result of the offence occurring to them. Because of this, the variable will be omitted in the next section. Unlike houses, an apartment was not more likely to be victimized if there was public housing nearby.

*Affluence*
The importance of household income and number of rooms in the apartment confirms that socio-economic status of the victim is generally higher than non-victim. Offenders, it appears, choose relatively wealthy residential targets in apartments as well as houses.

More expensive apartments tend to be in buildings with more floors, and the higher the floor level of the apartment, the higher the rent. Consequently, one would expect more victims in higher level apartments. However, it appears that other factors such as ease of access for offenders, and lack of doormen in apartment buildings with few floors, outweigh affluence. Significantly more victimized apartments than non-victimized were on the seventh floor or lower, and 61 per cent of the victimized apartments were in structures of less than 16 floors, compared to 38.9 per cent of the non-victimized structures. This also contradicts the findings of the New York City Housing Authority Police records for a variety of crimes (Newman, 1973b; 113-17).

**Key Characteristics and the Dwelling Survey Burglary Rate**

We now continue with our dwelling survey and those respondents living in census tracts with burglary rates above the median to examine which of the variables differentiating victims from non-victims seem to be the more important. In the previous section, social cohesion, surveillability, presence of subsidized public housing, and income were all related to the likelihood of victimization.

HOUSES

The independent effects of surveillability, income, social cohesion, and nearness to public housing on victimization were examined using stepwise multiple regression. The results are summarized in Table 5.5.

The order of selection of variables places nearness to public housing first, income second, occupancy third, and then surveillance. Income and surveillance add significantly to our prediction of victimization, affirming their status as independent factors. Social cohesion does not add significantly after the effects of other variables are considered.

In a supplementary analysis, we found occupancy to be the only factor that remained important near public housing (in a larger sample, income might still have an effect). In areas not near public housing, occupancy was less important than surveillability and income.

In summary then, for houses, our analysis suggests first, as a practical measure for those in either a single or attached dwelling and who live further than a few blocks from a public housing project, the improvement of surveillability would prevent burglary. While for those close to a project, whether rich or poor, means need to be found to avoid leaving the home unoccupied for more than a few hours a week.

APARTMENTS

It will facilitate the understanding of the analysis for apartments to look at how the variables were themselves linked together.

*Socio-economic Factors*

The socio-economic factors and occupancy were all closely interrelated. Household income was strongly associated with both number of rooms and number of persons in the household. Occupancy, as measured by hours vacant, was positively associated with income only in apartments. This is probably a reflection of the fact that incomes are high where two residents of an apartment are working, a situation necessitating in most instances leaving the apartment vacant for large parts of the day. Occupancy was also associated with the number of persons in the household.

TABLE 5.5

Summary of results of stepwise multiple regression on
victimization of houses

| Step | Variable name | $R^2$ (total variance explained) | $F$ | Probability associated with $F$ |
|---|---|---|---|---|
| 1 | Nearness to public housing | 0.252 | 49.59 | < 0.01 |
| 2 | Household income | 0.303 | 10.53 | < 0.01 |
| 3 | Hours vacant | 0.347 | 9.82 | < 0.01 |
| 4 | Surveillability | 0.378 | 7.24 | < 0.01 |

*Location Variables*
The floor level of the apartment, the number of floors in the building, the presence of a doorman, and the presence of industrial structures or churches on the block also form a constellation of variables which appears to be concerned with location. Not surprisingly, higher floor levels for apartments are found in buildings with more floors, and doormen are found almost exclusively in buildings with 16 stories or more.

The inter-associations of our 'location' variables could cause misinterpretations of individual associations with victimization. For example, large apartment complexes are generally situated on blocks where industrial structures or churches were likely to be present. Thus, the association between block structure and victimization which was earlier suggested as refuting an hypothesis based on defensible space may in fact be due to mixed blocks having larger buildings which have doormen who effectively reduce the likelihood of burglary. This problem will be confronted in the regression analysis below.

*Carelessness*
Carelessness was the one major variable associated with victimization which did not show any consistent associations with either constellation of variables associated with victimization. Thus, carelessness appears to be an independent contributor to victimization.

*The Importance of the Variables*
As shown in Table 5.6, a stepwise multiple-regression technique was used to identify the relative importance of the socio-economic, location, and carelessness variables.[6]

Household income as a measure of affluence of the apartment, presence of industrial structure on the block as a measure of location and so ease of opportunity to the offender, and carelessness were the three variables, each of which made an independent contribution to the explanation of burglaries in apartments. However, the second variable needs some discussion. Although

TABLE 5.6

Summary of stepwise multiple regression on victimization in apartments

| Step | Variable | $R^2$ (total variance explained) | $F$ | Probability associated with $F$ test |
|------|----------|------------------------------|-----|---------------------------------|
| 1 | Household income | 0.063 | 17.74 | < 0.01 |
| 2 | Presence of industrial structure on block | 0.096 | 9.63 | < 0.01 |
| 3 | Carelessness | 0.120 | 7.03 | < 0.01 |

presence of industrial structures on the block was selected, it was very strongly associated with apartments on high floors and presence of a doorman. For instance, none of the 24 apartments with a doorman was victimized, and in 21 out of 24 cases, apartments with doormen were located in blocks with industrial structures. It is these variables that provide the explanation of the importance of this factor.

In summary, it appears that burglars are interested in higher income apartments whose residents are careless (not locking doors, etc.), but they are less likely to burglarize an apartment on the highest floors of a high-rise building or in a building with a doorman. In addition, our data suggest that more detailed individual case research should be done before defensible-space approaches are used extensively and expensively.

NOTES TO CHAPTER 5

1 We used this standard technique where, following predetermined rules, the variable most closely associated with burglary rates is first selected by the computer; then the other variables are searched to find that variable which, combined in an equation with the first, gives the most effective 'prediction' of census tract burglary rates. This process goes on until the improvement in predictive power is not 'significant' ($p < .01$) or results in an increase of variance explained of less than 1 per cent.

2 Precise details of the scales are available, through the Centre of Criminology, University of Toronto.

3 Since there were different sampling ratios (strata) in these census tracts, the data were weighted to represent victims and non-victims for all census tracts above the median. The other areas were abandoned as there were too few victims in low burglary rate areas to justify comparisons. The victims were those 89 persons victimized in the residence in which the interview took place. Our tables should *not* be used to predict the likelihood of a given house or group of houses being victimized, as we did not allow for the different proportions of victims and non-victims to be found in the total population.

4 In addition, the sample interviewed relative to the census averages tended to have more households with lower incomes (less than $11,000) and heads of households born in Europe. Fuller details may be obtained through the Centre of Criminology, University of Toronto.

5 See chapter 4, particularly Table 4.1.

6 See note 1 above.

# 6

# Public Experience with the System of Justice

From the early 1960s onwards in the United States, people started to worry about crime and to identify it as one of the major issues of the time. More people began to demand tougher laws and harsher treatment of criminals to curb the trend towards lawlessness. A 1969 Gallup Poll for instance, showed that a majority of Americans wanted the courts to deal more severely with criminals, a double sentence for crimes committed with a gun, stricter parole laws, more use of capital punishment, and, in general, a hard line against offenders (Gallup, 1969). Although there are many theories, little is known of the origins of these attitudes or of what the public knew about the criminal justice system itself.

One aspect which probably affects attitudes to the justice system is the personal experience of people when they come in contact with parts of the system. Reiss (1967b) gives an example of this. He suggests that citizens' experiences as victims or witnesses to offences may lead to more awareness of the problem of rights in citizen-police transactions, and hence probably less willingness to permit police greater discretion in such encounters than the law or the courts may warrant. Some efforts have been made to assess victims' experiences with the police (for example, victimization surveys) and certainly court and correctional service data exist which give counts and breakdowns of persons processed through that part of the justice system.

More recently, the Knudtens and others have been studying victims and witnesses in the court situation (Knudten, 1974; Ash, 1972). Their work has underlined the need to consider the rights and responsibilities not only of offenders but also of victims and witnesses. They have shown how the criminal justice system largely revolves around the principal officials — judges, police, and lawyers. Recent trends have provided more protection for offenders. In all this, it is the victim and witness who tend to suffer.

However, relatively little empirical work has been done to ascertain the level of general public experience with the criminal justice system. In this chapter, we turn our focus from the victim to the general public and examine some of the effects that experience with the criminal justice system has on attitudes to crime and punishment in relation to residential burglary. These are based on a sample of 425 households, which includes all 116 victims, and a systematic sub-sample of 309 non-victims. The two sub-samples were combined and weighted to represent a cross-section of adults 18 and over in households across Metropolitan Toronto.[1] (The sample slightly underrepresents males under 24.[2])

## Contact and Experience with the Justice System

By the time the interviewer arrived at the questions concerning contact and experience with the justice system, as much rapport had probably been attained with the respondent as we could expect throughout the interview. Thus, the questions that form the basis of this chapter were phrased in relatively straightforward terms. The interviewer was instructed to simply comment, 'Now I'd like to ask you about any contact you've had with the police, courts, and so on.'

Forty-four per cent of the respondents reported having been to court. This is nearly as high as the 51 per cent who had at some point called the police. As we will see, most of these court appearances were to do with traffic incidents.[3] Only a small proportion of criminal incidents for which the police are summoned actually reach the courts (see Hann, 1973).

One in seven mentioned that, in the 16 months before the interview there was an incident other than a recent burglary where the respondent might or should have called the police but did not. About one in eight Torontonians had had some experience of an out-of-court settlement. These facts reveal the importance of non-court justice. In deciding to call the police or to settle out of court, the citizen determines both the workload of some sections of the justice system and the type of justice that can be meted out. In the following discussion, we examine the experience of citizens with the courts and the police in more detail.

As shown in Table 6.1, men are generally more likely to have court experience than women. This is understandable in criminal and traffic-related cases, since most offenders are male in both of those large categories. Less understandable was the tendency for males under 40 to have had more experience with the courts than those over 40. Two reasons may account for

TABLE 6.1

Court experience by selected social and demographic variables

| | Percentage with court experience | | |
| | Male | Female | $X^2$ |
|---|---|---|---|
| *Age of respondent* | | | |
| less than 26 | 58.7 | 43.5 | |
| 26–39 | 65.3 | 26.0 | |
| 40–59 | 53.4 | 36.3 | |
| 60+ | 33.5 | 39.7 | |
| *Income* | | | |
| less than $11,000 | 41.7 | | |
| $11.000+ | 46.6 | | NS |
| *Education* | | | |
| less than secondary | 42.6 | | |
| secondary school, post | | | |
| secondary, non-university | 50.2 | | |
| some university or more | 39.8 | | NS |
| *Burglary insurance coverage* | | | |
| yes | 48.6 | | |
| no | 37.3 | | 0.04 |
| *Birthplace* | | | |
| Canada | 43.8 | | |
| United States, United Kingdom, | | | |
| Australia | 53.7 | | |
| Other | 38.4 | | NS |

this: first, younger persons are more likely to be charged; and secondly, there has been a dramatic increase in the use of the automobile over the last twenty years. There is also in Canada (Canada, Canadian Committee on Corrections, 1969) a trend for the age-specific conviction rate to be increasing for persons under 25.

Neither income nor education was found to be related to the probability of court experience, though persons without insurance against burglary and those born outside the English-speaking nations were marginally less likely to have court experience.[4]

Of the 44 per cent of Metropolitan Toronto's population over 18 who had been in court, three-quarters mentioned that they had been to court within the last five years. Of those with relatively recent experience (as measured by court contact in the last 5 years) three-quarters had been to court only once in that period and most of the rest only twice. A small fraction of persons had been 3 times or more, some of whom were lawyers, judges, court clerks, and so on.

If a person had been to court, in 53 per cent of the cases it had been as a party in a civil case and in 27 per cent as a witness. Relatively few had been jurors, although one in five had been spectators. Fifteen per cent reported receiving compensation for their time in court. The majority, 56 per cent, of persons who have been in court had been involved in traffic violations. Twenty per cent reported being in court in relation to a civil, family, or divorce case. About 17 per cent have been involved in cases concerning criminal violations.[5] The court experience is brief for most citizens. Two-thirds of the persons spent half a day or less in court and only 15 per cent had spent more than one day in court. In terms of forming beliefs about Canada's court system, this is their only first-hand experience and so must compete to form part of their beliefs with the headlines and dramatized stories in the mass media.

Compared to those with actual court experience, only about a quarter of the number of people in Toronto have been involved in an incident settled out of court, which might have been heard in court. However, with increasing court work-loads and delays, we expect that out-of-court agreement on facts and actual settlement might become more frequent, especially in cases restricted to a relatively small property loss and less serious crime. In these cases, the victim may simply want return of the goods and perhaps a small amount of compensation to pay for the 'trouble' caused by the offender. The victim may feel that it is not worth the trouble to spend the time in court to prosecute a case if an out-of-court settlement can be reached, or he may not want the offender to be officially sanctioned, yet feel that some sort of compensatory action should be taken.

In our sample, over half of the people in Toronto who had settled cases without going to court mentioned a case involving a traffic incident (excluding parking violations). Civil matters were the second most frequently mentioned, with family or divorce settlements being mentioned by 10 per cent and other civil matters by 17 per cent. The number of people mentioning out-of-court settlement in a criminal case was low – about 1 in 20 mentioned burglary and the same proportion mentioned some other criminal matter.

We have seen that residential burglary is a property crime usually perpetrated by the offender to avoid violent confrontation. As such it is *prima facie* a good candidate for out-of-court settlement on economic and emotional grounds, yet such out-of-court settlement is rare. In contrast, traffic incidents where there are victims and known persons responsible, but usually no 'criminal' intent, are often settled out of court. Most traffic incidents that involve property damage involve insurance companies, who are trying to minimize their own costs and so will avoid the legal fees required for court appearances. In these cases action is taken to alleviate harm to victim, offender, and company, as opposed to punishing any individual for a wrong act. Thus the motive is restitution rather than retribution.

While there is a substantial literature on interaction between police and public, most of it has centred on the duties and discretion of the police officer. Until recently, little research had been done regarding experience with the police from the viewpoint of the public. Most of this recent work has stemmed from the studies by Ennis (1967), Biderman (1967b), Reiss and Black (1967a and b), and others for the President's Commissions in Washington, DC, in 1966 and in the United States in 1967. In this next section, we will concentrate on the exercise of 'discretion' by the public in calling the police.

We asked respondents the *last time* they had called the police for any reason. Almost half reported that they had never called the police. Eleven per cent reported calling the police in the first four months of 1974 prior to our survey, and 14 per cent remembered the latest incident as occurring in 1973. Twenty-five per cent reported the last time they called the police was before 1 January 1973. We estimate that between one in five and one in six persons call the police at least once each year.[6]

The police were called for a variety of reasons.[7] Table 6.2 shows both the proportion of incidents for which the police were most recently called, as well as the proportion for which respondents felt they might or should have called the police in 1973, but did not.

About one-quarter of all police calls were related to an incident in which the respondent either saw or suspected a crime was committed, or where the respondent reported victimization. Complaints against neighbours, such as a noisy party or a dog barking, or incidents involving domestic quarrels took up about one-fifth of the public calls to the police, while traffic-related calls – a traffic violation or accident – accounted for 17 per cent of the incidents. Information requests, or requests for additional police service, accounted for 13 per cent of the calls, as did calls for emergency help, first aid or fire reports.

By comparing calls made with those not made, it may be seen that the type of incident which raises most problems for potential police callers are those involving a complaint against a neighbour, or a domestic quarrel either within the family or elsewhere. In the case of neighbour complaints, the decision to call the police is offset probably by the fear of spoiling good neighbourly relations. While for the family quarrels, the problem was probably to determine whether police intervention was appropriate in an essentially private matter.

An examination of the reasons for not calling the police cited by those who did not call, but felt they might or should have, reveals that the two most common reasons were that they felt the incident was not a police matter (the police either would not want to be bothered about such things, or it was a private, not a criminal matter) or the police would not be effective (the police could not do anything about the matter). Relatively few persons mentioned fear of punishment or personal reprisal as reasons for not calling the police. These results are very similar to the reasons given by victims of

TABLE 6.2

Type of most recent incident resulting in a police call, and in most recent incident where police could have been but were not called

| | Police called | | Police not called | |
|---|---|---|---|---|
| Type of incident | Per-centage | Rank order | Per-centage | Rank order |
| Crime related incident | 23 | 1 | 25 | 2 |
| Neighbour complained, domestic quarrel | 21 | 2 | 41 | 1 |
| Traffic incident | 17 | 3 | 12 | 3 |
| Information, service requested | 13 | 4 | 1 | 4 |
| Emergency | 13 | 5 | 1 | 5 |
| Other | 13 | | 22 | |
| | 100 | | 100 | |

TABLE 6.3

Factors related to ever having called the police

| | Percentage who called police |
|---|---|
| Income | |
| Less than $9,000 | 45.7 |
| $9,000–$14,999 | 41.4 |
| $15,000–$24,999 | 67.7 |
| $25,000+ | 78.2 |
| $N = 383\ p < .01$ | |
| Education | |
| Less than high school | 43.5 |
| Less than university | 49.6 |
| Some university or more | 79.9 |
| $N = 418\ p < .01$ | |

residential burglary who do not call the police in Toronto, and to reasons given in Ennis (1967) and the National Crime Panel (1974a).

In Table 6.3 the effect of income and education is related to the likelihood of ever having called the police. Our data indicate that the higher the socio-economic level of the respondent as indicated either by education or by household income, the greater the likelihood of having called the police. Persons who lived in single (detached) houses tended to have called the police more often than those living in apartments, who in turn tended to have called the police more often than those living in attached homes. This difference, however, is probably related to income and geographical location in relation to the urban-suburban crime rate difference. The differences were statistically significant. The association between education and calling the police for victims is of particular interest. As we saw for victims, the higher the education, the less likely an immediate reaction of retribution.

However, the police are called for a variety of reasons not all of which are related to crime reporting or a desire for vengeance. For instance, 70 per cent of those saying that they were somewhat or more worried about residential victimization recalled having called the police, while only half of those expressing lesser amounts of worry had ever called the police. Are worry and calling the police part of a deeper constellation of attitudes and behaviours in relation to crime?

While our data indicate that variation in decision-making about reporting to the police is related to the type of incident, we found that three-quarters of the people in Toronto felt that people living on the same street or on the same apartment floor would call the police if they suspected someone might be trying to break into a dwelling. Thus, for residential burglary, there appears to be strong consensus that phoning the police would be the common reaction to a suspected burglary. Only 18 per cent of the weighted sample replied that they did not know, indicating that the decision to phone the police would be problematic with their neighbours. However, it was felt that only 15 per cent of neighbours would intervene in a burglary.

### Public Experience with Burglary Prevention Programs

The emergence of crime as a major issue in North American cities has led to the development of a number of programs undertaken by various citizen groups, private agencies, government departments, and also parts of the justice system to help prevent crime. The most comprehensive programs have been funded by the Law Enforcement Assistance Administration (a part of the United States Department of Justice) who have provided funds to various agencies, especially the police. Many of these programs have involved the development of strategies to increase public awareness of how to prevent such crimes as residential burglary.

In Toronto, the Metropolitan Toronto Police Force developed a program called Operation Checkmate which involved the use of pamphlets and film presentations showing the potential consequences to victims of crimes like burglary and suggesting ways of reducing its incidence.

Our data indicate that 72 per cent of Torontonians have seen or read something written in the past five years on how to protect their homes against burglary. Seventy-four per cent of those who had remembered such a program or article cited TV as the source. Magazine articles were mentioned by 44 per cent, and radio was the third most frequently mentioned source at 31 per cent. Police pamphlets were mentioned by 29 per cent of the population, and insurance pamphlets by 21 per cent. These data are similar to

those reported by Scarr (1973: 276) for a sample of victims an
in high and low burglary-rate areas in the Washington, DC are
found that television and magazine articles were the most freq
public had been informed on how to protect themselves against

Of those who had read or seen (or heard) anything on how
home against burglary, 26 per cent reported that they took some additional
precautions as a result of what they had seen or read. This positive payoff was
partly offset by the 13 per cent who reported an increase in fear or anxiety.
We have no idea of the 'success' of these programs and pamphlets in reducing
burglary in Toronto, though in the final chapters of this report we indicate
that the items suggested are not the most effective techniques that potential
victims can adopt.

### Self-report

Official police statistics on burglary offenders in Toronto are concerned with
less than 1 in 10 of burglary offences. The police feel they know more about
the unidentified offenders than they can prove in court. We have shown that
victims see the offender in one in five cases. However, a more complete and
systematic picture of both the offender and the nature of the event was
obtained from confidential interviews with those members of the public who
had themselves committed burglary.

Moreover, an important part of a person's reaction to the experience of
or threat of burglary may be whether he has committed that offence himself.
A strong reaction to a specific burglary that is generated by rumour or mass
media reporting of spectacular events may be dissipated by the realization
that the crime is more often minor and is also something ordinary persons
like oneself commit.

It seems that residential burglary might indeed be a common offence for
persons to commit. From analysis of an anonymous questionnaire mailed in
New York State, Wallerstein and Wyle (1954) estimated that 17 per cent of
adults in New York had committed what could be defined as burglary. The
Scandinavians found a similar proportion of military recruits — a representative sample of young adult males — admitting to burglary-type behaviour
(Hood and Sparks, 1970).

Beyond our interest in the relationship between being an 'offender' and
reaction to burglary, surveys of the general public to find out whether they
have committed criminal offences, or 'self-report' surveys as criminologists
refer to them, have been crucial in questioning whether crime, particularly
involving juveniles, is really restricted to the disadvantaged segments in the
population. Doleschal suggests from his review of such surveys that close to
100 per cent of all persons have committed some offence, although few have
been arrested (1970: 566).

Even when caught, the resources of the middle and upper classes in enabling their offspring to avoid official labelling processes may result in an exaggerated impression that most crime is committed by working-class persons. Short and Nye (reported in Doleschal, 1970) among others, have found that substantial numbers of high school students in midwestern and western United States communities had committed delinquencies, but that the major determinants of arrest were the frequency and seriousness of delinquent behaviour.

These surveys have been part of the evidence used to illustrate that discretion as exercised by the public in reporting crime and in the criminal justice system itself has tended to result in the more powerful and integrated members of society being diverted from the system (see Hood and Sparks, 1970; Waller, 1974). Official police statistics and demographic studies in the past have been interpreted to suggest that the great majority of crimes, especially property crimes, are committed by young male urban lower class denizens. For residential burglary, studies have shown a very strong association between class and offender experience in burglary for persons arrested by the police. In Canada, Chimbos (1973) found that almost all of the offenders arrested for breaking and entering in his small rural town were of working-class origin. West's participant observation on a sample of about 50 serious thieves in Cabbagetown, a part of downtown Toronto, also perpetuates the notion of the disproportionate distribution of offenders in the lower class area (West, 1974).

However, opportunities for residential burglary, like car theft, are commonplace and equally available to persons throughout the social structure. Indeed, in middle- and upper-class enclaves of society, tempting opportunities to burglarize, combined with local knowledge of residents' habits, would seem to favour the development of at least some amateur middle- and upper-class burglary, probably done only once or twice by local youths, possibly for thrills, and not necessarily resulting in much property loss.

Self-report surveys have certain methodological problems: the respondent must be asked if he committed a specific behaviour, whereas if he had been convicted, the police, witnesses, a prosecutor, and ultimately the court would have made that decision following complex rules; as in any discussion of whether an event took place, there may be problems of recall or distortion and, as well, there is no independent means of verification. In our survey, we asked a series of specific questions at a point in the interview when rapport was high. From these we were able to code whether a burglary had been committed. Like the Scandinavian or New York study, we were only interested in gross frequencies.

The over-all figures for Metropolitan Toronto suggest that 11 per cent of the population had been involved in an incident which might be classified as breaking and entering or 'unlawfully being in a dwelling.' The proportion of persons in Metropolitan Toronto, from our own interviews, reporting offender experience in any type of burglary (residential or not) was grouped by various demographic variables. The only items significantly related to involvement in burglary are income and sex. The richer the person, the more likely he is to report perpetrating a burglary incident.[8] This may be partly artifactual, as Gold and Gibson suggest that exaggeration in confessions of criminal acts are linked with higher social status. Also males, particularly between ages forty and sixty, are more likely to have reported their involvement than females. However there was a tendency for those living in areas with very high burglary rates to admit to burglary more often.

Of the 11 per cent of the general population who reported engaging in breaking and entering some sort of structure, 42 per cent admitted doing it only once, and 20 per cent only twice. However, 18 per cent admitted three to six times, and 12 per cent seven times or more. In the majority of cases (78 per cent) the latest incident was reported as occurring more than five years ago, but 17 per cent reported that it occurred two to five years ago, and 5 per cent within the last two years.

We did not confine our self-reporting of burglary strictly to residential burglary, as it appears that many persons may have engaged in similar behaviour in relation to schools, factories, etc. However, our interviews with incarcerated burglars suggested that many persons who end up in prison follow a career pattern starting with residential burglary, but then proceeding to other crimes. This is evidenced by the large number of juvenile residential breaking and entering arrests, but the small number of older men in prison for that offence. Our data for self-reports suggests that the commonest burglary experiences were with residences. Over half the offenders said their latest experience was with a residential dwelling, most specifying a single house. Thus, it looks as if single houses are the most common target of people, most of whom are amateurs, and many of whom will only commit burglary once or twice in their lives. Other targets mentioned were schools, gas stations, factories.

Our data further suggest that many of the crimes were of a nature unlikely to result in a report to the police. Only 22 per cent of the latest events reported by offenders involved the offender taking something, and only 12 per cent resulted in any damage being done. When we asked why the offenders had burglarized, 44 per cent mentioned thrills, fun, or excitement as the first reason to the interviewer. Curiosity was also frequently mentioned. Very few persons mentioned stealing as a reason for entering, which is consistent with the nuisance rather than criminal nature of many of the reported offences.

About one in every seven offenders had been caught. Of those caught, only a very small fraction reported being sentenced to jail or prison, or receiving a different sentence. Most said they were either let go by the victim, or, more often, let go by the police.

## Conclusion

In this chapter, we have seen that many members of the public have had contact with the courts and police, but often only once. Most of the court incidents involved traffic violations, while the police incidents were likely to be a crime or a family or neighbour dispute.

We have also seen that of the 11 per cent of the adult respondents who admitted to some personal involvement as an offender in a burglary offence, most remembered an incident taking place more than five years ago, not resulting in a theft or damage, and only very rarely resulting in some sort of formal action by the police; in short, the offence that we saw described by victims in chapter 4. Their typical reason for committing 'burglary' was for fun, thrills, or excitement, and this was usually done only once or twice. In the next chapter, we examine the public's attitudes to crime and punishment.

NOTES TO CHAPTER 6

1  Details on the design of this sample, including how it compares with data for Metropolitan Toronto along selected household variables, are available at the Centre of Criminology, University of Toronto. As in the 1665 cases in the screening sample, the major bias seemed to be the under-sampling of persons under 24, especially males. See also note 9, chapter 20.

2  The median and modal household income was between $11,000 and $15,000. This latter is comparable to known estimates for the census for the Metropolitan area of Toronto where the average income per family (a unit which over-all is slightly smaller than a household) in 1971 was $12,933. About 50 per cent of the weighted sample of persons had attained a completed secondary school level of education.

3  This issue was raised in question 92c, where no distinction was made between a traffic accident or traffic violation, nor among types of traffic violations.

4  Throughout this chapter we have used the chi-square test to give an approximate evaluation of the statistical significance of differences between groups. We have used a sample size ($N$) equal to the size of the unweighted sample, though strictly speaking the chi-square test is for random samples. Generally speaking, using disproportionately stratified samples increases the standard error of population estimates as compared to equally sized random samples. However, it gives us reasonable estimates of the significance of the differences presented, as the most important was just more than marginally significant.

5  Some rough calculations suggest that a maximum of 1.4 per cent of the adult population of Toronto have had court experience with burglary. In any given year, the police record about 17,000 cases of breaking and entering or other 'burglary' related offences. Of these about one in ten results in arrest, i.e., 1700 cases reach the courts. In five years, disregarding multiple victimization, about 8500 cases could reach the courts, which represent about 1.35 per cent of the households in Toronto in 1971. It is then assumed that both adults go to court in an average household.

6  We did not use the methods developed to identify when a burglary incident had occurred to pinpoint the exact date when the police were called. As a result, these data are subject to problems of 'telescoping' the event nearer the time of the interview and to lack of 'recall' so that events occurring further in the past are

likely to have been forgotten. Allowing for these distortions, probably near one in five call the police each year.

7   For a stimulating analysis of the calls received by the Metropolitan Toronto Police, see Shearing (1973).

8   Our findings, based on the small number of cases, tentatively suggest that persons with high socio-economic status have also had more frequent experience with burglary as an offender than those with low socio-economic status. For example, only three-tenths of those with less than secondary schooling reported involvement in two or more burglaries, compared to three-quarters of those with secondary non-university, and five-sixths of those with at least some university education. Also, one-quarter of those with present household incomes of less than $11,000 reported two or more involvements, compared to seven-tenths of those with higher household incomes. The findings are inconsistent with studies (Vaz, Short and Nye, cited in Doleschal, 1970) which have suggested that while there are no differences in percentages of persons reporting offences by socio-economic groups, persons from lower socio-economic groups who do commit crimes, commit them more frequently (and more often of a serious nature).

# 7

# The Attitude of the Public to Crime and Punishment

In the 1960s and 1970s, officials of the criminal justice system have been placing greater emphasis on using prison only as a last resort. Government ministers talk more of rehabilitation, particularly in the community, and less of punishment for its own sake. In this chapter we turn to an examination of public attitudes to crime and punishment in an attempt to discover not only what these attitudes are, but also some of the factors that are associated with them.

The development of the attitude survey technique as an accepted tool of the social scientist and the proliferation of societal concern with crime in the United States and Europe in the last two decades have resulted in many surveys dealing with various aspects of crime or the criminal justice system (Biderman, 1972; Fattah, 1975). Some studies have concentrated on the favourite areas of public concern and fear. Others have analysed socio-demographic factors, such as age, race, income, or education, that are related to variations in public attitudes. Still others have examined attitudes to the police and concern about appearing as a jury member or witness. Yet there has been no systematic analysis of a specific crime, even though criminologists have emphasized continually that 'crime' includes a wide variety of different events, so that one may expect different attitudes to particular types of crime.

From the earlier studies, there are indications that some specific factors would affect public attitudes to particular types of crimes. For instance in studies done for the President's Commission in the United States, it was found that the public fears crimes in which stranger-to-stranger violence is threatened or occurs (USA President's Commission, 1967a: 88). Such crimes are rare; thus the public fears most the crimes that occur least often.

Residential burglary is a common occurrence. The more exceptional events are covered by the mass media, and become the subject of stories from friends and neighbours. It is usually a property crime committed without intentional confrontation; and, as we have seen, there is rarely any physical injury to the victim even in cases of confrontation. In spite of this, there is a potential for violent confrontation in a person's home. Thus, burglary provides a good case study of public attitudes to crime within a broader context.

In the first section of this chapter, the level of societal fear of burglary is examined. This section includes a description of the type and number of precautions taken, the extent of insurance coverage, and the availability of potential weapons for warding off would-be intruders. The next section deals with the public confidence in the police as measured by their view of the proportion of residential burglars who are caught.

In the section following that, the views of the public on sentencing are analysed. The importance of aspects of the offence, as measured by items such as property taken or a history of personal violence by the offender, is contrasted with characteristics of the public such as their age, personal involvement in offences, and the precautions they take.

## Fear

Furstenberg (1971) has shown that a conceptual confusion has been involved in some of the polls which dealt with public fear or concern with a crime. Both the President's Crime Commission (USA, 1967a) and Harris (1968) used 'fear' and 'concern' interchangeably. Furstenberg suggests that we should differentiate the two, since an individual may be troubled by the problem of crime (concern) but may not be in the least afraid of being personally victimized (fear). Thus, for example, it is possible to account for Harris' paradoxical finding for Baltimore – that the people objectively in least danger are the most afraid – by assuming that his indicator of fear reflected more concern for crime as a social problem.

In this section, analysis is undertaken of the fear of victimization of a specific crime, residential burglary, and not the magnitude of concern with residential burglary as a social problem.

Fear of crime, that is of being a victim, can have very significant ramifications on the way of life of persons affected. In the *Life* magazine article (Rosenthal, 1969) which presented some of the Harris poll results, Rosenthal cited increasing use of locks and other means of protection, decreasing use of parks, decreasing downtown trips, and fear of strangers as the result of fear of crime. At the more extreme level, the increased possession of firearms, the development of the home as a fortress, and actually fleeing away from cities to suburbs are examples of what more pronounced fears can do to the way of life of ordinary people.

To measure fear of victimization for Toronto residents, we asked how much they worried about their houses being broken into, and how many Metro residents have ever moved or planned to move because of a fear of crime in general. We also examined the extent to which the public took special precautions against burglary, or carried a weapon that could be used to protect the home, as a measure of fear of crime. To measure the degree to which persons attempt to protect themselves against the material losses of burglary, we have attempted to ascertain the proportion of residents with insurance against theft or damage by thieves in the home and we have examined the proportion who keep records of identification marks of their possessions to facilitate claims or recovery.

Table 7.1 shows how worry about residential burglary is distributed in Toronto. We combined our five degrees of worry into three to allow comparisons with data collected by Ennis (1967) for the entire USA, and Scarr (1973) for selected victims and non-victims in the Washington, DC, area. One in seven white Americans, approximately the same proportion as Torontonians, were very concerned that their residence would be broken into. However, rates of intermediate fear are higher for white Americans than Torontonians. Non-white Americans generally show a higher degree of fear than white Americans and Torontonians. Comparisons between Toronto and the three counties studied in Scarr's study suggest that Torontonians worry less about residential burglary than their Washington counterparts.

The level of worry was cross-tabulated with the police-recorded burglary rate of the area, socio-demographic variables, and experience with the criminal justice system. For this we dichotomized the level of worry into those reporting somewhat, much, or very much worried, and others.

In contrast to the findings of Furstenberg (1972: 22) for Baltimore, we found no relation between level of worry and the police-recorded burglary rate for Toronto. It is possible that the higher levels of crime in Baltimore make it more visible compared to Toronto. Thus, the crime rate has to be above a certain level before fear is affected by real increases in recorded crime.

Those in Toronto, who had called the police (for whatever reason) at least once in their lives were found statistically significantly to worry more about victimization.[1] There was a similar tendency for those with court experience. Thus, consistent with Furstenberg, those who have been victims of a crime are more likely to be worried about victimization in the near future. An alternative explanation, which appears to be consistent with our analysis of police reporting, is that certain members of the public have broad

TABLE 7.1

Distribution of fear of residential burglary victimization in Metropolitan Toronto and the United States

*A. Toronto*

| Degree of worry | Percentage of total population |
|---|---|
| Very much | 6.8 |
| Much | 6.7 |
| Somewhat | 14.0 |
| A little | 31.2 |
| Not at all | 41.3 |
| | 100.0 |

*B. Percentage Comparison with other Studies*

| | Metro Toronto | USA (Ennis) | | | | Washington DC (Scarr) | | | |
|---|---|---|---|---|---|---|---|---|---|
| | | White | | Non-White | | Victim | | Non-Victim | |
| Degree of worry | | Male | Female | Male | Female | Day | Night | Day | Night |
| Very much or much | 13 | 11 | 14 | 22 | 25 | 21 | 22 | 21 | 18 |
| Somewhat | 14 | 36 | 38 | 29 | 37 | 27 | 18 | 16 | 23 |
| A little or none | 73 | 53 | 48 | 49 | 38 | 52 | 60 | 63 | 59 |

TABLE 7.2

Worry of victimization and socio-demographic variables

| Variable | Percentage somewhat or more worried |
|---|---|
| *Sex* | |
| Male | 9.5 |
| Female | 16.7 |
| *p* < .05 | |
| *Age* | |
| Under 25 | 10.6 |
| 26–39 | 14.2 |
| 40–59 | 19.6 |
| 60+ | 4.6 |
| *p* < .05 | |
| *Persons in household* | |
| One | 6.5 |
| Two | 9.6 |
| Three or four | 14.5 |
| Five or more | 24.0 |
| *p* < .01 | |

attitudes that reflect general worry about crime and so are more likely to call the police when faced with a 'suspicious' occurrence.

Income and education do not affect degree of worry. However, women are more likely to be worried by burglary victimization, as shown in Table 7.2. This is closely associated with the findings of the President's Commission which suggest that fear of victimization is basically a fear of (criminal) attack. The findings on sex differences were similar to those found in the Ennis study in Table 7.1. Once again, these tables do not clarify whether physical strength or a constellation of attitudes to do with attachment to the home is important. The relationship between age and degree of fear in Table 7.2 shows an increasing amount of worry as one gets older, followed by a sharp reduction after sixty.[2] This seems reasonable since one's family and possessions usually increase as one gets older, but upon retirement an increasing amount of time is spent with the home occupied and probably less vulnerable to burglary.

Perhaps the most interesting finding of Table 7.2 is the relationship between level of fear of residential burglary and the number of persons in the household. The more persons in the household, the more likely a high level of fear of victimization. This suggests that the worry of criminal victimization is not restricted to oneself, but also to those who are dependents. This finding also ties in with the relationship between age and degree of worry, since the number of dependents at home increases among adults up to late middle age. By retirement, most of the dependents have left home.

As we have seen, Torontonians show relatively low amounts of fear of residential burglary victimization compared to citizens of the United States. As a result, we would expect the proportion of the population who have either moved or intended to move because of fear to be smaller than in the United States (Rosenthal, 1969). Indeed, we found only 5.9 per cent of the respondents had moved or intended to move. Even this figure is probably an overestimate of the effect of fear of burglary in Toronto since a large number of persons now residing in Toronto are immigrants from other areas and may have come from areas where the perceived fear of residential burglary crime is higher. It is even conceivable that many persons move *to* Toronto to escape from the high crime rates of other areas yet still live in a cosmopolitan area.

We also asked the respondents which of a list of items were employed in the home. We felt that the conscientious use of these items represented a clear concern to prevent entry to the home by thieves. Thus, for example, we asked about *special* locks on doors or windows, rather than just locks. Table 7.3 shows the proportion of the households in Toronto that employed each item in the list. Whenever possible, results are compared to data on selected victims and non-victims in Scarr's Washington area study (Scarr, 1973).

The most common device, available to half our sample, was a chain lock which is usually standard in apartment buildings. Also frequently mentioned were dead bolt locks, which are standard equipment on many residences constructed recently, and which are frequently recommended in the crime prevention literature as a good means of preventing a burglar from slipping the lock. Dogs which were either strictly watchdogs (rare) or pets were found in 13 per cent of the households. Security guards, such as one might see in larger apartment buildings, including the private security firm employed in some of Toronto's public housing units, were mentioned by 9 per cent of the household respondents. However, burglar alarms are relatively rare in Toronto.

The indications are that Torontonians are not, in general, building technological fortresses in an attempt to prevent or deter burglars from entering. Fifty-four per cent of the population mentioned using none or only one item in this list of devices; 40 per cent mentioned only two or three devices; and only 6 per cent mentioned four or more ever being used.

We also measured other instrumental actions taken by the general public in response to possible victimization. Just over 3 in 10 household respondents reported keeping a list of serial numbers on goods like TV sets, stereos, etc. This strategy is a very important aid to police in tracking stolen goods to their original owners and has been emphasized by the police as a worthwhile precaution that the public should take. However, the low percentage of offences cleared by charge and the small number of persons who have their goods recovered suggests that this strategy is almost useless for residential burglary.

TABLE 7.3

Rank order of use of burglary and prevention devices in Toronto residences*

| Device | Percentage using device in Toronto | Percentage using device in Washington, DC area | |
|---|---|---|---|
| | | Victims | Non-Victims |
| 1  Chain locks | 49.1 | no similar category | |
| 2  Dead bolt locks | 29.6 | 44.4 | 27.8 |
| 3  Other special locks | 16.1 | 16.7 | 7.8 |
| 4  Special lighting (devices) | 10.2 | no similar category | |
| 5  Security guards | 8.6 | 7.8 | 7.8 |
| 6  Key locks on windows | 7.0 | 4.4 | 1.1 |
| 7  Bars on doors, windows | 5.5 | no similar category | |
| 8  Volunteers patrolling | 3.5 | – | – |
| 9  Burglar alarms | 1.0 | 7.8 | 6.7 |

* Based on 425 cases weighted to represent Toronto's household population.

One in five of the household respondents mentioned that there was a gun or rifle of some sort that could be used for the protection of the home, whether it was there for sport or not. One-third of the sample mentioned that some other sort of weapon (other than a kitchen utensil) could be used for this purpose, with many mentioning items like a baseball bat or hockey stick. Mace and other sprays that temporarily immobilize people were mentioned by less than 1 per cent of the population in spite of the publicity given such devices in the press in the months just previous to the survey.

Sixty-four per cent of the respondents reported that the contents of their dwelling were insured, while 32 per cent did not have insurance, and 4 per cent did not know for certain.[3] Seventy-six per cent of the single houses had insurance, compared to 59 per cent of the attached houses and 54 per cent of apartments.[4]

In our analysis of police records for 1971, we found that there was a higher rate of burglaries for houses than apartments. Thus, those more likely to be victimized were also more likely to be insured. Further, those who live in houses in Toronto are more affluent than those in apartments on the average, and those with higher household incomes are more likely to have insurance against residential burglary. At the upper end of the income scale, over 90 per cent of those whose household earnings were $25,000 or more had such insurance. Of course, these are the people who probably can afford to buy insurance and, at the same time, are likely to have expensive possessions and in this sense cannot afford not to have insurance.

We also found that for those in single or attached houses, over 9 out of 10 of those with household incomes above $11,000 compared to about half with the lower incomes had insurance. However, the proportion having insurance in apartments does not vary much with income. The low rates of insurance coverage here, even where insurance is affordable, suggests that taking this precaution is associated with a lower level of expectation or worry of victimization amongst apartment dwellers, an expectation which is not unrealistic. However, other factors are involved in whether or not burglary insurance is bought, including the requirement of buying insurance to obtain a mortgage.

### Belief in Police Efficiency

Public attitudes to police efficiency, may be related to actions such as calling the police and also to more deeply held views on retribution. At any rate, there is rarely any confrontation in residential burglaries reported to the police. As a result, it is difficult for the police to track down the offender. In addition, the goods taken tend to be cash or at least easily portable and turned into cash, so that it is unlikely that the police can do much to trace the offender through the stolen property. There are, however, a few cases where fingerprints can be used to identify or even convict an offender. If the public feels the police are not effective, they may stop calling the police or may call for long term sentences in the exceptional case, where the offender is caught.

Our questions were centred on a hypothetical example that represents the average residential burglary recorded by the police. It is also an offence for which the police would not be likely to let the offender go free. The question was, 'I would like you to consider a situation where a person breaks into your house while you are out by slipping the lock, and takes $250 in goods and cash. What percentage of persons committing such offences do you think the police would catch? _ per cent.'

The example involves a substantial material loss of $250, which is just below the average loss in police recorded burglary cases in Toronto of $285. It does not involve confrontation, which would greatly increase the chances of the offender being detained by the police, nor damage to the premises since in most cases little or no damage is done. The technique of slipping a lock clarified the element of criminal intent on the part of the offender.

About one-third of the respondents felt that the police would catch less than 10 per cent of the hypothetical offenders. Another third felt that the police would catch between 11 and 50 per cent of the offenders, and about one in ten felt that the police would catch half or more. Twenty per cent of the respondents did not reply to this question.[5] The actual clearance rate by charge for police-recorded burglaries in Toronto was 10 per cent and about half of these resulted in an arrest, both of which figures are probably high relative to other areas in North America. In general, then, even though the police are seen as more effective than they actually are, the public realize that only a small proportion of offenders is caught.

TABLE 7.4

Police effectiveness by demographic, socio-economic, and justice system experience
variables (opinion of the percentage of offenders police would catch in a typical
burglary [add to 100.0])

|  | 10% or less | 11-50% | Over 50% | $X^2$ |
|---|---|---|---|---|
| *Males* | | | | |
| Less than 25 | 33.8 | 60.3 | 5.8 | |
| 26-39 | 42.7 | 50.8 | 6.4 | |
| 40-54 | 73.9 | 18.5 | 7.6 | |
| Over 60 | 34.3 | 33.7 | 32.0 | |
| | | | | $p < .01$ |
| *Females* | | | | |
| Less than 25 | 23.7 | 61.8 | 14.5 | |
| 26-39 | 51.9 | 36.3 | 11.8 | |
| 40-54 | 41.9 | 47.8 | 10.4 | |
| Over 60 | 29.3 | 34.4 | 36.3 | |
| | | | | $p < .01$ |
| *Insurance coverage* | | | | |
| Yes | 39.8 | 52.0 | 8.2 | |
| No | 46.3 | 29.2 | 24.5 | |
| | | | | $p < .01$ |
| *Education* | | | | |
| Less than secondary | 39.7 | 40.9 | 19.5 | |
| Less than university | 43.7 | 47.6 | 8.6 | |
| Some university + more | 51.6 | 41.6 | 6.8 | |
| | | | | $p < .05$ |

In Table 7.4, the level of confidence in police effectiveness is
cross-tabulated with various demographic and other variables. A large
proportion of those who did not have insurance felt that the police would
catch over half the burglars in our typical incident. For these persons, their
lack of insurance coverage would seem to be consistent with their belief in
police effectiveness.

Persons who were between 25 and 55, better educated, and male were
more likely to have a pessimistic and therefore realistic view of police
effectiveness. Both men and women who were either young adults (under 25)
or old (over 55) and those with less education tended to feel that police
would be more effective. Studies in other countries have found that the
young overestimate their chances of getting caught (Willcock and Stokes,
1963; California, 1968).

These relationships are difficult to explain. It is possible that the young
have heard of people who are caught, the persons in the middle age ranges
have heard of crimes where the offender has not been caught, and, the old are
influenced perhaps by the mass media, by what they would like to be the
situation, or, by a belief that was generated before police statistics on

clearance rates were available. Whatever the explanation for these variations, the public is generally pessimistic about police efficiency and has not been fooled by assessments 'derived' from sensational television accounts in which nearly all crime is solved by effective detectives or patrolmen, nor from newspaper accounts of major robberies or other crime which are cleared up more frequently than typical police-recorded offences.

## Attitudes to Sentencing

Public views of sentencing are important not only as a measure of public concern, but also because they may provide an indication of the direction of law reform. While the connection may be tenuous, it is the representatives of the public who have the authority to fund or provide resources which bring about change in the structure of the law itself, and in the justice system or parts of it. Hogarth (1971) has systematically shown that even for a group as homogenous as judges, different sentences are given for similar cases, because the magistrates place different emphasis on reformation or justice as aims of the criminal justice system. An understanding of the views of the general public is important if public policy is to respond to the needs of society and not just to the demands of the vociferous few.

There are now several Gallup polls in both the United States and Canada suggesting that each year the public wants harsher sentencing, or at least believes that sentencing itself is becoming too lenient (Fattah, 1975). Our analysis will try to identify some of the factors behind such feelings. Simultaneously, within the justice system and in criminology itself, most of the progressive programs of the 1960's and 1970's focused on rehabilitative or humanitarian perspectives. Yet it is not known to what extent the public also accepts rehabilitation or indeed humanitarian constraints as important aims in sentencing.

Table 7.5 shows the distribution of the responses to the question, 'What do you think should be the most important aims in sentencing?' The interviewer was instructed to rank the aims if two or more were mentioned, and if the respondent answered in a general way, such as 'prevention,' to probe to distinguish between rehabilitating the offender or deterring others through punishment. The interviewer was also asked to probe for moral denunciation and retribution. The responses were written *verbatim* and coded later.

Moral denunciation (emphasis on the immoral nature of the crime) and retribution (punishment for a wrong-doing) were mentioned as the most important aims by relatively few persons. Over half the sample replied to the interviewer that in the case of burglary, rehabilitation is the most important aim. While it can be argued that this just reflects the respondents' desires to present themselves in a favourable light, it is interesting to note that this is how they did it. In contrast to the shorter and omnibus approach used in

TABLE 7.5

Most important aims in sentencing identified by respondents

| Aims | | Percentage of respondents | |
|---|---|---|---|
| **A.** *General rehabilitation* – to 'cure' offender | | | |
| e.g. | 'correction' | | |
| | 'find out why he committed crime' | | |
| | 'get him to go straight' | 48 | |
| | 'get him some help – psychiatric, family, etc.' | | |
| | 'make him a useful citizen' | | |
| | | | 57 |
| | *Rehabilitation through job training* | | |
| e.g. | 'give opportunity to learn a skill' | | |
| | 'go to a training school' | 9 | |
| | 'rehabilitation by a special school' | | |
| | 'I suppose if he is young we should try to re-train him' | | |
| **B.** *Retribution* – punishment for wrong done | | | |
| e.g. | 'if he had hurt somebody, he should get a beating' | | |
| | 'he deserves it (prison)' | 6 | |
| | 'give him a penalty according to what he did' | | |
| | 'punishment is necessary' | | |
| *Individual deterrence and denunciation* – keep individual away from society, to prevent him from further crime and emphasize that crime was wrong. | | | 28 |
| e.g. | 'to discourage the offender from further burglaries' | | |
| | 'to make offender well aware of his crime' | 22 | |
| | 'making sure he won't do that again' | | |
| | 'the fact that he can't go around breaking the law' | | |
| | 'to punish him so he doesn't repeat it' | | |
| **C.** *General deterrence* – to serve as an example or warning to others | | | |
| e.g. | 'the punishment should be an example to others' | | |
| | 'in order to deter others from committing this crime' | 9 | 9 |
| | 'prison. Just put him behind bars – it will discourage others from doing the same.' | | |
| **D.** *Restitution* – person should compensate victim | | | |
| e.g. | 'to make him work to pay off what he stole' | | |
| | 'if a man steals from me only, I want my money back' | 2 | 2 |
| | 'I like the idea of restitution' | | |
| | 'criminal should pay the victim back' | | |
| *Others* | | | 1 |
| *Don't know* | | | 3 |
| | | | 100 |

Gallup polls, substantial rapport had been established between the interviewer and the respondent; so we have grounds for placing some confidence in these findings. However, we do not know what the respondent meant by 'rehabilitation.' Did he mean to treat the offender humanely? Did he want to see the offender's motivation changed so that he would not commit offences again? If he meant the latter, is he aware of society's success so far? Would he follow the example of United States' Attorney General Saxbe, who attempted to argue for harsher sentences and speedier justice to deter the offender, as he believed that prison and probation were generally unable to reduce the likelihood of reconviction.

A sizeable minority felt that individual and general deterrence were the principal aims of the sentencing process. One suspects that if the levels of crime in Toronto rise to the proportions known in some of the other large North American cities, there might be an increase in the number who express views that deterrence is the principal aim of sentencing. If this resulted in the toughening of the sentencing practices, it is not at all clear that it would have any major effect on the level of crime.

How much use of prison do Torontonians want and what affects these views? To answer this, a specific 'typical' offender was depicted to the respondent. The respondent was then asked what sentence the offender should receive. The typical police-recorded burglary situation presented in the previous question on police effectiveness was used to focus attention. Thus, this situation involved a hypothetical break-in to the respondent's own house (salience); where entry was gained by slipping the lock (criminal intent, no damage); $250 in goods and cash were taken (serious enough to call police); the offender was an English Canadian (to avoid racial or ethnic interactions as much as possible), male (the usual case), 18 years old (average age of known burglars), with no previous criminal charge (not a professional or habitual criminal), who was convicted in court in Metropolitan Toronto (situates the crime locally). For Canada as a whole in 1972, nearly 75 per cent of first offenders in break-and-enter cases were placed on probation, given a suspended sentence, fined, or discharged.[6] Among the views expressed in our population, approximately 60 per cent felt such sentences should be used. Although the comparison is tentative, this suggests that the judge faced by the individual case is slightly less retributive than the general public would be. Fines would be used, however, more often by the general public than by judges.

Of the population in this study, 41 per cent felt that the offender should receive probation, 17 per cent would recommend a short prison term of less than six months, and 17 per cent favoured a longer prison term. Other answers included restitution (5 per cent), and hard labour, psychiatric care, and warnings were mentioned a few times. Three per cent of our weighted sample did not know what the sentence should be.

Table 7.6 is a summary table showing relationships between the severity of the sentence the respondent felt should be given the offender and fear of victimization and insurance coverage.[7] Persons who were 'much' or 'very

TABLE 7.6

Severity of sentence opinion by fear of victimization and insurance coverage
(in percentages)

|  | Severity of sentence | | | |
|---|---|---|---|---|
|  | Fine, probation, suspension | Short term in jail | Long term in jail | $X^2$ |
| *Fear of victimization* | | | | |
| Worry much, very much | 41.6 | 18.7 | 39.7 | |
| Worry somewhat, little, none | 63.8 | 17.5 | 18.6 | |
|  | | | | $p < .01$ |
| *Burglary insurance coverage* | | | | |
| Yes | 66.3 | 17.5 | 16.1 | |
| No | 51.3 | 17.2 | 31.5 | |
|  | | | | $p < .01$ |

much' worried about their residence being broken into were significantly more likely to feel that a more severe sentence should be given to the offender in the typical case than did those who were somewhat worried or less. Similarly, persons who were not covered by insurance against theft from their residence were significantly more likely to want a more severe penalty.

The relationship between fear of victimization and severity of sentence in the case of residential burglary fits in well with US surveys which show both an increasing concern with crime and lawlessness and community sentiments favouring new and tougher laws to deal with these problems.

Importantly, it shows a different picture from those actually experiencing burglary who were generally less interested in jail. Indeed, of the 116 victims 81 per cent suggested that the offender in the hypothetical case would receive probation, a fine, or a suspended sentence, compared to 62.6 per cent of the general public who were not victimized. Fear of victimization is more closely linked to retribution than is anger at actual victimization.

The finding that those not covered by insurance tend to have more severe attitudes to sentencing suggests that the relative gravity of the loss experienced affects sentencing attitudes. Insurance can thus be seen as having a mediating effect on public attitudes to burglary, tending to cushion the effect that an absolute loss of goods has on the severity of sentencing felt by the public. Consistent with this, one would also expect the rich to have a less retributive reaction, as the loss of $250 to a man earning over $25,000 is much less important than to a man earning $7,500. Those respondents whose total household income was $25,000 or more were almost unanimous in selecting the most lenient sentences (fines or probation or suspended sentence). Of those in lower income brackets, only about 60 per cent selected the most lenient sentence for our hypothetical case.

However those not covered by insurance may tend to be drawn from the less advantaged social groupings in terms of education, parental income, and occupation. Thus they may have more punitive views and feel that the offender should take more responsibility for his acts. It was not possible in this study to examine this hypothesis effectively. However sentencing attitudes were not related to education.

No significant differences were found in sentencing attitudes by sex or by experience with the criminal justice system (i.e., been to court or called the police). It was found, however, that over 90 per cent of those who were 25 or younger favoured a lenient sentence, compared to 64 per cent for the remaining categories of population. This seems to suggest that an 'empathy' effect operates in sentencing, since the typical offenders were described as being 18 and without a previous criminal charge. Possibly those who are young can put themselves more easily in the same position as the offender and thus are more likely to be lenient in sentencing in such cases. It is also possible that, since younger persons do not own as much, they are not so concerned about protecting property, and will not see property loss as a serious offence. They may not be as concerned about the invasion of privacy, or the threat of such an invasion that residential burglary poses, as in many cases they may have lived in a co-operative or even communal types of arrangements where privacy is not desired as much.

Two other items were included in attitudes to restitution by the offender, and in how the public would feel towards the adoption of a sentence of a period of unpaid work for the community. These are items being considered for inclusion in sentencing procedures in Canada, in part because of the tremendous cost and inefficiencies of a criminal justice system based predominantly on prison. Our typical example of residential burglary is a pivotal case where on the one hand the perpetrator is an amateur, the value of property taken is moderate, no violence is intended or involved, but on the other hand, such instances are common and so an expression of non-prison measures could have an important effect on criminal justice costs.

When we asked, 'Should the offender have to pay restitution?' in connection with our hypothetical case, about five-sixths of the weighted sample representing the adult population over 18 years of age in Metropolitan Toronto replied affirmatively. Unfortunately, however, the question was not phrased in such a way as to make clear whether the public would support restitution as an alternative to regular sentencing procedures, or as a supplement.

The majority did seem to favour the suggestion of adopting a sentence of unpaid work for the community as an alternative sentence in our hypothetical case. Seventy-four per cent replied yes, 23 per cent replied no, and 3 per cent replied something else to the question: 'If the offender could be sentenced to a number of weeks or days of unpaid work for the community, would you adopt such a sentence?'

It looks as if the public in Toronto is receptive to unpaid community work as an alternate sentence to fines, probations, or jail terms from a hypothetical case. However, if these opinions are matched with the feelings of victims in the face of real experiences, discussed in chapter 4, our analysis clearly suggests that, unlike capital punishment (Fattah, 1975), sentencing procedures and the criminal justice system are lagging behind what the public would tolerate.

### Factors Affecting the Public's Attitude

We have now shown how fear of victimization, income, and insurance coverage are linked to the desire for prison sentences. This next section turns to analysis of how variations in the burglary event itself can affect attitudes to sentencing.

We undertook to examine this aspect of sentencing by systematically changing, one at a time, hypothetical aspects of either the offence or the offender and then seeing whether a more or less severe sentence would be given compared to the hypothetical 'modal' offence described earlier. A five-point scale was used to determine the severity, with the categories being labelled 'much more severe,' 'more severe,' 'about the same,' 'less severe,' and 'much less severe': the midpoint of the scale, 'about the same,' was used in reference to the respondent's opinion of sentencing in the original question involving the hypothetical modal situation.

We based the severity measure on the respondent's opinion of the sentence that should be given in a 'modal' case and so examined the variation in opinions about the appropriate severity of sentencing rather than absolute levels. Thus, 'much more severe' does not mean that a long prison sentence was indicated, as in many instances it may refer to a jail sentence instead of probation or indeed the respondent may have only meant more severe probation.

In Table 7.7 the mean score is the average of all the scores given (weighted to represent the adult population of Toronto), while the standard deviation gives an indication of the consensus of opinion. The larger the standard deviation, the more the disagreement in relative severity of the sentence that should be given. The mean change in severity gives the average change from the 'about the same' sentence that each item elicited. Thus, changing the offence from one where the residence was entered by slipping the lock to one where the door was broken down increased the sentence severity score by an over-all average of .43, the direction being indicated by the plus sign. A decrease in severity is indicated by a negative sign.

TABLE 7.7

Relative rank of factors affecting public opinion on the severity of sentence

|  | Mean severity score* | Standard deviation |
|---|---|---|
| 1 Two previous assault convictions (none) | 1.44 | 0.57 |
| 2 Two previous shoplifting convictions (none) | 0.90 | 0.54 |
| 3 Offender aged 30 (older) | 0.68 | 0.60 |
| 4 $3000 taken (more valuable) | 0.60 | 0.64 |
| 5 Breaking down door (more damage) | 0.43 | 0.52 |
| 6 Warehouse or factory (compared to house) | 0.28 | 0.61 |
| 7 Victim pressing (none) | 0.09 | 0.40 |
| 8 Insurance coverage (none) | 0.05 | 0.38 |
| 9 Provincial compensation (none) | 0.02 | 0.32 |
| 10 Immigrant (less Canadian) | 0.02 | 0.34 |
| 1 Offender aged 14 (younger) | −0.45 | 0.66 |
| 2 Unlocked door (easier entry) | −0.38 | 0.61 |
| 3 More psychiatric help (none) | −0.17 | 0.48 |
| 4 Female (male) | −0.02 | 0.32 |

* Plus score indicates the public felt a more severe penalty should be given; negative score, a less severe penalty.

The two most important items affecting sentence severity scores are the existence of previous assault and shoplifting convictions.[8] Because of the especially high severity score given a previous assault conviction, it seems that major consideration is given to the probability of a confrontation involving violence, a finding which reinforces the notion that the crucial element in the public's attitude to sentencing is the fear of personal injury.

Age of the offender, unlike sex or immigrant status, is an important factor in the public's attitude to sentence severity. Offenders around age 14 were generally thought to deserve less severe sentences, while offenders around 30 were felt to deserve more severe penalties than the 'modal' 18-year-old offender. Whether the door was locked (a measure of carelessness by the victim) or broken down and the value of goods or cash taken were other items which were salient in producing changes in opinions of sentence severity in the directions expected. Surprisingly in view of the different maximum sentences available, most people felt that breaking into a warehouse or factory should be punished more severely. This finding may come from an assumption by the respondent that offences in warehouses involved larger sums of money.

**Insurance Coverage, Sentencing Attitudes, and Belief in Police Efficiency**

In this chapter, our findings indicate that the level of societal fear of residential burglary in Toronto is less than in the United States. Torontonians

TABLE 7.8

Principal relationships found in chapter 7

*Insurance*
- Those living in detached houses tend to have theft insurance more often than those in attached homes or apartments.
- Richer persons tend to have theft insurance more often than poorer ones.

*Fear of victimization*
- People who have called the police or had court experience tend to worry about victimization more than those who have not.
- People in larger households tend to worry more than those in smaller ones.
- Women worry more than men.
- People in middle age tend to worry more than people who are young or old.

*Confidence in the police*
- People not covered by insurance tend to think that the police catch more burglars than they actually do (and more than those with insurance estimate are caught).
- Women, persons over sixty, and those with less than secondary school education tend to feel unrealistically over-confident in the police more often than men, those sixty and under and those with more education.

*Sentencing*
- Those who worry more about victimization felt harsher sentences were appropriate more often than those who worry less.
- Poor persons and those who were not covered by insurance felt harsher sentences were appropriate more often than those who were rich or not covered.
- Young adults under 25 tended to feel *lenient* sentences were more appropriate more often than others.

are not building fortresses or moving because of crime. A sizeable minority, however, do keep lists of serial numbers or have guns or other weapons that can be used for household protection. A majority have insurance policies protecting them against residential theft.

Torontonians were found generally to overestimate how effective police are in catching burglars. When offenders are caught, most people felt that the conventional aims of imprisonment were most important. Most, however, were also in favour of some effective form of restitution and were generally lenient in their sentencing attitudes. Table 7.8 summarizes the main relationships found in this chapter.

Richer people were seen as being both able to afford insurance, and as having more (in our absolute sense) to lose without insurance. Apartment dwellers were at less risk of being seriously burglarized, and generally not as affluent as home-dwellers, and hence had less need of insurance.

The findings grouped under fear of victimization suggest that fear levels were increased by the presence of more persons who were vulnerable to violence. Fear of victimization and calling the police appear related. Those particularly vulnerable to the economic and possible physical consequences of burglary tend to be overconfident of police success in catching burglars. This

TABLE 7.9

Summary of stepwise multiple regressions showing the independent effects of insurance coverage explaining belief in police effectiveness

| Variable entered | $R^2$ | $\beta$ |
|---|---|---|
| *Belief in police effectiveness* | | |
| *(more recorded offences cleared by arrest)* | | |
| Age (older) | .055 | .277 |
| Court experience (had court experience) | .077 | .109 |
| Sex (female) | .078 | .056 |
| Income (poor) | .083 | −.028 |
| Insurance coverage (no coverage) | .117 | .197* |
| *F = 14.34 with 5,368 d.f. p < 0.01 | | |
| *Severity of sentence (harsher sentences requested by)* | | |
| Worry (fearful) | .008 | −.237 |
| Income (poor) | .014 | −.037 |
| Age (older) | .015 | .282 |
| Insurance Coverage (no coverage) | .041 | 1.60+ |
| *F = 3.67 with 4,344 d.f. p < .01 | | |

may involve a degree of wish-fulfilment or reflect the lack of relevant experience to make more realistic judgments.

Severity of sentence was seen to be affected by factors concerned with the relative effect of burglary on a household. Where fear levels were high (entailing a higher emotional cost to the victim in the event of burglary, it is assumed) or where no insurance is employed to offset the economic effect of burglary, or where the burglary is perceived as being substantial relative to one's income, more severe sentences are advocated.

As fear increases there will be a rising desire for more severe penalties for the offender. And so, as levels of burglary in Toronto rise, or are believed to rise, there will be a call for harsher sentences. Insurance coverage will also increase. As fear appears to be based on notions of potential injury or violence tied in with burglary, public knowledge of the rarity of such incidents even in cases involving confrontation might be effective in avoiding beliefs in non-existent crime waves and also reducing fear generally.

It was noted earlier in the chapter that persons not covered by insurance tended to believe that the police are more effective in solving burglaries than they really are. It was also found that those not covered by insurance were harsher in their sentencing attitudes. The importance of insurance to both sentencing attitudes *and* belief in police effectiveness is clearly illustrated in Table 7.9. Adding the variable of insurance coverage in both cases increased significantly our ability to predict a person's belief in police effectiveness and sentencing attitudes even after we had considered the effects of other explaining variables.

TABLE 7.10

Belief in police effectiveness by severity of sentence, for those with no insurance

| | | Belief in police effectiveness (% that would be caught) | | |
| --- | --- | --- | --- | --- |
| | | >10% | 11-50% | >50% |
| Severity of | Probation, etc. | 30 | 15 | 20 |
| sentence | Short term | 8 | 5 | 2 |
| | Long term | 13 | 9 | 3 |

$X^2 = 5.82$, not significant, $N = 105$

These findings suggest that having insurance is a good indicator of a constellation of attitudes regarding confidence in the police and sentencing. Particularly, these findings seem to suggest that there exist persons who do not take out insurance because of an unrealistic belief in police efficiency, and that when their idealistic views are violated, harsh reactions to the violators can be detected.

To test our hypothesis, we examined the relationship between belief in police effectiveness and public attitudes to sentencing, controlling for insurance coverage. The results indicate that attitudes about police effectiveness are unrelated to attitudes to sentencing, both for those insured and those not. Table 7.10 shows the results for those not covered by insurance.

Thus, our hypothesis, while intriguing, is not validated by our data for the abstract case.

NOTES TO CHAPTER 7

1   The percentage of those who had ever called the police who were somewhat or more worried was 18, and of those who had never called the police it was 8, $p < .01$.
2   The small number of persons over 60 worried is inconsistent with this; but our sample contained few people over 60 so that we have emphasized the broad trends only.
3   Fire and theft insurance (usually sold as a package) is often required to obtain mortgages. As most apartments are rented, apartment dwellers are less likely to have such coverage than house owners.
4   This difference was statistically significant using a chi-square test, $p < .01$.
5   These are not included in the remaining analysis.
6   The Law Reform Commission (1976) showed that sentences of first offenders in break-and-enter cases in September 1972 for Canada were distributed as follows: imprisonment (some of these were for only one day), 25.3 per cent; fine, or fine or days in default, 1.6 per cent; probation or suspended sentence, 67.4 per cent; discharge, 5.8 per cent ($n = 190$).
7   For the purposes of analysis, responses to this question were divided into three major categories. The least serious were those which did not involve a jail or prison term. In this category, were included fines, probation (suspended sentence with supervision), and suspended sentence without supervision, but not restitution. The

intermediate category was composed of prison sentences from a few days to a few months, while the serious category consisted of prison terms of six months or longer.

8   The findings in Table 7.7 concerning the relative importance of the different items in affecting sentence severity were confirmed when we asked the respondents to rank the items which the respondents felt *should be* most important in determining sentences. The first choice of 42 per cent of the population was the change from no charges to two previous assault convictions, followed by two previous shoplifting convictions (18 per cent) and age factors (14 instead of 18 by 10 per cent and 30 instead of 18 by 9 per cent).

# 8

# Conclusions and Implications

For the last decade, a widening schism has been apparent between the expectations of the public and the ability of the criminal justice system to meet them. On one hand, crime has been increasing and is now seen as a major social problem. Studies find the public increasingly concerned with crime and demanding more police and longer and tougher sentences — basically more of the same against the criminal (Gallup, 1969; Furstenberg, 1971; Gallup, 1974; Fattah, 1975).

On the other hand, as a result of systematic evaluative research, the extent to which crime is reduced through traditional law enforcement and criminal justice measures is being seriously questioned (Kelling, 1974; Hood and Sparks, 1970; Robison and Smith, 1971; Martinson, 1974; and Waller, 1974). In addition, costs for the provision of these services have been increasing dramatically. Police costs in Canada, for instance, have more than doubled within a decade. In reaction to this dilemma, criminal justice officials have been considering decriminalizing certain behaviour, encouraging the diversion of offenders out of the criminal justice system, and using alternatives to incarceration at time of sentence.

In the preceding seven chapters, we have focused attention on the victim's and the public's experience of residential burglary in Toronto. In this chapter, we will see how the results of this analysis have added to our general knowledge of crime, criminal justice, and the public reaction to both. We will also try to see what social action might rationally be taken, based on this understanding. We will try to make proposals that will meet not only the needs of individual victims in their conflicts with offenders, but also more general societal needs to prevent and alleviate harm, and that, at the same time, will continue to distinguish certain forms of behaviour as morally wrong.

## Burglary and the Public

### AN APPROACH

We have systematically examined data on the public's views and experiences of a 'pivotal' type of crime. We tried to understand the nature of the crime itself, the extent to which victims precipitated or were more vulnerable to this crime, its general impact on both victims and the public, and the factors associated with the retributive reaction of the public to both the offence and the offender.

The crime of residential burglary is pivotal for several reasons. Attitude surveys show that people are concerned about residential burglary, but relatively few take precautions against it. It involves intrusion into personal territory and fear of personal violence, yet personal injury rarely occurs. It results in persons being imprisoned for short periods and many being placed on probation, but the maximum penalty in Canada is life imprisonment. It is one of the commonest of serious crimes, accounting in 1971 for a total of over $40 million of recorded cases in Canada, but in any one burglary relatively little of dollar value is taken. It is, therefore, an offence where the public and legislators might be prepared to consider using police, criminal justice, and imprisonment less, but where feelings of vengeance and concern exist.

Our major analysis was carried out on the data from interviews with more than 1600 households in Metropolitan Toronto in 1974. We also studied in detail more than 5000 police records of burglary-related events that occurred in 1971 in Metro Toronto. These were linked with 1971 census data to enable us to analyse the distribution and demographic correlates of residential burglary victimization, and so develop an equation that might predict accurately the rates of burglary for Toronto's census tracts. A small survey of convicted residential burglars was organized in a non-systematic sample of both juveniles and adults, where we were interested in what aspects of the victim, his residence, or the neighbourhood led to their selection by the offender.

### THE EXTENT OF BURGLARY IN TORONTO

We found that in a 12-month period, 26.4 dwellings per 1000 may be expected to be burglarized in Toronto. If loss occurred, the individual event involved an average loss of $345 and rarely involved any threat or actual harm to the residents. It probably occurred when the dwelling was empty, at night or in the evening.

Sixty-two per cent of the events were reported to the police, compared to between 43 and 52 per cent in major cities in the USA. Even if this reporting rate was higher, the burglary rate itself was lower than cities examined in the USA. This was true for both police-recorded burglary rates and for independent survey rates, such as the 'National Crime Panel' (e.g., 1974a to 1974b). Toronto's victimization burglary rate is only 40 per cent of the lowest figure reported by the National Crime Panel for major cities.

The police-recorded burglary rate was also lower than in the case of cities in the USA. Over-all, Toronto's figures were about the same for average value of property stolen as reported to the police in the USA. A large amount of burglary reported to police was found to be petty, that is, resulting in a value of goods taken of less than $100. Toronto was found to be a little unusual in this respect as more petty burglary seemed to be reported here than, for instance, in Washington, DC, or in Montreal. In less than 1 per cent of the burglaries was $5000 or more netted.

The 'clearance rate' of residential burglaries is relatively low compared to other indictable criminal code infractions, with about 10 per cent of the reported occurrences resulting in a charge being laid. There was usually little or no restitution or recovery of property involved in residential burglary. Property stolen was likely to be covered by insurance more often for house dwellers than apartment dwellers. 'Big' jobs were more likely to occur in houses than in apartments, with entry through doors most of the time. Slightly fewer 'big' jobs were cleared than 'medium' and 'small' ones, but the likelihood of property stolen being covered by insurance was greater the larger the burglary. There did not appear to be any clear temporal patterns for residential burglary in Toronto.

**Reduction of Residential Burglary**

Traditionally both the police and social scientists have been trying to understand and prevent crime by looking at the captured offender or the reported offence. Their work has concentrated on why particular sorts of persons commit crime. We have continued some of this tradition by examining what sorts of areas of cities produce crime. We have confirmed the traditional findings that areas with more people who are unemployed and who are less established in the neighbourhood are likely to have more crime. However, we have shown for Toronto that areas with more immigrants and more minority racial groups do not have higher burglary rates. We have also shown that a city such as Toronto, going through rapid growth, has less crime than major US cities. In general, these facts are consistent with the theories of

crime, that it is encouraged by relative poverty and by situations v
relatively large number of persons without major social attachments.

Newman has argued that communities should be designed to
defensible space. It will take a long time to realize this goal as changes can be
made only in new housing developments. If planners are to modify the
physical structure, they should also consider the social structure. We have not
been able to examine all the reasons why Toronto has a lower crime rate than
cities in the United States. However, we have suggested that the cultural
heritage, the selective immigration policy, the high rates of employment, and
general affluence are all important. We also see the need to find more
effective ways of integrating younger men into the society, if reduction of
burglary is an important social goal.

Of course, burglary is a relatively rare event, causing little economic or
social harm when it occurs. At the societal level, it is the abstract fear of
confrontation that can affect people's lives and, indeed, for victims, distort a
relatively trivial event. Over-all the $40 million that are lost each year by
victims does not create a major social problem compared to inflation, traffic
deaths, or even flu. Before we consider how a largely inevitable, endemic
problem can be alleviated rather than cured, we shall first identify some
victim-related factors that can be easily influenced.

## HOUSES

For both houses and apartments, we found in Toronto that richer households
are proportionately more likely targets. However, where houses were located
in or near public housing, affluence lost its importance and those residences,
more often left unattended, were the more likely to be burglarized. Our
findings suggest that programs aimed at increasing residential security,
through educating the public to 'harden targets' by, for example, being more
careful in habits such as locking doors, will be ineffective in Canada. In
addition, taking other special precautions in the form of special locks, special
lighting, bars over windows, and so on does not seem to be of major
importance, though our findings are less precise here.

For houses, strategies of increasing surveillance and the number of hours
that a residence is occupied seem to be the most effective victim-related way
of reducing residential burglary in areas not near public housing. However, in
high crime-prone areas, particularly near public housing projects or in areas
with low social cohesion, the only effective means of protection is ensuring
that the house is occupied as much as possible.

Given the considerations of occupancy and surveillability, the risk of
victimization is probably reduced if the dwelling is occupied by the
conventional family of two parents and children with one parent working.
Not only is the likelihood of occupancy very much greater, but children

provide several more 'eyes' for surveillance, and child-related activities are efficient natural mechanisms for providing neighbourhood acquaintances and social cohesion. In addition, we have seen that fear of victimization increases with household size, suggesting that there is an increased motivation for persons with large families to protect their kin from the relatively remote chance of harm through residential burglary.

If we want to prevent burglary, we should be trying to mix residences in which occupants are largely absent within an area of houses with children. Similarly, it may be functional for prevention of crime to retain distinctly ethnic areas; where several generations occupy the same household, the house is unlikely to be vacant for long periods.

APARTMENTS

Our findings for apartments question the conclusions drawn from the 'defensible space' literature. The location of the apartment in the building, affluence, and the presence of a doorman were much more important factors in determining the likelihood of victimization than items such as social cohesion. There were other notions that the literature on defensible space suggested should be important to the likehihood of victimization but were not: being located in blocks with mixed industrial and residential usage, sharing a corridor with more units, being in an apartment with commercial uses, and, finally, less use of corridors for playing or informal meetings. These findings indicate that further research and testing needs to be done to ensure that the strategies of defensible space in crime prevention are appropriately focused if they are to be applicable to multiple-dwelling structures outside publicly subsidized projects of the cities studied by Newman. In view of the present popularity of the ideas entailed in defensible space, this research should be done in a variety of multiple dwelling structures at different socio-economic levels before general design principles are accepted.

The implementation of defensible-space mechanisms is also problematic in other senses. They involve very clearly a change in lifestyle, since what is advocated is architectural or design innovations which would not only improve surveillability and hence *decrease privacy*, but presumably also increase the likelihood or inevitability of more intimate social interactions with one's neighbours. These mechanisms also involve long periods of planning and construction and substantial funding.

While there is no doubt that strategies that reduce opportunity can reduce crime, it is questionable as to how effective defensible space is or whether the costs justify the benefits. These issues require more social scientific and public debate. For example, it is possible that the public is willing to trade off an increase in crime rates for privacy; particularly as such increases may be small in percentage terms, but still leave the absolute crime rate and probability of being victimized below tolerable limits.

On the positive side, our findings suggest that strategies of restricting entry in apartments are a particularly effective means of preventing burglary, especially through the employment of a doorman. Approximations to this, such as working intercom systems, might also provide some protection. A doorman, commissionaire, or security guard could be made mandatory in apartment buildings located in areas of high crime rates, or in buildings of vulnerable residents (e.g., where most residents are absent for a large part of the day). The costs of crime protection would then be met by the developers or owners rather than indirectly by the general public through support of the police.

A major reason given for reluctance to employ the opportunity-reduction approach advocated above is that crime is supposedly displaced rather than reduced. The argument is that if you make crime harder to commit in one area, it will increase in another. The usual forms of displacement cited are to other targets, to other forms of crime, and to other areas (Reppetto, 1976). Thus, if programs are instituted that make it difficult to burglarize private houses, there may be an increase in apartment burglaries; perhaps robberies will rise if burglaries are made harder; or the offenders will shift attention to an area where the targets are easier.

In all of these displacement arguments, there is a belief that most property crime is committed by offenders who examine the various risk-return ratios before deciding on a particular crime. The motivation of the offender is also assumed to be independent of the opportunities. However, from our interviews with incarcerated burglars and our self-report data we found that, in most instances, burglary is not an act involving lengthy planning or premeditation, but is rather one involving the seizure of inviting opportunities by relative amateurs. We suggest that reducing the opportunities of performing easy burglaries will tend to eliminate, rather than displace, a significant amount of this crime, since the choice is not seen by amateurs as one between illegal alternatives, but is essentially between an inviting illegal opportunity and no opportunity at all (i.e., legal alternatives for getting kicks or material possessions). Many of these amateurs would not housebreak if the act required sophisticated skills or a significant degree of commitment to crime.

### Alleviating Victim Concern and Harm

So we have seen that residential burglary is usually a minor offence which could be prevented by increased surveillability and presence of persons or by grander scale social policies that reduce economic disparities and involve young males more effectively in society. It seems that some progress could be made with the former, but it is unlikely that residential burglary is a sufficiently major problem to warrant the latter and so perhaps we should accept it as endemic. But what is the nature of the harm done to victims, how are they concerned, and what might be done to alleviate such harm?

## PUBLIC CONCERN

Our findings indicate that one in seven persons was very worried about their residence being broken into. This is a finding similar to those in the USA, though the number with intermediate fear levels in Toronto was lower. Since the proportion of dwellings burglarized in Toronto is significantly lower than in most American cities, this high degree of worry may reflect the amount of US crime coverage in the Canadian media. In terms of the spiral of increasing crime and increasing fear, we found that the more people worry about being victimized, the more likely they are to want longer prison sentences. And we found Canadians to be much more severe in their sentencing attitudes than one would expect from the real level of crime in Canada. Similarly, we have seen that those not insured tend to be more severe in their views.

We have also discovered from the data that the victims' immediate reaction tended to be surprise, followed by an unspecific feeling of being upset, and then anger and fear. Female respondents mentioned fear much more often than did males. We also found that a very large proportion of those victimized, especially women, suffered from minor but long-term effects as a result of victimization. The most frequent was a general increase in suspicion or distrust, followed by fear of being alone, and fear of entering the residence or rooms within the residence. However, only 30 per cent of the victims felt at the time of the interview (as opposed to the event) that they would like to see the offender in prison. This suggests that, while victims have strong emotional reactions to victimization possibly based on what *could* have happened, the *actual* behaviour involved and the relatively trivial loss usually sustained (as evidenced for example by 41 per cent of the victims reporting no loss) mitigates against a desire to see the offender imprisoned. Even of those who suffered a property loss or damage, who had not recovered goods, two-thirds said they would be prepared to settle the case out of court at the time of the interview.

Our survey findings also suggest that police reports or research based on police data underemphasize the extent of confrontation that occurs in residential burglary. Rates of confrontation are important aspects of crime for planners, since it is fear of criminal attack which seems to be the basis of public fear of crime. In 44 per cent of the burglaries reported in our study, the respondent recalled that someone was home at the time, and in 21 per cent of the cases an actual confrontation between victim and offender occurred. However, most of the confrontations involved only some sort of verbal exchange, in which the offender tried to justify his presence.

The generally peaceful nature of burglary is consistent with its amateurish nature. More than one person in ten reports having committed a burglary. Our victim-survey findings reinforce notions based on police data that most burglars use relatively unsophisticated techniques to get into a home. Most just walk in, or break open a door or window. Cash, electronic items, and jewellery were, in that order, the most popular items taken. In many cases, nothing is actually stolen, or the attempt is thwarted.

This study has suggested that the fear of crime may be as important a problem as actual crime. Thus efforts must be made to avoid processes that increase this anxiety, such as the dramatization of slowly increasing crime rates by police departments or politicians in attempts to obtain more resources (Weis, 1974), the presentation of dramatic cases and global statistics by the press, or efforts to induce the public to take precautions by focusing on extreme threats of crime.

Some reduction in this fear might be achieved by more frequent publicity of the peaceful nature of residential burglary. The police officer called to the house could do more to provide reassurance to the victim by explaining the amateur and non-violent nature of most residential burglars. Further a major preoccupation of the police is to respond to calls for assistance in an effective manner. In most burglaries reported to the police, however, there is little that they can do to recover goods or catch the offender. Although only a small percentage of the cases resulted in an offender being caught, two-thirds of those in our victim sample who called the police were satisfied with police action, usually because fingerprints were taken or the case was followed-up in person. This suggests that a policy of deliberate follow-up of cases to inform the public what to expect and what happened may have beneficial 'public relations' effects for the police in the short run.

Faced by rising costs of policing and an expectation that crime will be reduced by police, the public and its selected representatives will be continually dissatisfied. Money, public frustration, and victim fear and property loss could all be saved, if police departments changed their response to burglary. It would seem the public would be better served by a reassuring explanation of what the police can do, what the chances are of the offence re-occurring, and whether a follow-up of police action is worth taking. While this may appear to give a licence to the petty offender, it would enable police to concentrate more on ensuring conviction of those more serious offenders who are committed to crime, who steal large sums of money, or who use threats of personal injury. It is also an area where the armed and highly trained 'law enforcement officer' is needed only if the event is in progress. For most burglaries, a civilian or at most a 'peace officer,' would be ideal. As the goal of police action would become one of recording the details of property lost, it would appear that much more recording could be done over the telephone with civilian employees. A telephone call back to report progress or admit no action would provide positive feedback to the public.

COMPENSATION THROUGH INSURANCE

This study indicated factors that are associated with a higher likelihood of burglary. If insurance rates were to be tied to risk, who would pay more than the average? Fortunately for equity, richer persons are the more likely victims and so would pay higher insurance rates. Persons who stay at home during the week or pay the extra cost of doormen would pay lower premiums. However, the other factors pose more of a moral dilemma. Households located near publicly subsidized housing or in an area with a high proportion of single males over 15 are substantially more likely to be victimized and so might be requested to pay higher premiums. In this case, state subsidized insurance or compensation would make more sense.

Should the state require and provide minimum insurance to provide compensation for the first $100 or $1000 stolen? Such insurance would have covered more than 92 and 96 per cent respectively, of the incidents in this study. This could be combined with a small deductible amount to avoid expensive overhead on many minor incidents. Individuals would then be able to supplement the state insurance if they had goods of outstanding value. Safeguards, of course, would have to be built into any scheme to prevent fraudulent collection of insurance and to prevent a large increase in 'reported' burglary.

As Fooner (1969, 1971a and b) has shown, travellers' cheques can reduce actual losses of cash and ease recovery substantially. People might be encouraged by the state or financial incentives or both to use more travellers' cheques in place of cash that they need for emergencies.

As we have seen, the principal financial costs of burglary in Canada are a minimum of $40 million in property transfers associated with an estimated 400,000 residential burglary events each year. Of these, approximately 250,000 are recorded by the police, and about 10 per cent or 25,000 reported crimes are cleared by charge. We have not tried to estimate the costs of police or lawyers, courts or corrections time, but it would not be unreasonable to assume they exceed $100 per case or a total of $25,000,000.

Already there have been efforts through bail reform acts to avoid the pre-trial incarceration costs. Should residential burglary involving only theft still be punishable in the Criminal Code? Should it become an administrative offence, if the property damage is less than $50, that only becomes a crime the third time the offender is caught? Should it be a typical candidate for pre-court diversion? Should it be the subject of alternatives to incarceration?

The fact that 38 per cent of the residential burglaries in Metropolitan Toronto are not reported to the police indicates that some citizens prefer to avoid the criminal justice system for some residential burglary offences. Yet 44 per cent of the general public had been to court at some time and 51 per cent had called the police for other reasons.

Reporting to police was more likely if the event was thought to have occurred very recently, if entry had been through a window, if the value of the property stolen was at leas $100, if any damage was done, and if there was much disarrangement of the victim's belongings.

Our findings also suggest that the public wants to activate the criminal justice system when there is something to be gained or when the event involves an element of physical force. As so many events are not reported to the police and many others are reported only out of moral duty, the legal definition of the criminal offence might be brought more closely into line with the public's view. In addition, only one in four of the victims recalled any feeling that they wanted to see the offender punished in the criminal justice system, thus suggesting that trends in public policy towards decriminalization and less use of the criminal justice system are strongly supported for this type of crime.

For the majority of the less serious events (under $200 in property stolen and damage done) the crime might be made exclusively a 'summary offence,' requiring restitution to the victim, but with only a fine as a general deterrent and to denounce the act generally. Further, the discretion exercised by both the public and police in not prosecuting should be given more publicity, so that those who feel only morally bound to report are free to drop legal action. This should free expensive police time for more effective investigation of those cases where there is a probability of catching the offender or where the seriousness of the offence warrants special measures.

For more serious offences involving larger sums of money, the main concerns of the public are to provide restitution and discourage burglary in general. In the individual case, some financial or possibly compulsory work penalty for the community would appear to meet public needs for denunciation of the act, provide possible general deterrence of other potential offenders, and allay the mild concerns for vengeance. In those rare instances where violence is threatened or occurs, this study has not been able to suggest appropriate action. However, these cases should be treated by police and courts in a clearly different manner, so that the public fear of physical harm is not generalized to the typical amateurish property crimes.

The public also mentioned frequently that they reported to the police because of their insurance policy required it or to get their goods returned. With a wider use of insurance both these functions could be handled by the insurance companies in conjunction with a central data bank for lost property.

This could lead to a substantial saving in police time and could be improved by a change in the Criminal Code, so that an indictable offence could be deemed to occur only when there had been threat of physical injury or the loss or damage was $200 or more. If the public knew who had committed a lesser burglary they would report to the police. When three such reports had been made to the police, the offender could be arrested and charged. Thus minor burglary for the third time would become an offence. For these lesser offences there would be civil compensation procedures.

The previous section has argued ways of alleviating public concern through deliberate action to reduce fear of victimization by public information. It is possible that the vision of wider insurance would also lead to a more tolerant view of sentencing, which in turn would enable the reduction of costs in imprisonment and over-all savings to society in dollars alone as well as human suffering. Unfortunately, in a survey, it is not possible to distinguish cause from effect, but such policies can be justified on their own and should be tried with an evaluation component.

Does the fact of not being insured result in beliefs that insurance is a waste of money, over-confidence in the police, and a desire for harsher sentences, or, are these beliefs just part of a set of personality attributes that leads one not to take out insurance? If so would the provision of insurance or state compensation change all these views? Alternatively would views be changed by information on the relative ineffectiveness of harsh sentences or police activity in relation to burglary? This is probably an area where further experimentation by social psychologists, perhaps in laboratories or tightly controlled experiments, might lead to a clearer understanding of the causal nexus.

### Further Research

In examining the implications of the findings of this report for legislation, policy, and operations in criminal justice, we have suggested a number of areas where the frontiers of knowledge can be advanced only by deliberate experiments undertaken by the public or private sectors. These experiments would have to follow controlled designs and include a systematic component to evaluate effectiveness of the new program. They would provide more effective understanding of the impact of various alternative strategies not only on the incidence and extent of harm from burglary, but also the needs, fears, and reactions of the public.

The study itself has been exploratory in nature and has shown some of the questions that can be answered through a survey of a sample of representatives of households and offenders. However, it has identified many more questions than it has answered and, we hope, will stimulate interest among researchers to pursue knowledge that is not only of interest in itself, but can be relevant to a society obsessed, concerned, and in some cases frightened by crime. If public policy is to be guided by a thorough understanding of why the public reacts in the way it does, or why burglary occurs, then the tools of the experimental psychologist and laboratory experiments must be used. There is also knowledge that can only be developed from cooperation between architects and social scientists in understanding the relationship between surveillability, occupancy, and territorial imperatives to the structuring of human settlements.

This reasearch forms a small part of a broader area of interest. The analysis of defensible space that we have undertaken was part of the broader issue of the relation between social science and architecture. Ravetz (1973) has suggested that the architectural research on defensible space has underlined the potent effect of structure on criminal behaviour. Sociological research has questioned the environmental determinism that some architects have espoused. Research, examining experimentally designed human settlements which reduce residential crime, should advance our understanding of the effect of environmental changes on personal relations.

The research on defensible space has also raised the question of the mechanisms by which strangers are recognized and inhibited from aberrant or threatening behaviour and entry into another person's territory. The survey material gathered in this study provides a preliminary basis for some re-thinking of the personal space theorems developed by Sommer (1969) and the analysis of the extrapolation of the existence of territorial or aggressive urges in man, such as has been put forward by Ardrey (1966), Lorenz (1966), and Morris (1969). While the demands of public policy may require action that will improve a bad situation, these broader and more theoretical issues must be further investigated if we are to avoid squandering millions of dollars on ad hoc experiments at little more than stabs in the dark.

Our study indicated that one's experience with the various aspects of the criminal justice system had a marked effect on attitudes to such crucial variables as belief in police efficiency or desire for retribution. The lack of salience of vicarious experience compared to even a small amount of real life exposure is fascinating and leads to a number of questions which deserve further analysis. How do the public resolve media stereotypes with their experiences with the real situation? How much knowledge is required for the public to develop an independent assessment? How does uncertainty relate to fear of crime and concern?

Some of the questions raised in this study concerned with the effect of social cohesion on the reduction of opportunities for burglary can be examined in other natural social contexts. In particular, there are still many tightly knit communities where the level of social cohesion far exceeds those of the residential areas that were examined in Metropolitan Toronto. These tightly knit village communities may provide other advantages or disadvantages as a form of human settlement. However, they provide models that should be examined further.

Although of more technical interest, the theory and methodology of drawing conclusions from disproportionate sampling frames must be improved. The study has shown that effective victimization surveys can be carried out without using expensive samples. Although a disproportionate sampling frame enabled us to reach many useful conclusions, it decreased the reliability of absolute levels and measures of incidence of the offence and made difficult the use of statistical tests for drawing conclusions. Our data should provide a natural testing ground for those interested in developing statistical methodology on these issues.

## Conclusion

This text has taken us from a crisis in criminal justice to some alternatives that might reduce the harm to the victim and reduce the social costs associated with society's traditional reaction to burglary. We have also seen the sorts of planning that would be required to reduce burglary.

Although the analysis has deliberately been limited to residential burglary, many of our conclusions would apply without substantial modifications to other offences, where the acquisition of another person's property is one of the principal motivations of the offender.

If we want to reduce the negative effects of crime, then we must start before the crime occurs in order to influence a wide range of social policies. We must also examine our Criminal Code to remove dead letters and to realize the reasons behind the public's reactions to crime. We must do more to inform the public how they can help themselves to provide protection against the typical amateur offender. Above all we should refocus our concern in crime to protect the victim, find more appropriate ways to denounce crime, and resolve conflicts between victim and offender in a just, humane, equitable, and cost-effective manner.

# Appendices

APPENDIX A

INSTITUTE FOR BEHAVIOURAL RESEARCH
SURVEY RESEARCH CENTRE
667-3022 AREA CODE 416

4700 KEELE STREET,
DOWNSVIEW, ONTARIO M3J 1P3

March, 1974

Dear Sir or Madam:

In a few days an interviewer from the Survey Research Centre of York University will visit your home in connection with a study on burglary which we are conducting in Metropolitan Toronto. We are writing to request your participation in this study.

We enclose a letter from Professor John Edwards, Director, Centre of Criminology, University of Toronto. This letter explains the purpose of the study. The Survey Research Centre is conducting the survey on behalf of the Centre of Criminology.

Our surveys are based on samples of addresses which are scientifically selected. As your address has been selected, we wish to inform you of the forthcoming visit of our interviewer. In order to avoid any misunderstanding, each interviewer carries an identification card as an employee of the Survey Research Centre of York University. It will be shown to you upon request.

I wish to reassure you of the complete confidentiality and anonymity of this study. All information given to our interviewer is treated with the most careful attention in this regard. All information which might identify any particular respondent will be destroyed well before any report is published. All reports will contain only statistical information.

Please accept this word of appreciation in advance for your participation in this study.

Sincerely,

C. Michael Lanphier
Director
Survey Research Centre

CML/rp
#146

CENTRE OF CRIMINOLOGY
UNIVERSITY OF TORONTO
607-609 SPADINA AVENUE
TORONTO, CANADA M5S 1A1

March, 1974.

Dear Sir or Madam:

In a new effort to prevent crime and reduce its costs, the Centre of Criminology of the University of Toronto is conducting a major study of burglary in Metropolitan Toronto.

Your household has been selected by scientific sampling methods to take part in this study. An interviewer will be calling at this residence to ask some general questions about crime prevention and the criminal justice system. We are also interested to know about any incident of breaking and entering that may have been experienced in your household since January 1st, 1973. As part of this project, the Survey Research Centre of York University will be carrying out a survey of 2,800 households throughout Metropolitan Toronto. Your co-operation in this study will help to improve our understanding of burglary, its prevention, its impact on the public, and to systematically assess the public's views on the way it is handled by police, the courts and other agencies.

Any information that you give the interviewer is entirely voluntary and will be kept strictly confidential. You may also choose not to answer any individual question the interviewer may ask you, though full responses will be much more useful. Moreover, the Centre of Criminology's research policy is to take steps, at and after the conclusion of the survey interviews, to ensure that all means of identifying the names and addresses of the persons interviewed are destroyed.

Should you have any further enquiries about this study, please contact:

Norm Okihiro, Senior Research Assistant,
Centre of Criminology,
University of Toronto,
928-8678.

Thank you for your co-operation.

Yours sincerely,

J. Ll. J. Edwards,
Director.

JLJE:at
#146

BURGLARY AND THE PUBLIC

A STUDY OF

VICTIMIZATION IN BURGLARY

IN

METROPOLITAN TORONTO

THE INTERVIEW SCHEDULE FOR THE HOUSEHOLD FIELD SURVEY

A Research Project
of
The Centre of Criminology
University of Toronto

Principal Investigator:        Irvin Waller, Ph.D.

Senior Research Assistant:  Norm Okihiro, M.A.

Implementation of Survey:  The Survey Research Centre
                                              York University

Director:                            C.M. Lanphier, Ph. D.

. . . . . . . . . . . . . . . . . . . . . . . . . . . . . . . . . . . . . . . . . . . . . .

*(Tear Off Label)*

SURVEY RESEARCH CENTRE

YORK UNIVERSITY

APRIL, 1974

PROJECT #146

BURGLARY AND THE PUBLIC

Hello. My name is _____. I represent the Centre of
Criminology of the University of Toronto and the Survey Research Centre
of York University. We hope you have received the letter that was sent
to you regarding the burglary study in Metropolitan Toronto which we are
conducting. Although we want to obtain as representative a sample as
possible, I would just like to reassure you that participation in this
survey is entirely voluntary and you are quite free to refuse to answer any
of the questions that I ask you. The information is confidential, and this
is the only record we keep of your address. *(INTERVIEWER: TEAR OFF ADDRESS
LABEL AND HAND IT TO RESPONDENT).*

Basically this survey concerns the effect of breaking and entering on
householders. As the letter suggests, this survey will improve our understanding of the crime itself, its prevention, and the relative effectiveness of
different ways of controlling burglary. The survey may take up to an hour, and
you may be interested to know that this type of survey has never been done
before in Canada.

Would you please give me a list of persons in your household?
*(Enter on page 2)*

| RECORD OF CALLS | | | | |
|---|---|---|---|---|
| | Day | Month | Time | Results |
| 1 | | | | |
| 2 | | | | |
| 3 | | | | |
| 4 | | | | |
| 5 | | | | |

Interviewer's Signature:_____

Length of Interview:_____

Editing time:_____ min.

*INTERVIEWER:*

1. *# of H.H.'s at this
   address:*  _____

2. *Type of interview:*

   *Screening only* . .
   *Victim* . . . . . . .
   *Non-victim* . . . .
   *Refusal (fill out
   page 9.)* . . . . .

3. *TYPE OF STRUCTURE:*

   *Single house.* . . . . . . . . . . . .
   *Single house attached (to non-resident
   structure* . . . . . . . . . . . . . .
   *Semi-detached or double house* . . . . .
   *Row house* . . . . . . . . . . . . . .
   *Duplex.* . . . . . . . . . . . . . . .
   *Apartment, triplex, multi-dwelling.* . . .
   *Mobile, trailer, houseboat.* . . . . . .
   *Rooming house* . . . . . . . . . . . .
   *Boarding house.* . . . . . . . . . . .
   *Other (specify)*
   _____ . . . . . . .

*List additional H. H. members on opposite page.*

| Relation to Head | Age | Sex | M.S. | Eligible? * | Person Number | Selected? | Selection Table # _____ |
|---|---|---|---|---|---|---|---|
| (Head) | | | | | | | |
| | | | | | | | |
| | | | | | | | |
| | | | | | | | |
| | | | | | | | |
| | | | | | | | |
| | | | | | | | |
| | | | | | | | |

*\*Eligible: 18 years and over and residing with H.H. since January 1973.*

| INTERVIEWER ONLY: |

4. *Is respondent willing to be interviewed alone?*

Yes . . . . . . . . . . . . . . . . . 1

No. . . . . . . . . . . . . . . . . 2

*Specify relationship to selected respondent of persons present during interview.* _____

5. *To your knowledge, does this respondent know about the subject of the study at this point?*

Yes - Read letter.(Proceed with questionnaire Part A, page 3. ). . . . . 1

Yes - Heard about it. (Proceed with Questionnaire Part A, page 3). . . 2

No. (Briefly state study purpose and proceed to Part A, page 3). . . . . 3

D.K.(Briefly state study purpose and proceed to Part A, page 3.) . . . . 4

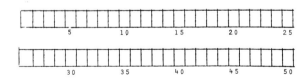

PART A

6.  How much do you worry that your house/apartment may be
    broken into?  Do you worry . . .

    . . . Very much . . . . . . . . . . . . . 1
    . . . Much. . . . . . . . . . . . . . . . 2
    . . . Somewhat. . . . . . . . . . . . . . 3
    . . . A little. . . . . . . . . . . . . . 4
    . . . Not at all. . . . . . . . . . . . . 5
    D.K.. . . . . . . . . . . . . . . . 8

7a. Have you ever moved or do you plan to move because of
    fear of crime?

    ┌─Yes - Have moved. . . . . . . . . . 1
    └─Yes - Plan to move. . . . . . . . . 2
    No. . . . . . . . . . . . . . . . . 3
    D.K.. . . . . . . . . . . . . . . . 8

b.  Why?

    _____    ___
    _____    ___

8a. Do you carry any insurance against theft or damage by
    thieves on your home, furnishings or possessions other
    than a vehicle or boat?

    Yes *(Go to Q. 9a)* . . . . . . . . . 1
    No. . . . . . . . . . . . . . . . . 2
    D.K.*(Go to Q. 9a)* . . . . . . . . . 8

b.  If <u>No</u>, could you tell me the principal reason why you don't
    carry insurance?

    Costs too much, can't afford it . . 1
    No goods worth insuring . . . . . . 2
    Never thought of it; never got
    around to it. . . . . . . . . . . . 3
    I take other precautions. . . . . . 4
    Other (specify)

    _____

    _____. . 5

    D.K.. . . . . . . . . . . . . . . . 8

I would like to ask you about some things which might have happened to you any time in the <u>last 3 years</u> or so. Please take your time and think carefully, and if anything occurred which might fit the description I give, please let me know. It doesn't matter who else was involved, or whether you think it was serious or not. By home, we include farm, cottage, apartment or hotel room, or second home, which you were living in at the time".

9a.  Has anyone broken into your home?

                                Yes . . . . . . . . . . . . . . . 1
                                No *(Go to Q. 10a)* . . . . . . . . 2

b.  How many times?

> INTERVIEWER: *If Yes to Q. 9a., add "Other than that" to Q. 10a ,*
> *Q. 11a, Q.12a and Q. 13a to ensure same incident*
> *is not recorded twice.*

10a.  (Other than that) Has anyone tried or attempted to break in?

                                  Yes . . . . . . . . . . . . . . . 1
                                No *(Go to Q. 11a)*. . . . . . . . 2

b.  How many times?

11a.  (Other than that) Have you found a door jimmied, a lock forced, a window open or broken or anything similar?

                                  Yes . . . . . . . . . . . . . . . 1
                                No *(Go to Q. 12a.)*. . . . . . . . 2

b.  How many times?

12a.  (Other than that)  Has anyone entered your home illegally or without you or someone else who lives here giving consent?  *(Neighbours or relatives entering without knocking is considered as tacit consent)*

                                  Yes . . . . . . . . . . . . . . . 1
                                No *(Go to Q. 13a.)* . . . . . . . . 2

b.  How many times?

13a. (Other than that)  Has anyone come into your home for
the purpose of theft?  *(Do not include thefts in the residence
by a member of the household, e.g. maid)*

Yes . . . . . . . . . . . . . . . 1

No. . . . . . . . . . . . . . . . 2

b. How many times?  _____

If *Yes* to Q. 9 - Q. 13, go to Q. *14a.*

If *No* to *all* of Q. 9 - Q. 13:

1. *If respondent fulfills criteria for intensive interview,
go to Part C. (See selection sheet or log.)*

2. *If respondent does not fulfill criteria, go to Part A1, p.7.
( See selection sheet or log.)*

14a. Did the latest incident take place in this dwelling?

Yes *(Go to Q. 15a)*  . . . . . . . . 1

No. . . . . . . . . . . . . . . . 2

b. In what type of dwelling did it take place?

Single house. . . . . . . . . . . .01
Single house attached (to non-
resident structure, e.g. store) . .02
Semi-detached or double house . . .03
Row house . . . . . . . . . . . .04
Duplex. . . . . . . . . . . . . .05
Apartment, triplex, multi-dwelling.06
Mobile, trailer, houseboat. . . . .07
Rooming house . . . . . . . . . .08
Boarding house. . . . . . . . . .09
Other (specify)

_____ . . .10
D.K.. . . . . . . . . . . . . . .98
INAP. . . . . . . . . . . . . . .99

c. Where?

Other dwelling in Metro Toronto . . 1
*(Show Census Tract Map of Metro
Toronto and code exact Census Tract
Number)*
Census tract number _____

Ontario, outside Metro. . . . . . . 2
Canada, outside Ontario. . . . . . 3
Elsewhere (specify)

_____ . . . 4
D.K.. . . . . . . . . . . . . . . 8
INAP. . . . . . . . . . . . . . . 9

a. Do you recall exactly in which month the latest incident
occurred?

Yes. . . . . . . . . . . . . . . 1
No . . . . . . . . . . . . . . . 2

A date can often be confusing. We would like to try to
pinpoint the date by getting you to recall some of
the things which might have happened about the same time
as the latest incident.

*Try to get exact dates of any events near the time of the
incident and record below. Use probes such as weather
(e.g. snow storms), holidays, birthdays, illness, job
changes, births, deaths and marriages.
If necessary, try to get R. to pinpoint events in relation
to items on Card A.*

_____

_____

_____

b. Which month was that?

D.K. . . . . 9 8

c. Which year was that?     1971
   *(Circle appropriate year)*     1972
                            1973
                            1974

D.K. . . . . 8

*(If unable to recall month, ask:)*
d.  Do you recall the season?

Spring (Apr., May) . . . . . . . . 1
Summer (June, July, Aug., Sept.) . 2
Fall (Oct., Nov.). . . . . . . . . 3
Winter (Dec., Jan., Feb., Mar.). . 4
No . . . . . . . . . . . . . . . . 5
INAP . . . . . . . . . . . . . . . 9

---

1.  *If incident occurred after January 1, 1973:*

    | Yes |
    | R. *not sure* | ———→ *Go to Part B*

2.  *If incident occurred before January 1, 1973 and R. fulfills criteria
    for intensive interview, go to Part C. (See selection sheet or log.)*

3.  *If incident occurred before January 1, 1973 but R. does not fulfill
    criteria, go to Part AI, p. 7. (See selection sheet or log.)*

---

PART A1

16a. Have you <u>ever</u> called the police because you knew or suspected
that someone had broken into, or attempted to break into, your
own residence or the residence of a neighbour?

```
                                        ┌Yes - Own . . . . . . . . . . . . 1
                                        └Yes - Neighbour . . . . . . . . . 2
    │                                    No (Go to Q. 17). . . . . . . . . 3
    │                                    D.K.. . . . . . . . . . . . . . . 8
    │
    ↓
```

b. How long ago was the <u>last</u> incident?

```
                        This year . . . . . . . . . . . . 1
                        Last year . . . . . . . . . . . . 2
                        2 - 5 years ago . . . . . . . . . 3
                        More than 5 years . . . . . . . . 4
                        D.K.. . . . . . . . . . . . . . . 8
                        INAP. . . . . . . . . . . . . . . 9
```

17. I would like your general impressions on present sentences for
<u>crimes against residences</u> such as theft, robbery, or break-and-
enter. Do you feel these sentences, as they are given now, are
generally . . .

```
                . . . too severe. . . . . . . . . . . . 1
                . . . fairly severe . . . . . . . . . . 2
                . . . about right . . . . . . . . . . . 3
                . . . fairly lenient. . . . . . . . . . 4
                . . . too lenient . . . . . . . . . . . 5
                        D.K.. . . . . . . . . . . . . . . 8
```

Now I'd like to ask you some questions about yourself and your
family.

18a. What level did you obtain in school?

```
                        None. . . . . . . . . . . . . . . 01
                        Some elementary school. . . . . . 02
                        Complete elementary school. . . . 03
                        Some secondary school . . . . . . 04
                        Complete secondary school . . . . 05
                        Some post secondary school (non-
                        university) . . . . . . . . . . . 06
                        Complete post secondary school
                        (non-university). . . . . . . . . 07
                        Some university . . . . . . . . . 08
                        Complete university . . . . . . . 09
                        Post-graduate university. . . . . 10
```

b. How many years is that?            _____

*(Hand R. Card B)*

Within which of the following categories did the income <u>before</u>
taxes from <u>all</u> sources of all persons living here in 1973 fall?
This includes lodgers, partners, employees or others occupying
this dwelling.

| | | |
|---|---|---|
| A. | Less than 3,000. . . . . . . . | 01 |
| B. | 3,000 - 4,999. . . . . . . . . | 02 |
| C. | 5,000 - 6,999. . . . . . . . . | 03 |
| D. | 7,000 - 8,999. . . . . . . . . | 04 |
| E. | 9,000 - 10,999 . . . . . . . . | 05 |
| F. | 11,000 - 14,999. . . . . . . . | 06 |
| G. | 15,000 - 24,999. . . . . . . . | 07 |
| H. | 25,000 - 39,999. . . . . . . . | 08 |
| I. | 40,000 and over. . . . . . . . | 09 |
| | D.K. . . . . . . . . . . . . . | 98 |
| | Ref. . . . . . . . . . . . . . | 99 |

Thank you for taking time to answer these questions.

*END OF SCREENING INTERVIEW*

| FOR REFUSALS ONLY |

R1. *Reason for refusal:*

_____

_____  ___ ___

R2. *Estimate income of all persons in household:*

| | |
|---|---|
| *Low (below $6,000)* . . . . . . . . | *1* |
| *Medium ($6,000 to $18,000)* . . . . | *2* |
| *High (Over $18,000)* . . . . . . . . | *3* |
| *Could not estimate* . . . . . . . | *4* |

R3. *Estimate age group of R.:*

| | |
|---|---|
| *0 - 17* . . . . . . . . . . . . . | *1* |
| *18 - 25*. . . . . . . . . . . . . | *2* |
| *26 - 35*. . . . . . . . . . . . . | *3* |
| *36 - 45*. . . . . . . . . . . . . | *4* |
| *46 - 55*. . . . . . . . . . . . . | *5* |
| *56 - 65*. . . . . . . . . . . . . | *6* |
| *Over 65*. . . . . . . . . . . . . | *7* |
| *Could not estimate* . . . . . . . | *8* |

R4. *Sex:*

| | |
|---|---|
| *Male* . . . . . . . . . . . . . . | *1* |
| *Female* . . . . . . . . . . . . . | *2* |
| *Could not determine*. . . . . . . | *3* |

R5. *Estimate ethnic origin: (If could not estimate, code 99)*

_____

_____  ___ ___

R6. *Estimate No. of families in dwelling:* _____  ___ ___

R7. *Estimate ability to speak English:*

| | |
|---|---|
| *Excellent*. . . . . . . . . . . . | *1* |
| *Good* . . . . . . . . . . . . . . | *2* |
| *Fair* . . . . . . . . . . . . . . | *3* |
| *Not at all* . . . . . . . . . . . | *4* |
| *Could not estimate* . . . . . . . | *5* |

R8. *Type of dwelling:*

| | |
|---|---|
| *Single house* . . . . . . . . . . | *01* |
| *Single house attached (to non-resident structure)*. . . . . . . . | *02* |
| *Semi-detached or double house*. . . | *03* |
| *Row house*. . . . . . . . . . . . | *04* |
| *Duplex* . . . . . . . . . . . . . | *05* |
| *Apartment, triplex,multi-dwelling*. | *06* |
| *Mobile, trailer, houseboat* . . . . | *07* |
| *Rooming house*. . . . . . . . . . | *08* |
| *Boarding house* . . . . . . . . . | *09* |
| *Other (specify)* | |
| _____ . . . . . | *10* |

PART B

LATEST INCIDENT REPORT  -   *(Enter month & year in tab)* →

Could you give me a brief description of the latest incident
and then I will ask you some specific questions.

*(Make brief note, do not write verbatim)*

_____
_____
_____
_____
_____

I'd like to go back over your description of the incident now and
ask some specific questions. *(Where answers are obvious from
description given, fill in by reading response, but do not repeat
question.)*

**.** What was the day of the week?

Monday . . . . . . . . . . . . . . . . 01
Tuesday. . . . . . . . . . . . . . . . 02
Wednesday. . . . . . . . . . . . . . . 03
Thursday . . . . . . . . . . . . . . . 04
Friday . . . . . . . . . . . . . . . . 05
Saturday . . . . . . . . . . . . . . . 06
Sunday . . . . . . . . . . . . . . . . 07

Weekend (Fri. 6:00p.m. to Sunday
11:59 p.m.). . . . . . . . . . . . . 08

Weekday. . . . . . . . . . . . . . . . 09

D.K. . . . . . . . . . . . . . . . . . 98

1a. Do you recall the time of the day (of the latest incident)?

Yes. . . . . . . . . . . . . . . . . 1
No *(Go to Q. 22)* . . . . . . . . . . 2

b.  When?

Between _____a.m./p.m. and _____a.m./p.m.     __ __

Go to Q. 23                                                       __ __

2.  *(If No in Q. 21a., ASK:)*
Was it during the morning, afternoon, evening or night?

Morning(7:00 a.m. to 11:59 a.m.) . . . 1
Afternoon (12:00 noon to 4:59 p.m.). . 2
Evening (5:00 p.m. to 9:59 p.m.) . . . 3
Night (10:00 p.m. to 6:59 a.m.). . . . 4
D.K. . . . . . . . . . . . . . . . . . 8
INAP . . . . . . . . . . . . . . . . . 9

23. How did the offender (or offenders) actually get in?

```
┌──────────────────────────── Door . . . . . . . . . . . . . . 1
│                              Window (Go to Q. 25a.) . . . . . . 2
│                              ┌─────────────────────────────────────┐
│                              │ Wall or roof (Go to Q. 26) . . . . . 3 │
│                              │ Other (specify). . . . . . . . . . 4 │
│                              └─────────────────────────────────────┘
│                              D.K. . . . . . . . . . . . . . . 8
↓
```

24a. Was the door shut, partly open or wide open?

```
┌──────────────────────────── Shut . . . . . . . . . . . . . . 1
│                              ┌─────────────────────────────────────┐
│                              │ Partly open (Go to Q. 24c.). . . . . 2 │
│                              │ Wide open. . . . . . . . . . . . . 3 │
│                              │ D.K. . . . . . . . . . . . . . . 8 │
│                              └─────────────────────────────────────┘
│                              INAP . . . . . . . . . . . . . . 9
↓
```

b. Was it locked?

```
                              Yes. . . . . . . . . . . . . . . 1
                              No . . . . . . . . . . . . . . . 2
                              D.K. . . . . . . . . . . . . . . 8
                              INAP . . . . . . . . . . . . . . 9
```

c. Was this the front or main door, side door, or back door?

```
                              Front (main) . . . . . . . . . . . 1
                              Side . . . . . . . . . . . . . . 2
                              Back . . . . . . . . . . . . . . 3
                              Other (specify) _____ . 4
                              D.K. . . . . . . . . . . . . . . 8
                              INAP . . . . . . . . . . . . . . 9
```

d. How did he actually get in? *(Probe for details to distinguish
between force and no force)*

```
                              Just walked in open door . . . . . 01
                              Opened door wider. . . . . . . . . 02
                              Turned knob or opened unlocked
                              closed door. . . . . . . . . . . 03
                              Slipped the lock . . . . . . . . . 04
                              Picked the lock. . . . . . . . . . 05
                              Used duplicate key . . . . . . . . 06
                              Pried door open. . . . . . . . . . 07
                              Broke glass in door and unlocked
                              door . . . . . . . . . . . . . . 08
                              Opened milk box and unlocked door. 09
                              Otherwise forced or broke door . . 10
                              Other (specify) _____ . 11
                              D.K. . . . . . . . . . . . . . . 98
                              INAP . . . . . . . . . . . . . . 99
```

┌─────────────────┐
│ *Go to Q. 27a.* │
└─────────────────┘

25a. *(If Window in Q. 23, ASK:)*
　　　Was there a screen over the window at the time?

|                          |   |
|--------------------------|---|
| Yes . . . . . . . . . . . . . . | 1 |
| No. . . . . . . . . . . . . . . | 2 |
| D.K.. . . . . . . . . . . . . . | 8 |
| INAP. . . . . . . . . . . . . . | 9 |

b. Was window shut, partly open or wide open?

|                          |   |
|--------------------------|---|
| Shut. . . . . . . . . . . . . . | 1 |
| Partly open . . . . . . . . . . | 2 |
| Window open (or no glass in window) . . . . . . . . . . . . | 3 |
| D.K.. . . . . . . . . . . . . . | 8 |
| → *(Go to Q. 25d.)* ← | |
| INAP. . . . . . . . . . . . . . | 9 |

c. Was it locked?

|                          |   |
|--------------------------|---|
| Yes . . . . . . . . . . . . . . | 1 |
| No. . . . . . . . . . . . . . . | 2 |
| D.K.. . . . . . . . . . . . . . | 8 |
| INAP. . . . . . . . . . . . . . | 9 |

d. Was it a front, back or side window?

|                          |   |
|--------------------------|---|
| Front . . . . . . . . . . . . . | 1 |
| Back. . . . . . . . . . . . . . | 2 |
| Side. . . . . . . . . . . . . . | 3 |
| Other (specify) _____ | 4 |
| D.K.. . . . . . . . . . . . . . | 8 |
| INAP. . . . . . . . . . . . . . | 9 |

　　*(If Apartment, go to Q. 25f.)*

　　*(If House, ASK: )*
e. Was it a basement, 1st floor, 2nd floor window?

|                          |   |
|--------------------------|---|
| Basement. . . . . . . . . . . . | 1 |
| 1st Floor . . . . . . . . . . . | 2 |
| 2nd Floor . . . . . . . . . . . | 3 |
| 3rd Floor or higher . . . . . . | 4 |
| D.K.. . . . . . . . . . . . . . | 8 |
| INAP. . . . . . . . . . . . . . | 9 |

f. How did the offender(s) actually get in?

|                          |   |
|--------------------------|---|
| In open window (absolutely no force). . . . . . . . . . . . . | 1 |
| Just removed or forced screen . . | 2 |
| Physically opened unlocked shut or partly open window . . . . . . | 3 |
| Pried locked window . . . . . . | 4 |
| Broke or otherwise forced window. | 5 |
| Other (specify) _____ | 6 |
| D.K.. . . . . . . . . . . . . . | 8 |
| INAP. . . . . . . . . . . . . . | 9 |

*Go to Q. 27a.*

26. *(If Wall or Roof or Other in Q. 23, ASK: )*
    How was it done?

    _____

    _____

    _____                    ____

                                                    D.K. . . . . . . . 8
                                                    INAP . . . . . . . 9

27a. Were you or anyone else home at the time of the incident?

                                        ── Yes. . . . . . . . . . . . . . . . 1
    ┌─────────────────────────────────────┐
    │                                   No *(Go to Q. 30)* . . . . . . . . . . 2
    │                                   D.K. . . . . . . . . . . . . . . . 8
    ↓

b. Was there a confrontation?

                                        ── Yes. . . . . . . . . . . . . . . . 1
    ┌─────────────────────────────────────┐
    │                                   No *(Go to Q. 30)* . . . . . . . . . . 2
    │                                   D.K. . . . . . . . . . . . . . . . 8
    │                                   INAP . . . . . . . . . . . . . . . 9
    ↓

c. What happened?  *(Probe for details)*

    _____

    _____                    ____ ____

                                                    INAP . . . . . . . 99

28a. How many offenders were there? *(Specify exact number)*      ____ ____
                                                    INAP . . . . . . . 99

b.  Was the offender(s) armed?

                                        Yes – Gun or rifle · · · · · · · · 1
                                        Yes – knife. . . . . . . . . . . . 2
                                        Yes – Other (specify) _____ . 3
                                        No . . . . . . . . . . . . . . . . 4
                                        D.K. . . . . . . . . . . . . . . . 8
                                        INAP . . . . . . . . . . . . . . . 9

c. Did you or anyone else (other than the police) try to apprehend
   the offender(s) personally?

                                        ── Yes (Who? – specify) _____ . 1
    ┌─────────────────────────────────────
    │                                   No *(Go to Q. 29a.)* . . . . . . . . . 2
    │                                   INAP . . . . . . . . . . . . . . . 9
    ↓

d. Were you/they successful?

                                        Yes. . . . . . . . . . . . . . . . 1
                                        No . . . . . . . . . . . . . . . . 2
                                        INAP . . . . . . . . . . . . . . . 9

29a. Could you describe your feelings during the confrontation?

_____     ____

_____     ____

_____     ____

INAP . . . .999

b. Did anyone in the household suffer physical injuries as a result of this incident?

Yes - Self . . . . . . . . . . . . 1
Yes - Others . . . . . . . . . . . 2
Yes - Both self & others . . . . . 3

No . . . . . . . . . . . . . . . 4
D.K. . . . . . . . . . . . . . . 8
INAP . . . . . . . . . . . . . . 9
→ *(Go to Q. 32.)* ←

c. Could you describe details of injury (injuries) received?

_____     ____

_____

_____

INAP . . . . . 9

|  | YES | NO | D.K. | INAP |
|---|---|---|---|---|
| d. (i) Did anyone call a doctor? . . . . . . . | 1 . . | 2 . . | 8 . . . | 9 |
| (ii) Was anyone hospitalized?. . . . . . . . | 1 . . | 2 . . | 8 . . . | 9 |
| (iii) Was anyone prescribed medicines or drugs?. . . . . . . . . . . . . . . . | 1 . . | 2 . . | 8 . . . | 9 |
| (iv) Did anyone undergo any other medical treatment?. . . . . . . . . . . . . | 1 . . | 2 . . | 8 . . . | 9 |
| (v) Did anyone miss work because of this incident? . . . . . . . . . . . . . | 1 . . | 2 . . | 8 . . . | 9 |

e. Could you estimate the total cost of the injuries received by persons in the household, including wages lost?

$ _____ or between $ _____ and $ _____     __ __ __

INAP. . . . . . 999

Go to Q. 31a.

30. Who was the first to discover the incident?

Self . . . . . . . . . . . . . . . 1
Other member of household. . . . . 2
Neighbour. . . . . . . . . . . . . 3
Police . . . . . . . . . . . . . . 4
Relative . . . . . . . . . . . . . 5
Caretaker, Superintendent. . . . . 6
Other (specify) _____ . 7
D.K. . . . . . . . . . . . . . . . 8
INAP . . . . . . . . . . . . . . . 9

31a. What was your reaction <u>immediately</u> after you found your residence was broken into?  Describe as fully as possible.

*(Probe for annoyance, fear, anger, surprise, etc.)*

_____    ___  __

_____    ___  __

_____    ___  __

                                             INAP . . . . . 999999

b. What did you feel, at that time, should happen to the offender, (if caught)?

_____    ___  __

_____

                                             INAP . . . . . . 99


c. Would you have liked to see him imprisoned (or sent to jail)?

                        Yes . . . . . . . . . . . . . . . . . 1
                        No. . . . . . . . . . . . . . . . . . 2
                        D.K.. . . . . . . . . . . . . . . . . 8
                        INAP. . . . . . . . . . . . . . . . . 9

32.  Why do you think the offender(s) entered your dwelling?  Was it. . .

     *(Code all that apply)*

|  | YES | NO |
|---|---|---|
| . . . a. For thrills. . . . . . . . | 1 . . . . . . . | 2 |
| . . . b. To steal something . . . . | 1 . . . . . . . | 2 |
| . . . c. Sexual intent (specify) | | |
| _____. . 1 . . . . . . . | | 2 |
| . . . d. For revenge. . . . . . . . | 1 . . . . . . . | 2 |
| . . . e. For some other reason (specify) | | |
| _____. . 1 . . . . . . . | | 2 |

3a. Was anything taken in this incident?

Yes . . . . . . . . . . . . . . . 1

No *(Go to Q. 38)*. . . . . . . . . 2

D.K.. . . . . . . . . . . . . . . 8

b. What? *(Code "Yes" for all that apply)*

| | | YES | NO | DK | TABLE FOR Q. 37 |
|---|---|---|---|---|---|
| a. | Cash. . . . . . . . . . . | 1 | 2 | 8 | $_____ or btwn. $_____ and $_____ |
| b. | T.V.. . . . . . . . . . . | 1 | 2 | 8 | $_____ or btwn. $_____ and $_____ |
| c. | Radio . . . . . . . . . . | 1 | 2 | 8 | $_____ or btwn. $_____ and $_____ |
| d. | Hi-fi or stereo equipment . . . . . . . | 1 | 2 | 8 | $_____ or btwn. $_____ and $_____ |
| e. | Jewellery . . . . . . . . | 1 | 2 | 8 | $_____ or btwn. $_____ and $_____ |
| f. | Furs. . . . . . . . . . . | 1 | 2 | 8 | $_____ or btwn. $_____ and $_____ |
| g. | Beer, wine or spirits . | 1 | 2 | 8 | $_____ or btwn. $_____ and $_____ |
| h. | Stocks, bonds . . . . . | 1 | 2 | 8 | $_____ or btwn. $_____ and $_____ |
| i. | Travellers cheques. . . | 1 | 2 | 8 | $_____ or btwn. $_____ and $_____ |
| j. | Credit cards. . . . . . | 1 | 2 | 8 | $_____ or btwn. $_____ and $_____ |
| k. | Other (specify) _____ . . | 1 | 2 | 8 | $_____ or btwn. $_____ and $_____ |

[ ][ ][ ][ ][ ][ ][ ][ ][ ][ ][ ][ ][ ][ ][ ][ ][ ][ ][ ]

[ ][ ][ ][ ][ ][ ][ ][ ][ ][ ][ ][ ][ ][ ][ ][ ][ ][ ][ ]

4a. Was there an insurance evaluation?

Yes . . . . . . . . . . . . . . . . 1

No *(Go to Q. 35a.)*. . . . . . . . . 2

D.K.. . . . . . . . . . . . . . . . 8

INAP. . . . . . . . . . . . . . . 9

b. What estimate of goods, cash or documents was <u>accepted</u> by the insurance company?

$_____ or between $_____ and $_____      ___ ___ ___

INAP . . . . . 9 9 9

Go to Q. 37

35a. Was there a police estimate?

```
                                            Yes . . . . . . . . . . . . 1
  ┌──────────────────────────────────┐    ┌─────────────────────────────────┐
  │                                        │ No (Go to Q. 36a) . . . . . . . . 2 │
  │                                        │ D.K.. . . . . . . . . . . . . . 8 │
  │                                        └─────────────────────────────────┘
  │                                          INAP. . . . . . . . . . . . . 9
  ↓
```

b. What was it?

$_____ or between $_____ and $_____   ___ ___ ___

                                                    INAP . . . 9 9 9

┌─────────────────┐
│  *Go to Q. 37*  │
└─────────────────┘

36a. Did you make a personal estimate of the replacement value
of the things taken, including cash?

```
                                            Yes . . . . . . . . . . . . . 1
  ┌──────────────────────────────────┐    ┌─────────────────────────────────┐
  │                                        │ No (Go to Q. 37.) . . . . . . . . 2 │
  │                                        │ D.K.. . . . . . . . . . . . . . 8 │
  │                                        └─────────────────────────────────┘
  │                                          INAP. . . . . . . . . . . . . 9
  ↓
```

b. What was it?

$_____ or between $_____ and $_____   ___ ___ ___

                                                    INAP . . . 9 9 9

37. For each item, what is the estimate of its value?

*Fill in the estimates in Table on page 16., Q. 33b.*

*Use the following procedure:*

*1. Take Insurance Evaluation if available.*

*2. If Insurance Evaluation not available, take Police Estimate.*

*3. If neither of the above is available, take Personal Estimate
of Replacement Cost.*

38a. Was there any damage done to your dwelling or its contents during the incident?

Yes . . . . . . . . . . . . . . 1
No *(Go to Q. 38d.)*. . . . . . . . 2

b. If <u>Yes</u>; *(Probe for details)*

_____

_____         ___  ___

_____

INAP . . . 99

c. What would you estimate as the cost of this damage?

$ _____ or between $_____ and $ _____         ___  ___  ___

INAP . . . 9 9 9

d. Were any of your possessions disarranged or otherwise scattered about during this incident?

Yes, extensive disarrangement,
scattered everywhere. . . . . . . 1
Yes, a little disarrangement,
a few things scattered about. . . 2
No. . . . . . . . . . . . . . . 3
D.K.. . . . . . . . . . . . . . 8

e. Did <u>you</u> suffer any other inconvenience as a result of this incident?

Yes . . . . . . . . . . . . . . 1
No *(Go to Q. 39a.)*. . . . . . . . 2

f. If <u>Yes</u>; *(Probe for details)*

_____

_____         ___  ___

_____

INAP . . . 99

39a. Apart from your first reactions, have you or your children
 suffered from any of the following as a result of this
 incident . . .

SELF     CHILDRE

(a) . . .fear of being alone

Yes . . . . . . . . . . 1 . . . . . . 1
No . . . . . . . . . . 2 . . . . . 2
INAP. . . . . . . . . 9 . . . . . 9

(b) . . .fear of entering your
 residence or rooms
 within your residence

Yes . . . . . . . . . . 1 . . . . . . 1
No. . . . . . . . . . 2 . . . . . 2
INAP. . . . . . . . . 9 . . . . . 9

(c) . . .sleeplessness

Yes . . . . . . . . . . 1 . . . . . . 1
No. . . . . . . . . . 2 . . . . . 2
INAP. . . . . . . . . 9 . . . . . 9

(d) . . .headaches

Yes . . . . . . . . . . 1 . . . . . . 1
No. . . . . . . . . . 2 . . . . . 2
INAP. . . . . . . . . 9 . . . . . 9

(e) . . .general increase in
 suspicion or distrust

Yes . . . . . . . . . . 1 . . . . . . 1
No. . . . . . . . . . 2 . . . . . 2
INAP. . . . . . . . . 9 . . . . . 9

(f) . . .anything else? _____

Yes . . . . . . . . . . 1 . . . . . . 1
No. . . . . . . . . . 2 . . . . . 2
INAP. . . . . . . . . 9 . . . . . 9

*(If Yes to any item in Q. 39a., ASK:)*

b. Have you sought medical assistance?

Yes . . . . . . . . . . . . . . . . . 1
No *(Go to Q. 40a.)*. . . . . . . . . 2
INAP. . . . . . . . . . . . . . . . . 9

c. Could you estimate the cost, including lost wages?

$_____ or between $_____ and $_____   ___ ___

INAP . . 9 9

40a. Was the incident reported to the police?

```
┌─────────────────────────────────────────── Yes . . . . . . . . . . . . . . . 1
│                                            No (Go to Q. 50a.). . . . . . . 2
↓
```
b. By whom?

```
                        Self. . . . . . . . . . . . . . . 1
                        Other household member. . . . . 2
                        Neighbour . . . . . . . . . . . 3
                        Other (specify)__. _____ . . 4
                        D.K.. . . . . . . . . . . . . . . 8
                        INAP. . . . . . . . . . . . . . . 9
```

c. How long after the **incident** occurred was it reported to the police?

```
                        Right away (within 2 minutes) . 1
                        Just a few minutes (5 minutes). 2
                        6 – 15 minutes. . . . . . . . . 3
                        16 minutes to half an hour. . . 4
                        31 minutes to 1 hour. . . . . . 5
                        More than 1 hour. . . . . . . . 6
                        D.K.. . . . . . . . . . . . . . 8
                        INAP. . . . . . . . . . . . . . 9
```

d. Was there any special reason you had in mind when you reported the incident to the police? *(Probe "anything else")*

|   |   | YES | NO | INAP |
|---|---|---|---|---|
| A. | It was the right thing to do; it was my duty . . . . | 1 | 2 | 9 |
| B. | It was necessary to claim insurance. . . . . . . . . | 1 | 2 | 9 |
| C. | To prevent the offender from committing similar acts in the future . . . . . . . . . . . . . . . . . | 1 | 2 | 9 |
| D. | To get the goods back. . . . . . . . . . . . . . . | 1 | 2 | 9 |
| E. | It was just instinct; never even thought about it. . | 1 | 2 | 9 |
| F. | Nobody else to call. . . . . . . . . . . . . . . . | 1 | 2 | 9 |
| G. | Other (specify) _____ . . . | 1 | 2 | 9 |

*(Hand R. Card C)*

e. Could you rank these reasons for notifying police about this incident in order of their importance? *(Code 3 only)*

```
                        1st choice . . . . . . . . . . ____
                        2nd choice . . . . . . . . . . ____
                        3rd choice . . . . . . . . . . ____
                        INAP . . . . . . . . . . . . . 999
```

41a. Were you, or whoever notified the police, hesitant to call them?

> Yes . . . . . . . . . . . . . . . 1
>
> No *(Go to Q. 42a.)*. . . . . . . . 2
> D.K.. . . . . . . . . . . . . . . 8
> INAP. . . . . . . . . . . . . . . 9

b. Was there any particular reason? *(Probe "anything else")*

|  |  | YES | NO | D.K. | INAP |
|---|---|---|---|---|---|
| A. | Did not want to take the time. Might mean time spent in court or lost from work | 1 | 2 | 8 | 9 |
| B. | Did not want harm or punishment to come to the offender. | 1 | 2 | 8 | 9 |
| C. | Afraid of reprisal | 1 | 2 | 8 | 9 |
| D. | Thought it was a private, not criminal matter | 1 | 2 | 8 | 9 |
| E. | Police couldn't do anything about the matter | 1 | 2 | 8 | 9 |
| F. | Police wouldn't want to be bothered about such things. | 1 | 2 | 8 | 9 |
| G. | Didn't know how to notify them or know that they should be notified. | 1 | 2 | 8 | 9 |
| H. | Fear of trouble from police (including fear of own offences being discovered) | 1 | 2 | 8 | 9 |
| I. | Too confused or upset to notify them | 1 | 2 | 8 | 9 |
| J. | Not sure the real offenders would be caught | 1 | 2 | 8 | 9 |
| K. | Fear of insurance cancellation or increased rates. | 1 | 2 | 8 | 9 |
| L. | Do not speak English well enough | 1 | 2 | 8 | 9 |
| M. | Other (specify) _____ | 1 | 2 | 8 | 9 |

*(Hand R. Card D)*

c. Could you rank these reasons for being hesitant to call the police about this incident in order of their importance.

*(Code 3 only)*

> 1st choice . . . . . . . . . . . . _____
>
> 2nd choice . . . . . . . . . . . . _____
>
> 3rd choice . . . . . . . . . . . . _____
>
> INAP . . . . . . . . . . . . . . . 999

a. How long did it take for police to arrive after they
   were notified?

<pre>
                          Right away (within 2 minutes) . . . . 01
                          Just a few minutes (5 minutes). . . . 02
                          6 - 15 minutes. . . . . . . . . . . . 03
                          16 minutes to half an hour. . . . . . 04
                          31 minutes to 1 hour. . . . . . . . . 05
                          More than 1 hour. . . . . . . . . . . 06
                          Did not come that day . . . . . . . . 07
                         ┌─────────────────────────────────────────┐
                         │ Did not come at all (Go to Q. 51.) . 08 │
                         │ D.K.. . . . . . . . . . . . . . . . . 98 │
                         └─────────────────────────────────────────┘
                          INAP. . . . . . . . . . . . . . . . . 99
</pre>

b. Did they complete an occurrence form?  *(Show sample)*

<pre>
                          Yes . . . . . . . . . . . . . . . . . 1
                          No. . . . . . . . . . . . . . . . . . 2
                          D.K.. . . . . . . . . . . . . . . . . 8
                          INAP. . . . . . . . . . . . . . . . . 9
</pre>

3. Did they take **notes** in a notebook?

<pre>
                          Yes . . . . . . . . . . . . . . . . . 1
                          No. . . . . . . . . . . . . . . . . . 2
                          D.K.. . . . . . . . . . . . . . . . . 8
                          INAP. . . . . . . . . . . . . . . . . 9
</pre>

. What other action was taken in the dwelling?  *(Code all that apply)*

|  | YES | NO | D.K. | INAP |
|---|---|---|---|---|
| . . .fingerprinting . . . . . . . . | 1 | 2 | 8 | 9 |
| . . .took other samples & evidence. | 1 | 2 | 8 | 9 |
| . . .asked questions. . . . . . . . | 1 | 2 | 8 | 9 |
| . . .inspected residence . . . . . | 1 | 2 | 8 | 9 |
| . . .other (specify)_____ . | 1 | 2 | 8 | 9 |

5a. Did the police question whether a crime had occurred?

<pre>
─────────────────────────────────── Yes . . . . . . . . . . . . . . . . . 1
│                                   ┌─────────────────────────────────────┐
│                                   │ No(Go to Q. 46.). . . . . . . . . . 2 │
│                                   │ D.K.. . . . . . . . . . . . . . . . 8 │
│                                   │ INAP. . . . . . . . . . . . . . . . 9 │
│                                   └─────────────────────────────────────┘
↓
</pre>

b. Could you give the details of that?

_____

_____

<pre>
                                              INAP . . . . 9 9
</pre>

46. Was the case followed up by another policeman?

```
                                    Yes - on phone . . . . . . . . . . 1
                                    Yes - in person. . . . . . . . . . 2
                                    Yes - by letter. . . . . . . . . . 3
                                    No . . . . . . . . . . . . . . . . 4
                                    D.K. . . . . . . . . . . . . . . . 8
                                    INAP . . . . . . . . . . . . . . . 9
```

47. Did you or anyone in the H.H. emphasize to the police that every effort should be made to have the offender arrested?

```
                                    Yes. . . . . . . . . . . . . . . . 1
                                    No . . . . . . . . . . . . . . . . 2
                                    D.K. . . . . . . . . . . . . . . . 8
                                    INAP . . . . . . . . . . . . . . . 9
```

48a. Was the offender arrested?

```
                                    Yes. . . . . . . . . . . . . . . . 1
                                    No (Go to Q. 49a). . . . . . . . . 2
                                    D.K. . . . . . . . . . . . . . . . 8
                                    INAP . . . . . . . . . . . . . . . 9
```

b. What sentence did he receive? *(Do not read out)*

```
                                    Fine . . . . . . . . . . . . . . . .01
                                    Probation (suspended with
                                       supervision) . . . . . . . . . . .02
                                    Suspended without supervision. . . .03
                                    Prison for a few days. . . . . . . .04
                                    Prison for a few weeks . . . . . . .05
                                    Prison for a few months. . . . . . .06
                                    Prison for 6 months to a year. . . .07
                                    Prison for up to 2 years (less a
                                       day) . . . . . . . . . . . . . . .08
                                    Prison for 2 years or longer . . . .09
                                    Other. . . . . . . . . . . . . . . .10
                                    D.K., not settled yet. . . . . . . .98
                                    INAP . . . . . . . . . . . . . . . .99
```

49a. In the end, were you satisfied with the police action?

```
                                    Yes (Go to Q. 51 ) . . . . . . . . 1
                                    No . . . . . . . . . . . . . . . . 2
                                    INAP . . . . . . . . . . . . . . . 9
```

b. In what way were you not satisfied?

_____

_____

_____

```
                                    INAP. . . . . . .9999
```

    Go to Q. 51 .

*(If "No" to police notification in Q. 40a., ASK:)*

50a. Why not?   *(Probe "anything else")*

|  | | YES | NO | D.K. | INAP |
|---|---|---|---|---|---|
| A. | Did not want to take the time. Might mean time spent in court or lost from work | 1 | 2 | 8 | 9 |
| B. | Did not want harm or punishment to come to the offender. | 1 | 2 | 8 | 9 |
| C. | Afraid of reprisal | 1 | 2 | 8 | 9 |
| D. | Thought it was a private, not criminal matter. | 1 | 2 | 8 | 9 |
| E. | Police couldn't do anything about the matter | 1 | 2 | 8 | 9 |
| F. | Police wouldn't want to be bothered about such things. | 1 | 2 | 8 | 9 |
| G. | Didn't know how to notify them or know that they should be notified. | 1 | 2 | 8 | 9 |
| H. | Fear of trouble from police (including fear of own offences being discovered) | 1 | 2 | 8 | 9 |
| I. | Too confused or upset to notify them | 1 | 2 | 8 | 9 |
| J. | Not sure the real offenders would be caught. | 1 | 2 | 8 | 9 |
| K. | Fear of insurance cancellation or increased rates. | 1 | 2 | 8 | 9 |
| L. | Do not speak English well enough | 1 | 2 | 8 | 9 |
| M. | Other (specify)_____ | 1 | 2 | 8 | 9 |

*(Hand R. Card D)*

b.   Could you rank these reasons for not calling police about this
incident in order of their importance?   *(Code 3 only)*

    1st choice . . . . . . . . . . .  _____
    2nd choice . . . . . . . . . . .  _____
    3rd choice . . . . . . . . . . .  _____
    INAP . . . . . . . . . . . . . .  999

*If something was taken, some damage was done, or any injuries, ASK Q. 51. if not, go to Q. 58a.*

51. Was the incident reported to the insurance company?

```
                                              Yes . . . . . . . . . . . . . . . . 1
                                              No (Go to Q. 55.) . . . . . . . . . 2
                                              D.K.. . . . . . . . . . . . . . . . 8
                                              INAP. . . . . . . . . . . . . . . . 9
```

52. Did you receive any compensation?

```
                                              Yes - full. . . . . . . . . . . . . 1
                                              Yes - partial . . . . . . . . . . . 2
                                              Not yet, but expected . . . . . . . 3
                                              No. . . . . . . . . . . . . . . . . 4
                                              D.K.. . . . . . . . . . . . . . . . 8
                                              INAP. . . . . . . . . . . . . . . . 9
```

53. Have you had to change insurance companies or do you expect your insurance premium to rise because of this incident?

```
                                      Yes - premium has already risen . . 1
                                      Yes - expect it to rise . . . . . . 2
                                      Yes - had to change companies . . . 3
                                      No. . . . . . . . . . . . . . . . . 4
                                      D.K.. . . . . . . . . . . . . . . . 8
                                      INAP. . . . . . . . . . . . . . . . 9
```

54. Did the insurance company advise you to report the incident to police?

```
                                              Yes . . . . . . . . . . . . . . . . 1
                                              No. . . . . . . . . . . . . . . . . 2
                                              Yes, but already had. . . . . . . . 3
                                              D.K.. . . . . . . . . . . . . . . . 8
                                              INAP. . . . . . . . . . . . . . . . 9
```

55. Did you receive any financial compensation or restitution other than from the insurance company?

```
                                      Yes - Criminal Injuries
                                      Compensation Board. . . . . . . . . 1
                                      Yes - other . . . . . . . . . . . . 2
                                      No. . . . . . . . . . . . . . . . . 3
                                      D.K.. . . . . . . . . . . . . . . . 8
                                      INAP. . . . . . . . . . . . . . . . 9
```

---

*If something was stolen from the residence, ASK Q. 56a.*
*If nothing taken, Go to Q. 58a.*

---

56a. Were any of the goods recovered?  By whom?
     *(Code first way only)*

```
                          ┌─ Yes - police recovered . . . . . . . 1
                          ├─ Yes - offender gave back . . . . . . 2
  ────────────────────────┤  Yes - found by friend or neighbour . 3
                          └─ Yes - other recovery . . . . . . . . 4

                          ┌─────────────────────────────────────────┐
                          │ No (Go to Q. 57a.) . . . . . . . . . 5   │
                          │ D.K. . . . . . . . . . . . . . . . . 8   │
                          └─────────────────────────────────────────┘

                            INAP . . . . . . . . . . . . . . . 9
```

b. What was that?

| | | YES | NO | D.K. | INAP |
|---|---|---|---|---|---|
| A. | Cash. . . . . . . . . . . . . | 1 | 2 | 8 | 9 |
| B. | T.V. . . . . . . . . . . . . | 1 | 2 | 8 | 9 |
| C. | Radio . . . . . . . . . . . . | 1 | 2 | 8 | 9 |
| D. | Hi-fi or stereo equipment . | 1 | 2 | 8 | 9 |
| E. | Jewellery . . . . . . . . . . | 1 | 2 | 8 | 9 |
| F. | Furs . . . . . . . . . . . . | 1 | 2 | 8 | 9 |
| G. | Beer, wine or spirits . . . | 1 | 2 | 8 | 9 |
| I. | Stocks, bonds . . . . . . . . | 1 | 2 | 8 | 9 |
| J. | Travellers cheques. . . . . | 1 | 2 | 8 | 9 |
| K. | Credit cards. . . . . . . . | 1 | 2 | 8 | 9 |
| L. | Other (specify) _____ | 1 | 2 | 8 | 9 |

c. What value would you say that was worth in total?

$_____ or between $_____ and $_____     ___ ___ ___

```
                    ┌──────────────────┐        INAP . . . 9 9 9
                    │ (Go to Q. 58a.)  │
                    └──────────────────┘
```

---

*If something was taken, or damage done, but no insurance compensation*
*or recovery, ASK:*

---

57a. Would you be prepared to settle the case out of court if the
     offender returned the goods, cash or documents taken and repaired
     damages?  (i.e. terminate any criminal or civil proceedings)?

```
                          Yes (Go to Q. 57c.). . . . . . . . .1
                       ┌─ Depends on circumstances . . . . . 2
                       └─ No . . . . . . . . . . . . . . . . 3

                          D.K. (Go to Q. 58a.) . . . . . . . 8
                          INAP . . . . . . . . . . . . . . . 9
```

b. Why?

_____

_____     ___ ___

_____     INAP . . .99

57c. What compensation in addition to the goods, cash or
documents returned would you require in order to settle
the case out of court?

No amount . . . . . . . . . . . 0 0 1

$_____ . . . . . . . . ___ ___ ___

INAP. . . . . . . . . . . . . . . 9 9 9

58a. Did you or someone in the household turn to anyone for
assistance other than police or insurance agents immediately
after the incident?

Yes . . . . . . . . . . . . . . . 1

No *(Go to Q. 59a)* . . . . . . . . 2
D.K.. . . . . . . . . . . . . . . 8

b. Who was that? *(1st mentioned)*

Spouse. . . . . . . . . . . . . . 1
Other household member. . . . . . 2
Family member not in dwelling . . 3
Landlord or superintendent. . . . 4
Neighbour or friend . . . . . . . 5
Lawyer. . . . . . . . . . . . . . 6
Private police or Community
Guardians . . . . . . . . . . . . 7
Other (specify) _____ . . 8
INAP. . . . . . . . . . . . . . . 9

c. What help did you get?

_____

_____

INAP. . . . . 99

d. Who else? *(2nd mentioned)*

Spouse. . . . . . . . . . . . . . .01
Other household member. . . . . . .02
Family member not in dwelling . .03
Landlord or superintendent. . . .04
Neighbour or friend . . . . . . .05
Lawyer. . . . . . . . . . . . . .06
Private police or Community
Guardians . . . . . . . . . . . .07
Other (specify)_____ . .08
No one. . . . . . . . . . . . . .09
INAP. . . . . . . . . . . . . . .99

e. What help did you get?

_____

_____

INAP. . . . . 99

59a. Do you know or have any ideas, hunches or suspicions as to the
     identity of the person/persons who entered your dwelling?

                                    ┌ Yes – offender(s) was caught . . . . 1
──────────────────────────────────┼ Yes – offender(s) was seen . . . . . 2
│                                   └ Yes – idea, hunch, suspicion only. . 3
│                                     No *(Go to Q. 60. )* . . . . . . . . 4
↓

b. If <u>Yes</u>:  Considering only the leader (or only offender) would
                you say he was . . .

                        . . .less than 12 years old . . . . . . . 1
                        . . .12 – 16 years old. . . . . . . . . . 2
                        . . .17 – 25 years old. . . . . . . . . . 3
                        . . .over 25 years old. . . . . . . . . . 4
                        D.K. . . . . . . . . . . . . . . . . . 8
                        INAP . . . . . . . . . . . . . . . . . 9

c. Was the person male or female?

                        Male . . . . . . . . . . . . . . . . . 1
                        Female . . . . . . . . . . . . . . . . 2
                        D.K. . . . . . . . . . . . . . . . . . 8
                        INAP . . . . . . . . . . . . . . . . . 9

d. Did he or she live within ½ a mile of here?

                        Yes. . . . . . . . . . . . . . . . . . 1
                        No . . . . . . . . . . . . . . . . . . 2
                        D.K. . . . . . . . . . . . . . . . . . 8
                        INAP . . . . . . . . . . . . . . . . . 9

e. Was he or she . . .    *( Code all that apply)*

| | YES | NO | D.K. | INAP |
|---|---|---|---|---|
| . . . a friend . . . . . . . . . . . . . . . . | 1 | 2 | 8 | 9 |
| . . . an acquaintance. . . . . . . . . . . . | 1 | 2 | 8 | 9 |
| . . . a friend of someone you know . . . . . | 1 | 2 | 8 | 9 |
| . . . a neighbour. . . . . . . . . . . . . . | 1 | 2 | 8 | 9 |
| . . . a relative . . . . . . . . . . . . . . | 1 | 2 | 8 | 9 |
| . . . someone you had trouble with before. . | 1 | 2 | 8 | 9 |
| . . . an employee or hired person. . . . . . | 1 | 2 | 8 | 9 |
| . . . a stranger, other(specify) _____ . | 1 | 2 | 8 | 9 |

f. Would you guess he or she was under the influence of alcohol at
   the time of the offence?

                        Yes – definitely known . . . . . . 1
                        Yes – probably . . . . . . . . . . . 2
                        No . . . . . . . . . . . . . . . . . 3
                        D.K. . . . . . . . . . . . . . . . . 8
                        INAP . . . . . . . . . . . . . . . . 9

59g. What about drugs?

```
                          Yes - definitely known . . . . . . 1
                          Yes - probably . . . . . . . . . . 2
                          No . . . . . . . . . . . . . . . . 3
                          D.K. . . . . . . . . . . . . . . . 8
                          INAP . . . . . . . . . . . . . . . 9
```

h. What would you guess as to his/her ethnic origin?

```
          _____        _____  ____

                                              INAP. . . 99
```

i. Was this person unemployed?

```
                          Yes - definitely known . . . . . . 1
                          Yes - probably . . . . . . . . . . 2
                          No . . . . . . . . . . . . . . . . 3
                          D.K. . . . . . . . . . . . . . . . 8
                          INAP . . . . . . . . . . . . . . . 9
```

j. Was there more than one offender?

```
   ┌─────────────────────── Yes. . . . . . . . . . . . . . . 1
   │                        No . . . . . . . . . . . . . . . 2
   │                        D.K. . . . . . . . . . . . . . . 8
   │                        INAP . . . . . . . . . . . . . . 9
   │
   ↓
```

k. How many? _____

```
                                              INAP. . . . 9
```

60. To what extent would you say that this incident was the
    result of the carelessness of someone who lives here?

```
                    . . . fully. . . . . . . . . . . . . . . 1
                    . . . partly . . . . . . . . . . . . . . 2
                    . . . not at all . . . . . . . . . . . . 3
                          D.K. . . . . . . . . . . . . . . . 8
```

*Latest Incident*

*(Hand R. Card E)*

61. What steps do you think you <u>could have taken</u> to prevent this
incident? *(Code first 3 mentioned in order of importance)*

| CODES | | Order of Importance - 1,2,3 |
|---|---|---|
| None . . . . . . . . . . . . . | 01 | |
| Stronger door. . . . . . . . . | 02 | |
| Stronger window. . . . . . . . | 03 | |
| Better windows . . . . . . . . | 04 | |
| Alarm. . . . . . . . . . . . . | 05 | |
| Lock doors . . . . . . . . . . | 06 | |
| Lock windows . . . . . . . . . | 07 | |
| Leave inside lights on . . . . | 08 | |
| Leave outside lights on. . . . | 09 | |
| Cancel deliveries. . . . . . . | 10 | |
| Ask neighbours to check house. . | 11 | |
| Use timer for lights, etc. . . . | 12 | |
| Other (specify) | | |
| 1. _____ . . | 13 | |
| 2. _____ . . | 14 | |
| 3. _____ . . | 15 | |
| D.K. . . . . . . . . . . . . . | 98 | |
| INAP . . . . . . . . . . . . . | 99 | |

_____ (Month)

_____ (Year)

____ ____

____ ____

____ ____

62. What precautions do you <u>now take</u> as a direct result of this
incident?

*(Record first 2 mentioned in order of importance using codes
in Q. 61. if applicable)*

1. _____    ____ ____

2. _____    ____ ____

---

*CONTINUE INTERVIEW WITH PART C,
QUESTION 63.*

PART C

Now I'd like to ask you some questions about things you may
or may not do which affect the security of your home.

63. Would you say it was easy or difficult to break into your
house/apartment?

Easy . . . . . . . . . . . . . . . 1
Difficult. . . . . . . . . . . . 2
Not sure, D.K. . . . . . . . . . 8

64. Could you tell me if you take the following precautions usually,
sometimes or never?

| Usually, | Sometimes, | Never, | INAP. |
|---|---|---|---|
| 1 | 2 | 3 | 9 |

a. Are the doors kept locked. . .

. . . when someone is home during the daytime? . . . . . . . . . ._____

. . . when someone is home during the evening? . . . . . . . . . ._____

. . . when you are asleep at night?. . . . . . . . . . . . . . . ._____

. . . when your home is left vacant for less than an hour? . . . ._____

. . . when your home is left vacant for more than an hour? . . . ._____

b. Do you leave at least one interior light on when no one is home
after dark?. . . . . . . . . . . . . . . . . . . . . . . . . . ._____

c. Do you leave at least one outdoor light on all night after
dark? *(If apartment, code 9 for INAP)*. . . . . . . . . . . . . ._____

d. Do you ask delivery men, repairmen, or meter readers to produce
identification?. . . . . . . . . . . . . . . . . . . . . . . . ._____

e. Do you accompany them while they are performing their tasks? . . ._____

f. Do you stop all deliveries if away for more than 2 or 3 days?. . ._____

g. Do you have friends or relatives cut the grass, shovel snow,
or remove papers and pamphlets while you are away for more than
2 or 3 days? . . . . . . . . . . . . . . . . . . . . . . . . . ._____

h. Do you ask police to check your home periodically while you are
away?. . . . . . . . . . . . . . . . . . . . . . . . . . . . . ._____

i. Do you discuss vacation dates with relative strangers or distant
acquaintances? . . . . . . . . . . . . . . . . . . . . . . . . ._____

j. When no one is home, is there a radio left on? . . . . . . . . ._____

k. When you lose a key or move into a new residence, do you have
the lock(s) changed? . . . . . . . . . . . . . . . . . . . . . ._____

*(Hand R. Card F)*

65. Which of the special precautions against burglary listed
    on this card are employed in this dwelling? *(Code all that apply)*

|  | YES | NO |
|---|---|---|
| . . . burglar alarms . . . . . . . . . . . . . . . . . . . . . . | 1 | 2 |
| . . . special door locks: i) Chain lock. . . . . . . . . . | 1 | 2 |
| ii) Dead bolt lock. . . . . . . . | 1 | 2 |
| iii) Other special door lock or lock system . . . . . . . . | 1 | 2 |
| . . . bars over doors or windows . . . . . . . . . . . . . . | 1 | 2 |
| . . . special lighting equipment (timer, outside flood-lighting, etc.) . . . . . . . . . . . . . . . . . . . | 1 | 2 |
| . . . key locks on windows . . . . . . . . . . . . . . . . | 1 | 2 |
| . . . volunteers patrolling area . . . . . . . . . . . . . | 1 | 2 |
| . . . security guards, private police, community guards. . | 1 | 2 |
| . . . other precautions (specify) _____ . . | 1 | 2 |

66a. Do you have a dog?

    Yes . . . . . . . . . . . . . 1
    No *(Go to Q. 67)* . . . . . . . . 2

b. Is this strictly a pet or is it also a watch dog?

    Pet only . . . . . . . . . . . . 1
    Watch dog also . . . . . . . . . 2
    Watch dog only . . . . . . . . . 3
    INAP . . . . . . . . . . . . . . 9

67. Do you keep a list of serial numbers on goods like a
    television set, stereo, etc.?

    Yes. . . . . . . . . . . . . . . 1
    No . . . . . . . . . . . . . . . 2
    D.K. . . . . . . . . . . . . . . 8

68. Is there a gun or rifle of some sort that could be used
    for the protection of your home even though it may also
    be used for sport?

    Yes. . . . . . . . . . . . . . . 1
    No . . . . . . . . . . . . . . . 2
    D.K. . . . . . . . . . . . . . . 8

69a.   Is there some other sort of weapon (other than a kitchen
       utensil) that could be used for this purpose?

                                          Yes . . . . . . . . . . . . . . 1
                                          No *(Go to Q. 70)*. . . . . . . . . 2

  b.   What sort of weapon?

                               Baseball bat,hockey stick, golf
                               club, etc.. . . . . . . . . . . . 1
                               Mace, other sprays. . . . . . . . 2
                               Other (specify)_____. . 3
                               INAP. . . . . . . . . . . . . . . 9


       Now I'd like to ask you some questions about your feeling towards
       living in this neighbourhood.

70.    What type of structure was your last dwelling?

                               Single house. . . . . . . . . . . 01
                               Single house attached (to a non-
                               residential structure,e.g. store) . 02
                               Semi-detached, or double house. . . 03
                               Row house . . . . . . . . . . . . 04
                               Duplex. . . . . . . . . . . . . . 05
                               Apartment, triplex, multi-dwelling. 06
                               Mobile,trailer, houseboat . . . . . 07
                               Rooming house . . . . . . . . . . 08
                               Boarding house. . . . . . . . . . 09
                               Other collective dwelling . . . . . 10
                               Other (specify) _____. . 11
                               D.K.. . . . . . . . . . . . . . . 98
                               INAP (no last dwelling)*(Go to Q.72)* 99


71.    Was this . . .

                           . . . in Toronto (Metropolitan) . . . . . 1
                           . . . in Ontario outside Toronto. . . . . 2
                           . . . in Canada outside Ontario . . . . . 3
                           . . . in the U.S.A. . . . . . . . . . . 4
                               Elsewhere . . . . . . . . . . . . 5
                               INAP. . . . . . . . . . . . . . . 9

72.    How long do you plan to live in this dwelling?

                               Less than one year. . . . . . . . 1
                               1 or 2 years. . . . . . . . . . . 2
                               A few years . . . . . . . . . . . 3
                               5 years or longer . . . . . . . . 4
                               D.K.. . . . . . . . . . . . . . . 8

73a. Was fear of crime one of the factors in helping you decide
to move into this neighbourhood?

Yes . . . . . . . . . . . . . . 1
No *(Go to Q. 74)*. . . . . . . . 2
D.K.. . . . . . . . . . . . . . 8

b. How important a factor was fear of crime?

Most important. . . . . . . . . 1
Important factor, but not princi-
pal one . . . . . . . . . . . . 2
Of minor importance . . . . . . 3
INAP. . . . . . . . . . . . . . 9

74. Is your closest friend outside this residence one of your
neighbours?

Yes . . . . . . . . . . . . . . 1
No. . . . . . . . . . . . . . . 2

75. Do you know the name of your next door neighbour . . .

. . . on the left?
Yes . . . . . . . . . . . . . . 1
No. . . . . . . . . . . . . . . 2
Nobody next door, INAP. . . . . 9

. . . on the right?
Yes . . . . . . . . . . . . . . 1
No. . . . . . . . . . . . . . . 2
Nobody next door, INAP. . . . . 9

. . . opposite you?
Yes . . . . . . . . . . . . . . 1
No. . . . . . . . . . . . . . . 2
Nobody opposite, INAP . . . . . 9

76. How often do you visit or talk to your immediate
neighbours?

Daily or more frequently. . . . . 1
Several times a week. . . . . . . 2
From time to time . . . . . . . . 3
Seldom. . . . . . . . . . . . . . 4
Never . . . . . . . . . . . . . . 5
INAP (no immediate neighbours). . 9

77. How many person(s) (on this block/in this apartment building)
could you arrange to have a parcel delivered to?

Exact number _____ ____

D.K.. . . . . . . . . . . . . . 8

78.  How often do you ask neighbours to keep an eye on your
     residence while you are away for more than a couple of
     days?  Would you say . . .

                              . . . all the time . . . . . . . . . . 1
                              . . . sometimes. . . . . . . . . . . . 2
                              . . . rarely . . . . . . . . . . . . . 3
                              . . . never. . . . . . . . . . . . . . 4
                                    D.K. . . . . . . . . . . . . . . 8

79a.  How likely are your neighbours to notice strangers
      loitering about your residence during the daytime
      while you are away?  Would you say . . .

                              . . . very likely. . . . . . . . . . . 1
                              . . . likely . . . . . . . . . . . . . 2
                              . . . not likely . . . . . . . . . . . 3
                                    D.K. . . . . . . . . . . . . . . 8

  b.  How about at night . . .

                              . . . very likely. . . . . . . . . . . 1
                              . . . likely . . . . . . . . . . . . . 2
                              . . . not likely . . . . . . . . . . . 3
                                    D.K. . . . . . . . . . . . . . . 8

80.  How likely are your neighbours to approach these strangers?
     Would you say . . .
                              . . . very likely. . . . . . . . . . . 1
                              . . . likely . . . . . . . . . . . . . 2
                              . . . not likely . . . . . . . . . . . 3
                                    D.K. . . . . . . . . . . . . . . 8

81a.  Is there a ratepayers' association, tenant's council, block
      association or other civic group in this area?

                              Yes. . . . . . . . . . . . . . . . 1
                              No *(Go to Q. 82a.)* . . . . . . . 2
                              D.K. . . . . . . . . . . . . . . . 8

  b.  Have any of these associations discussed or taken steps to
      increase neighbourhood protection or security against burglary?

                              Yes. . . . . . . . . . . . . . . . 1
                              No *(Go to Q. 82a.)* . . . . . . . 2
                              D.K. . . . . . . . . . . . . . . . 3
                              INAP . . . . . . . . . . . . . . . 9

  c.  What were these steps?

     _____

     _____
                                                   INAP . . . . 9 9

a.  Is this a publicly subsidized dwelling?

                    Yes  *(Go to Q. 83.)*. . . . . . . 1
    ┌──────────────────────────── No . . . . . . . . . . . . . . 2
    │
    ↓
b.  How far away is the nearest public housing project
    located? Would you say . . .

                    . . . within a few blocks. . . . . . . 1
                    . . . further. . . . . . . . . . . . 2
                    D.K. . . . . . . . . . . . . . . 8
                    INAP . . . . . . . . . . . . . 9

.   Are there any persons or groups of persons in this area
    whom you feel may contribute to the likelihood of your
    residence being broken into?

                    Yes (specify)
                    _____  ___ ___
                    No . . . . . . . . . . . . . . . 01
                    D.K. . . . . . . . . . . . . . . 98

    Now I'd like to ask you some questions about the occupancy
    pattern of your household.

a.  Thinking back to last week, how many mornings/afternoons/evenings/
    nights  during the week was this dwelling unoccupied?
    *(If dwelling vacant for more than one hour during the time period,
    count as unoccupied)*

| Number of Mornings/week 7:00a.m. - 11:59a.m. | Number of Afternoons/week 12:00p.m. - 5:59p.m. | Number of Evenings/week 6:00p.m. - 9:59p.m. | Number of Nights/week 10:00p.m.-6:59a.m. |
|---|---|---|---|
| 0 | 0 | 0 | 0 |
| 1 | 1 | 1 | 1 |
| 2 | 2 | 2 | 2 |
| 3 | 3 | 3 | 3 |
| 4 | 4 | 4 | 4 |
| 5 | 5 | 5 | 5 |
| D.K.. . 8 | D.K.. . 8 | D.K.. . 8 | D.K. . 8 |

b.  Now consider last weekend.  How many mornings etc. was this dwelling
    unoccupied?

| Mornings 7:00a.m. - 11:59a.m. | Afternoons 12:00p.m. - 5:59p.m. | Evenings 6:00p.m. - 9:59p.m. | Nights 10:00p.m.- 6:59a.m. |
|---|---|---|---|
| 0 | 0 | 0 | 0 |
| 1 | 1 | 1 | 1 |
| 2 | 2 | 2 | 2 |
| D.K.. . 8 | D.K.. . 8 | D.K.. . 8 | D.K. . 8 |

84c.  Still considering last week, how many hours was the house
unoccupied during each day of the week?  *(Code to nearest hour)*

|  | No. of Hours |
|---|---|
| Monday . . . . . . . . . . . . . | ___ ___ |
| Tuesday. . . . . . . . . . . . | ___ ___ |
| Wednesday. . . . . . . . . . . | ___ ___ |
| Thursday . . . . . . . . . . . | ___ ___ |
| Friday . . . . . . . . . . . . | ___ ___ |
| Saturday . . . . . . . . . . . | ___ ___ |
| Sunday . . . . . . . . . . . . | ___ ___ |

85a.  Compared to last week, would you say that this residence
is <u>un</u>occupied during the spring (April, May) . . .

|  |  |
|---|---|
| . . . much more often. . . . . . . . . . | 1 |
| . . . more often . . . . . . . . . . . . | 2 |
| . . . about the same . . . . . . . . . . | 3 |
| . . . less often . . . . . . . . . . . . | 4 |
| . . . much less often. . . . . . . . . . | 5 |
| D.K. . . . . . . . . . . . . . . | 8 |

*(Using codes as above, ASK:)*

b.  How about for summer? (June - Sept.)                    _____

c.  How about for Fall? (Oct., Nov.)                        _____

d.  How about for Winter? (Dec. - Mar.)                     _____

86.  How often during the different seasons did everyone who lives
here go away for weekends last year, leaving the dwelling
unoccupied?  Was this frequently, sometimes, rarely, never?

|  | Frequently | Sometimes | Rarely | Never | D.K. |
|---|---|---|---|---|---|
| a. Spring . . . . . . . . . . | 1 | 2 | 3 | 4 | 8 |
| b. Summer . . . . . . . . . | 1 | 2 | 3 | 4 | 8 |
| c. Fall . . . . . . . . . . . | 1 | 2 | 3 | 4 | 8 |
| d. Winter . . . . . . . . . | 1 | 2 | 3 | 4 | 8 |

87. During which month did you take your annual vacation last
    year? *(If month cannot be specified, probe for season)*

|                                              |    |
|----------------------------------------------|----|
| January                                      | 01 |
| February                                     | 02 |
| March                                        | 03 |
| April                                        | 04 |
| May                                          | 05 |
| June                                         | 06 |
| July                                         | 07 |
| August                                       | 08 |
| September                                    | 09 |
| October                                      | 10 |
| November                                     | 11 |
| December                                     | 12 |
| Spring (Apr., May)                           | 13 |
| Summer (Jun., Jul., Aug., Sep.)              | 14 |
| Fall (Oct., Nov.)                            | 15 |
| Winter (Dec., Jan., Feb., Mar.)              | 16 |

Split vacation into several times
during year . . . . . . . . . . . 17
Other(specify) _____ . 18
INAP (no vacation) *(Go to Q.89a)*. 99

88. Was your residence unoccupied then?

|                        |   |
|------------------------|---|
| Yes                    | 1 |
| No                     | 2 |
| D.K.                   | 8 |
| INAP (no vacation)     | 9 |

Now I'd like to ask you about any contact you've had with the
police, the courts and so on .

89a. Have you ever been to court?

Yes . . . . . . . . . . . . . . . 1
No *(Go to Q. 91a)* . . . . . . . . 2

b. How **many** times within the last five years? _____  ___ ___

INAP. . 99

90a. When you were in court, were you involved personally as
one of the parties in a case, a witness, a spectator, a
juror, or anything else? *(Code all that apply)*

|  | | YES | NO | INAP |
|---|---|---|---|---|
| a. | Court appearance for burglary incident described in Section <u>B</u> . . . . . . . . . . . . | 1 | 2 | 9 |
| b. | Party (or representing a party). . . . . . . | 1 | 2 | 9 |
| c. | Witness . . . . . . . . . . . . . . . . . | 1 | 2 | 9 |
| d. | Spectator. . . . . . . . . . . . . . . . . | 1 | 2 | 9 |
| e. | Juror. . . . . . . . . . . . . . . . . . . | 1 | 2 | 9 |
| f. | Other (specify) _____ . . . | 1 | 2 | 9 |

b. What kind of case(s) was this? *(Code all that apply)*

|  | YES | NO | D.K. | INA |
|---|---|---|---|---|
| Burglary incident described in Section B. . . . . . . . . . . . . . . | 1 | 2 | 8 | 9 |
| . . . parking tickets. . . . . . . . . . . . | 1 | 2 | 8 | 9 |
| . . . traffic accident or violation. . . . . | 1 | 2 | 8 | 9 |
| . . . criminal case - burglary . . . . . . . | 1 | 2 | 8 | 9 |
| . . . other criminal case. . . . . . . . . . | 1 | 2 | 8 | 9 |
| . . . family or divorce case . . . . . . . . | 1 | 2 | 8 | 9 |
| . . . other civil matter . . . . . . . . . . | 1 | 2 | 8 | 9 |
| . . . other (specify)_____ . . | 1 | 2 | 8 | 9 |

c. How much time was spent in court altogether?

$\frac{1}{2}$ day or less . , . . . . . . . . . . 1
More than $\frac{1}{2}$ day to 1 day. . . . . . 2
2 or 3 days . . . . . . . . . . . . 3
4 or 5 days (1 week). . . . . . . . 4
More than 5 days. . . . . . . . . . 5
D.K.. . . . . . . . . . . . . . . . 8
INAP. . . . . . . . . . . . . . . . 9

d. Did you receive any compensation?

Yes . . . . . . . . . . . . . . . . 1
No *(Go to Q. 91a.)*. . . . . . . . . 2
D.K.. . . . . . . . . . . . . . . . 8
INAP. . . . . . . . . . . . . . . . 9

e. How much?

$ _____ or between $ _____ and $_____      ___ __

INAP . . 99

91a. Have you ever been involved in anything which might have gone to court but was settled without going to court? *(Do not include parking tickets)*

Yes . . . . . . . . . . . . . 1
No *(Go to Q. 92a.)* . . . . . . 2

b. How many times within the last five years? _____    _____

INAP. . . 9

c. What type of case was the latest one?

|  | YES | NO | D.K. | INAP |
|---|---|---|---|---|
| Burglary incident described in Section B. . . . . . . . . . . . . . . . | 1 | 2 | 8 | 9 |
| . . . parking tickets. . . . . . . . . . . . | 1 | 2 | 8 | 9 |
| . . . traffic accident or violation. . . . | 1 | 2 | 8 | 9 |
| . . . criminal case - burglary . . . . . . | 1 | 2 | 8 | 9 |
| . . . other criminal case. . . . . . . . . | 1 | 2 | 8 | 9 |
| . . . family or divorce case . . . . . . . | 1 | 2 | 8 | 9 |
| . . . other civil matter . . . . . . . . . | 1 | 2 | 8 | 9 |
| . . . other (specify) _____ | 1 | 2 | 8 | 9 |

92a. When was the <u>last time</u> you called the police?

After Jan. 1, 1974 . . . . . . . . . 1
After Jan. 1, 1973. . . . . . . . . 2
Before Jan. 1, 1973 . . . . . . . . 3
Never called them *(Go to Q. 93a.)* . 4
D.K.. . . . . . . . . . . . . . . . 8

| ASK VICTIMS ONLY |
|---|

b. Was the last time the burglary incident already described?

Yes . . . . . . . . . . . . . . . . 1
No. . . . . . . . . . . . . . . . . 2

| ASK EVERYONE |
|---|

INAP. . . . . . . . . . . . . . . . 9

c. (Other than that) What was the most recent incident?

Traffic violation or traffic accident. . . . . . . . . . . . . . . .01
Domestic quarrel. . . . . . . . . . .02
Saw crime committed . . . . . . . .03
Emergency help, first aid . . . . .04
Fire. . . . . . . . . . . . . . . . .05
Information wanted. . . . . . . . .06
Other (specify)_____ .07
D.K.. . . . . . . . . . . . . . . . .98
INAP. . . . . . . . . . . . . . . . .99

93a.  Was there an incident since the start of last year for which you felt you might or should have called the police, but did not? *(Do not include burglary incident reported in Section B)*

                                              Yes . . . . . . . . . . . . . 1
                                              No *(Go to Q. 94.)* . . . . . . . 2

b.  What type of incident was that?

                                              Traffic accident. . . . . . . 01
                                              Domestic quarrel. . . . . . . 02
                                              Saw crime committed . . . . . 03
                                              Emergency help, first aid.. . . 04
                                              Fire. . . . . . . . . . . . . 05
                                              Information wanted. . . . . . 06
                                              Other (specify)

                                              _____. . 07
                                              D.K.. . . . . . . . . . . . . 98
                                              INAP. . . . . . . . . . . . . 99

*(Hand R. Card D)*

c.  For which of these reasons were police not called?
    *(Code all that apply)*

|   |   | YES | NO | INAP |
|---|---|---|---|---|
| A. | Did not want to take the time . Might mean time spent in court or lost from work . . . . . . . . . . . . . . . . . . . . . | 1 | 2 | 9 |
| B. | Did not want harm or punishment to come to the offender . . . . . . . . . . . . . . . . . . | 1 | 2 | 9 |
| C. | Afraid of reprisal . . . . . . . . . . . . . . . | 1 | 2 | 9 |
| D. | Thought it was a private, not criminal matter. | 1 | 2 | 9 |
| E. | Police couldn't do anything about the matter . | 1 | 2 | 9 |
| F. | Police wouldn't want to be bothered about such things . . . . . . . . . . . . . . . . . | 1 | 2 | 9 |
| G. | Didn't know how to notify them or know that they should be notified. . . . . . . . . . . . | 1 | 2 | 9 |
| H. | Fear of trouble from police (including fear of own offences being discovered). . . . . . . | 1 | 2 | 9 |
| I. | Too confused or upset to notify them . . . . . | 1 | 2 | 9 |
| J. | Not sure the real offenders would be caught. . | 1 | 2 | 9 |
| K. | Fear of insurance cancellation or increased rates. . . . . . . . . . . . . . . . . . . . . | 1 | 2 | 9 |
| L. | Do not speak English well enough . . . . . . . | 1 | 2 | 9 |
| M. | Other (specify) _____ . | 1 | 2 | 9 |

94. Generally, on this street (on this apartment floor) would
the people call the police if they suspected someone might
be trying to break into a dwelling?

                          Yes . . . . . . . . . . . . . . . 1
                          No. . . . . . . . . . . . . . . . 2
                          D.K.. . . . . . . . . . . . . . . 8

95. Would they try to intervene directly?

                          Yes . . . . . . . . . . . . . . . 1
                          No. . . . . . . . . . . . . . . . 2
                          D.K.. . . . . . . . . . . . . . . 8

96a. Within the last 5 years, have you ever read anything , or seen
anything on T.V. or on film or heard anything on radio, on how to
protect your home against burglary?

                          Yes . . . . . . . . . . . . . . . 1
                          No *(Go to Q. 97)*. . . . . . . . 2
                          D.K.. . . . . . . . . . . . . . . 8

b. Which? . . .     *(Code all that apply)*

|  | YES | NO | INAP |
|---|---|---|---|
| . . . police pamphlet . . . . . . | 1 . | . . . 2. | . . . 9 |
| . . . insurance pamphlet. . . . . | 1 . | . . . 2. | . . . 9 |
| . . . T.V. . . . . . . . . . . . | 1 . | . . . 2. | . . . 9 |
| . . . film . . . . . . . . . . . | 1 . | . . . 2. | . . . 9 |
| . . . radio . . . . . . . . . . . | 1 . | . . . 2. | . . . 9 |
| . . . magazine. . . . . . . . . . | 1 . | . . . 2. | . . . 9 |
| Other(specify) _____ . | 1 . | . . . 2. | . . . 9 |

c. As a result, did you take any additional precautions?

                          Yes . . . . . . . . . . . . . . . 1
                          No. . . . . . . . . . . . . . . . 2
                          D.K.. . . . . . . . . . . . . . . 8
                          INAP. . . . . . . . . . . . . . . 9

d. Did you experience an increase in fear or anxiety
regarding burglary?

                          Yes . . . . . . . . . . . . . . . 1
                          No. . . . . . . . . . . . . . . . 2
                          D.K.. . . . . . . . . . . . . . . 8
                          INAP. . . . . . . . . . . . . . . 9

This next section deals with your attitudes towards crime and punishment.

97. I would like you to consider a situation, where a person breaks into your house while you are  out by slipping the lock, and takes $250 in goods and cash.  What percentage  of persons committing such offences do you think the police would catch?  _____ %

_____ _____

*(Hand R. Card G)*

98a. Let us assume that an offender is caught for this offence.  He is an English-Canadian aged 18 years who has not been charged with a criminal offence before and is convicted  for the offence by a court in Metropolitan Toronto.  What sentence do you think he should receive?

```
Fine . . . . . . . . . . . . . . . . 01
Probation (suspended with
   supervision) . . . . . . . . . . . 02
Suspended without supervision. . . . 03
Prison for a few days. . . . . . . . 04
Prison for a few weeks . . . . . . . 05
Prison for a few months. . . . . . . 06
Prison for 6 months to a year. . . . 07
Prison for up to 2 years (less a day)08
Prison for 2 years or longer . . . . 09
Other (specify)
   _____ . 10
D.K. . . . . . . . . . . . . . . . 98
```

b. How much?  $ _____

_____ _____

*(Hand R. Card H)*

99. Now for the offence already described, I would like to obtain your own views if certain aspects of the offence and the offender were different.
Would  you tell me if the sentence should be much more severe, more severe, less severe, much less severe, or about the same in the following instances . . .

| Much more severe 1 | More severe 2 | About the same 3 | Less severe 4 | Much less severe 5 |
|---|---|---|---|---|

01. . . if the door had been broken down instead of the lock slipped?
02. . . if the door had been unlocked?
03. . . if the value of goods taken had been $3,000 instead of $250?
04. . . if it had been a warehouse or factory instead of your residence?
05. . . if the offender had been 30 instead of 18?
06. . . if the offender had been 14 instead of 18?
07. . . if the offender had been female?
08. . . if the offender was an immigrant?
09. . . if the offender had been previously convicted twice of shoplifting?
10. . . if the offender had been previously convicted twice of assault?
11. . . if the victim had complete insurance coverage of all that was taken?
12. . . if the victim was pressing for a severe penalty?
13. . . if there was a provincial scheme to compensate for losses from burglary?
14. . . if more psychiatric help were available to offenders?

100. Could you rank the items on Card H which you feel <u>should be</u> most important in determining sentences?

                             1st choice. . . . . . . . . \_\_\_\_ \_\_\_\_

                             2nd choice. . . . . . . . . \_\_\_\_ \_\_\_\_

                             3rd choice. . . . . . . . . \_\_\_\_ \_\_\_\_

101. Should he have to pay restitution?
*(Refer back to Q. 97 and Q. 98.if necessary)*

                             Yes . . . . . . . . . . . . 1

                             No. . . . . . . . . . . . . 2

                             D.K.. . . . . . . . . . . . 8

102a. If the offender could be sentenced to a number of weeks or days of unpaid work for the community, would you adopt such a sentence? *(Refer to Q. 97 and 98 if necessary)*

                             Yes . . . . . . . . . . . . 1

                             No. . . . . . . . . . . . . 2

                             D.K.. . . . . . . . . . . . 8

  b. How many days? _____

                                          INAP . . 99

103. What do you think should be the most important aims in sentencing? *(If more than one aim is mentioned, get the R. to rank the aims. If <u>prevention</u> is mentioned, probe to distinguish between rehabilitating the offender or deterring others through punishment. Probe for <u>moral denunciation</u> and <u>retribution</u>.)*

  _____ \_\_ \_\_

  _____ \_\_ \_\_

  _____ \_\_ \_\_

104. Are there any forms of sentence that we have not discussed, which you think should be available for residential burglary?

  _____

  _____

  _____ \_\_ \_\_

Many people have gone into someone else's residence without their consent, particularly as a child, or teenager. Have you ever been personally involved, either alone or as part of a group, in any of the following events?

105a. Have you ever broken **into** somebody **else's** house, garage, shed or apartment, even if it was vacant?

$$
\begin{array}{ll}
\text{Yes} & . . . . . . . . . . . . . . . 1 \\
\text{No.} & . . . . . . . . . . . . . . . 2 \\
\text{Ref..} & . . . . . . . . . . . . . . 3
\end{array}
$$

b. Have you ever tried to break into one of those?

$$
\begin{array}{ll}
\text{Yes} & . . . . . . . . . . . . . . . 1 \\
\text{No.} & . . . . . . . . . . . . . . . 2 \\
\text{Ref..} & . . . . . . . . . . . . . . 3
\end{array}
$$

c. Have you ever just walked into someone else's residence without the consent of someone there? *(Do not include simply dropping into a friend's, or relative's or neighbour's residence unannounced)*

$$
\begin{array}{ll}
\text{Yes} & . . . . . . . . . . . . . . . 1 \\
\text{No.} & . . . . . . . . . . . . . . . 2 \\
\text{Ref..} & . . . . . . . . . . . . . . 3
\end{array}
$$

d. Have you ever done any of the above in connection with a school, factory, warehouse or any other building?

$$
\begin{array}{ll}
\text{Yes} & . . . . . . . . . . . . . . . 1 \\
\text{No.} & . . . . . . . . . . . . . . . 2 \\
\text{Ref..} & . . . . . . . . . . . . . . 3
\end{array}
$$

---

*If "No" to all of above, go to Part D, Q. 108a, page 48*

*If "Yes" to any of the above, ASK:*

---

106. How many times altogether? _____                    ____

INAP . . . 9

*(For Q.107 A - G, consider only the latest incident)*

107a. How long ago was the latest incident?

$$
\begin{array}{ll}
\text{In last two years} & . . . . . . . 1 \\
\text{2 - 5 years ago} & . . . . . . . . 2 \\
\text{More than 5 years ago} & . . . . . 3 \\
\text{D.K..} & . . . . . . . . . . . . . 8 \\
\text{INAP.} & . . . . . . . . . . . . . 9
\end{array}
$$

107b. What type of premises was this?

```
                                    Single house . . . . . . . . . . 01
                                    Single house attached (to non-
                                    resident structure). . . . . . 02
                                    Semi-detached. . . . . . . . . 03
                                    Row house. . . . . . . . . . . 04
                                    Duplex . . . . . . . . . . . . 05
                                    Apartment. . . . . . . . . . . 06
                                    Mobile . . . . . . . . . . . . 07
                                    Hotel. . . . . . . . . . . . . 08
                                    Motel. . . . . . . . . . . . . 09
                                    Hospital.. . . . . . . . . . . 10
                                    Staff residence. . . . . . . . 11
                                    Institution. . . . . . . . . . 12
                                    Military camp. . . . . . . . . 13
                                    Work camp. . . . . . . . . . . 14
                                    Mission. . . . . . . . . . . . 15
                                    Rooming house. . . . . . . . . 16
                                    Boarding house . . . . . . . . 17
                                    School . . . . . . . . . . . . 18
                                    Factory. . . . . . . . . . . . 19
                                    Store. . . . . . . . . . . . . 20
                                    Gas station. . . . . . . . . . 21
                                    Other. . . . . . . . . . . . . 22
                                    D.K. . . . . . . . . . . . . . 98
                                    INAP . . . . . . . . . . . . . 99
```

c. Why did you do that?

_____

_____                      ___  __

                                                        INAP. . 99

d. Did you take anything?

```
                                    Yes  . . . . . . . . . . . . . 1
                                    No.. . . . . . . . . . . . . . 2
                                    D.K. . . . . . . . . . . . . . 8
                                    INAP . . . . . . . . . . . . . 9
```

e. Was there any damage done?

```
                                    Yes. . . . . . . . . . . . . . 1
                                    No . . . . . . . . . . . . . . 2
                                    D.K. . . . . . . . . . . . . . 8
                                    INAP.. . . . . . . . . . . . . 9
```

107f. Were you caught?

```
                                    Yes . . . . . . . . . . . . . . 1
                                    No (Go to PART D) . . . . . . . 2
                                    INAP. . . . . . . . . . . . . . 9
```

g. What happened to you?

```
                                    Let go by victim. . . . . . . . 1
                                    Let go by police. . . . . . . . 2
                                    Cleared in court. . . . . . . . 3
                                    Suspended sentence. . . . . . . 4
                                    Jail or prison. . . . . . . . . 5
                                    Other sentence. . . . . . . . . 6
                                    D.K.. . . . . . . . . . . . . . 8
                                    INAP. . . . . . . . . . . . . . 9
```

## PART D

Now I'd like to ask you some background questions.

108a. What level did you obtain in school?

```
                          None. . . . . . . . . . . . . . . . . . 0
                          Some elementary school. . . . . . . . . 0
                          Complete elementary school. . . . . . . 0
                          Some secondary school . . . . . . . . . 0
                          Complete secondary school . . . . . . . 0
                          Some post-secondary non-university. . . 0
                          Complete post-secondary non-university. 0
                          Some university . . . . . . . . . . . . 0
                          Complete university . . . . . . . . . . 0
                          Post-graduate university. . . . . . . . 1
```

b. How many years is that? _____

109. What is your religious preference?

```
                          Roman Catholic. . . . . . . . 01
                          Anglican. . . . . . . . . . . 02
                          United. . . . . . . . . . . . 03
                          Presbyterian. . . . . . . . . 04
                          Baptist . . . . . . . . . . . 05
                          Ukrainian Catholic. . . . . . 06
                          Greek Orthodox. . . . . . . . 07
                          Jewish. . . . . . . . . . . . 08
                          Other (specify) _____ 09
                          No preference . . . . . . . . 99
```

110. What language did you first learn to speak and still understand?

_____

111a. Where were you born?

| | |
|---|---|
| Toronto (Metro) *(Go to Q. 112a)*. . . | 01 |
| Ontario (outside Toronto). . . . . . | 02 |
| Other Canada . . . . . . . . . . . | 03 |

| | |
|---|---|
| U. K.. . . . . . . . . . . . . . . | 04 |
| U.S.A. . . . . . . . . . . . . . . | 05 |
| Italy. . . . . . . . . . . . . . . | 06 |
| Germany. . . . . . . . . . . . . . | 07 |
| The Ukraine. . . . . . . . . . . . | 08 |
| Portugal . . . . . . . . . . . . . | 09 |
| Greece . . . . . . . . . . . . . . | 10 |
| Other Europe.. . . . . . . . . . . | 11 |
| China. . . . . . . . . . . . . . . | 12 |
| Other Asia . . . . . . . . . . . . | 13 |
| Africa . . . . . . . . . . . . . . | 14 |
| S. America, Central America. . . . . | 15 |
| New Zealand, Australia . . . . . . . | 16 |
| West Indies. . . . . . . . . . . . | 17 |
| Other. . . . . . . . . . . . . . . | 18 |

b. *(If "Not" born in Canada, ASK:)*

How old were you when you first came to Canada? _____      ___ ___

INAP . . . 99

112a. What level did head of household obtain in school?

| | |
|---|---|
| None . . . . . . . . . . . . . . . | 01 |
| Some elementary school . . . . . . . | 02 |
| Complete elementary school . . . . . | 03 |
| Some secondary school. . . . . . . . | 04 |
| Complete secondary school. . . . . . | 05 |
| Some post-secondary non-university . . | 06 |
| Complete post-secondary non-university | 07 |
| Some university. . . . . . . . . . . | 08 |
| Complete university. . . . . . . . . | 09 |
| Post-graduate university . . . . . . | 10 |
| D.K. *(Go to Q. 113)*. . . . . . . . | 98 |

b. How many years is that? _____      ___ ___

D.K.. . . . 98

*(Hand R. Card B)*

113.  Within which of the following categories did the income <u>before</u>
      taxes from <u>all</u> sources of all persons living here in 1973 fall?
      This includes lodgers, partners, employees or others occupying
      this dwelling.

                                A.  Less than 3,000. . . . . . . 01
                                B.  3,000 - 4,999. . . . . . . . 02
                                C.  5,000 - 6,999. . . . . . . . 03
                                D.  7,000 - 8,999. . . . . . . . 04
                                E.  9,000 - 10,999 . . . . . . . 05
                                F.  11,000 - 14,999. . . . . . . 06
                                G.  15,000 - 24,999. . . . . . . 07
                                H.  25,000 - 39,999. . . . . . . 08
                                I.  40,000 and over. . . . . . . 09
                                    D.K. . . . . . . . . . . . . 98

114.  How many rooms are there in this house/apartment/flat?
      (Do not include bathrooms, closets, pantries, halls or
      rooms used only for business purposes). _____

115a. Do you own or rent this residence?

                                ────── Rent . . . . . . . . . . . . . . 1
                                      ┌─────────────────────────────────┐
                                      │ Own *(Go to Q. 116)* . . . . . . 2 │
                                      │ Residence provided by business, │
                                      │ church, etc. . . . . . . . . . 3 │
                                      │ Other. . . . . . . . . . . . . 4 │
                                      └─────────────────────────────────┘

   b. How long is your lease for?  *(Obtain length, <u>not</u> amount left)*

                                One week or less . . . . . . . . 01
                                One month or less. . . . . . . . 02
                                One month up to 6 months . . . . 03
                                6 months . . . . . . . . . . . . 04
                                Up to 1 year . . . . . . . . . . 05
                                1 year . . . . . . . . . . . . . 06
                                Up to 2 years. . . . . . . . . . 07
                                2 years. . . . . . . . . . . . . 08
                                More than 2 years. . . . . . . . 09
                                D.K. . . . . . . . . . . . . . . 98
                                INAP. (no lease) . . . . . . . . 99

116.  How many years have you lived at this address?

                                Less than one year . . . . . . . 1
                                1 - 2 years .. . . . . . . . . . 2
                                3 - 5 years . . . . . . . . . . 3
                                6 - 10 years . . . . . . . . . . 4
                                More than 10 years . . . . . . . 5

17. Have you done any major alterations to this residence
    since you moved in  other than routine painting and
    upkeep?   (Repainting upon moving in not considered).

                              Yes . . . . . . . . . . . . . . 1
                              No. . . . . . . . . . . . . . . 2
                              D.K.. . . . . . . . . . . . . . 8

18. Is this dwelling also used for business purposes?

                              Yes – see clients . . . . . . . 1
                              Yes – store or commercial . . . 2
                              Yes – other . . . . . . . . . . 3
                              No. . . . . . . . . . . . . . . 4
                              INAP. . . . . . . . . . . . . . 9

---

*If surveillance (Section E) can be completed without R's co-operation,
thank R. for interview and depart.*

*If not, ask for R's co-operation in gathering a few details on the
physical aspects of the dwelling.*

PART E

*INTERVIEWER ONLY*

> If *apartment*, go to page 56, Q. 126a.
>
> If *house* (single house, single house attached to a non-resident structure, semi-detached, row house, duplex, mobile home, **rooming** house or boarding house), answer the following questions:

119a. *Number of stories:* _____          _____

                                                        INAP. . . 9

   b. *Which floor do you occupy?*

                        Basement . . . . . . . . . . . . . . 1
                        Main floor . . . . . . . . . . . . . 2
                        2nd, 3rd and up. . . . . . . . . . . 3
                        Occupy whole dwelling. . . . . . . . 4
                        INAP . . . . . . . . . . . . . . . . 9

120.  *Is this a corner-lot or second to a corner-lot?*

                        Corner-lot . . . . . . . . . . . . . 1
                        Second to corner-lot . . . . . . . . 2
                        Other (specify)_____. 3
                        INAP . . . . . . . . . . . . . . . . 9

> *Front surveillance:*

121a. *How far from the street is the front of the dwelling?  (Estimate in number of single driveway widths)* _____          ____

                                                        INAP . . .99

   b. *Is the main outside door in the front of the dwelling?*

                        Yes. . . . . . . . . . . . . . . . . 1
                        No . . . . . . . . . . . . . . . . . 2
                        INAP . . . . . . . . . . . . . . . . 9

   c. *Considering the view of the house obtained from the street or the sidewalk in front of the house, code the following if they pose an obstruction as far as the front door or window is concerned:  Is this a slight obstruction, a fairly large one, or a total obstruction? (That is, can it camouflage a potential intruder?) (Code all that apply)*

| | Slight Obstruction | Fairly large Obstruction | Total Obstruction | INAP |
|---|---|---|---|---|
| a. Wall . . . . . . . . . . . . . . | 1 | 2 | 3 | 9 |
| b. Fence. . . . . . . . . . . . . . | 1 | 2 | 3 | 9 |
| c. Hedge. . . . . . . . . . . . . . | 1 | 2 | 3 | 9 |
| d. Bushes, trees. . . . . . . . . . | 1 | 2 | 3 | 9 |
| e. Garage or other building . . . | 1 | 2 | 3 | 9 |
| f. Landscaping . . . . . . . . . . | 1 | 2 | 3 | 9 |
| g. Other (specify)_____. | 1 | 2 | 3 | 9 |

121d.*Describe surveillability of front from residence across street:*

> No residence across the street . . 1
> Excellent. . . . . . . . . . . . 2
> Slight obstruction(s). . . . . . 3
> Fairly large obstruction(s). . . . 4
> Total obstruction (s), no
> surveillance opportunity at all. . 5
> Other (specify) _____ . 6
> D.K. . . . . . . . . . . . . . . 8
> INAP . . . . . . . . . . . . . . 9

---
*Side Surveillance: To the Right side - looking at the residence*

---

122a.*Does the R's residence have: (Code all that apply)*

|  | YES | NO | INAP |
|---|---|---|---|
| a. Right side door(s) . . . | 1 | 2 | 9 |
| b. Right side basement window(s). . . . . . . | 1 | 2 | 9 |
| c. Other right side window(s). . . . . . . | 1 | 2 | 9 |

---
*If none of above, Go to Q. 123a.*

---

b.*How far is the next residence?* _____ *Driveway widths* ___ ___

> No residence or attached residence
> (Go to Q. 123a.) . . . . . . . . . . . 00
>
> INAP . . . . . . . . . . . . . . . . 99

c.*Does dwelling next door (to the right) have surveillance points with respect to this dwelling? (i.e. bedroom, hall windows, etc.)*

> Yes. . . . . . . . . . . . . . . 1
> No . . . . . . . . . . . . . . . 2
> D.K. . . . . . . . . . . . . . . 8
> INAP . . . . . . . . . . . . . . 9

| (Code all that apply) | Slight Obstruction | Fairly large Obstruction | Total Obstruction | INAP |
|---|---|---|---|---|
| a. Wall . . . . . . . . . . . . . | 1 | 2 | 3 | 9 |
| b. Fence . . . . . . . . . . . | 1 | 2 | 3 | 9 |
| c. Hedge . . . . . . . . . . | 1 | 2 | 3 | 9 |
| d. Bushes, trees. . . . . . . . | 1 | 2 | 3 | 9 |
| e. Garage, or other building . . | 1 | 2 | 3 | 9 |
| f. Landscaping . . . . . . . . | 1 | 2 | 3 | 9 |
| g. Hidden recesses. . . . . . . | 1 | 2 | 3 | 9 |
| h. Other (specify) _____ . | 1 | 2 | 3 | 9 |

122d. *Describe surveillability:*

No residence next door (right side) . 1
Excellent . . . . . . . . . . . . . 2
Slight obstruction(s) . . . . . . . . 3
Fairly large obstruction(s) . . . . . 4
Total obstruction(s), no
surveillance opportunity at all . . . 5
Other (specify) _____ . . 6
D.K. . . . . . . . . . . . . . . . . 8
INAP . . . . . . . . . . . . . . . . 9

---
| Side Surveillance: To the left side -(looking at the residence) |
---

123a. *Does the R's residence have: (Code all that apply)*

|  | | YES | NO | INAP |
|---|---|---|---|---|
| a. | Left side door(s) . . . . | 1 . | . 2 . | . 9 |
| b. | Left side basement window(s) . . . . . . . . . | 1 . | . 2 . | . 9 |
| c. | Other left side window(s) | 1 . | . 2 . | . 9 |

---
| If none of above, go to Q. 124a. |
---

b. *How far is the next residence?*

_____ *Driveway widths* ___ ___

No residence or attached residence
(Go to Q. 124a.). . . . . . . . . . . 00

INAP . . . . . . . . . . . . . . . . 99

c. *Does dwelling next door (to the left) have surveillance points with respect to this dwelling? (i.e. bedroom, hall windows, etc.)*

Yes . . . . . . . . . . . . . . . . 1
No. . . . . . . . . . . . . . . . . 2
D.K. . . . . . . . . . . . . . . . . 8
INAP. . . . . . . . . . . . . . . . 9

| (Code all that apply) | Slight Obstruction | Fairly large Obstruction | Total Obstruction | INAP |
|---|---|---|---|---|
| a. Wall. . . . . . . . . . . . . | .1 . . . | . 2 . . . | . . . 3 | . . . .9 |
| b. Fence . . . . . . . . . . . . | .1 . . . | . 2 . . . | . . . 3 | . . . .9 |
| c. Hedge . . . . . . . . . . . . | .1 . . . | . 2 . . . | . . . 3 | . . . .9 |
| d. Bushes, trees . . . . . . . . | .1 . . . | . 2 . . . | . . . 3 | . . . .9 |
| e. Garage or other building. . | .1 . . . | . 2 . . . | . . . 3 | . . . .9 |
| f. Landscaping . . . . . . . . . | .1 . . . | . 2 . . . | . . . 3 | . . . .9 |
| g. Hidden recesses . . . . . . . | .1 . . . | . 2 . . . | . . . 3 | . . . .9 |
| h. Other (specify) _____ | .1 . . . | . 2 . . . | . . . 3 | . . . .9 |

23d. *Describe surveillability:*

| | |
|---|---|
| No residence next door (left side). . | 1 |
| Excellent . . . . . . . . . . . . . . | 2 |
| Slight obstruction(s) . . . . . . . . | 3 |
| Fairly large obstruction(s) . . . . . | 4 |
| Total obstruction(s), no | |
| surveillance opportunity at all . . . | 5 |
| Other (specify) _____ . . | 6 |
| D.K. . . . . . . . . . . . . . . . . | 8 |
| INAP. . . . . . . . . . . . . . . . . | 9 |

---

| *Back Surveillance:* |
|---|

24a. *Does the R's residence have: (Code all that apply)*

|  | | YES | NO | INAP |
|---|---|---|---|---|
| a. | Back door(s) . . . . . . . | 1 | 2 | 9 |
| b. | Back basement window(s) . | 1 | 2 | 9 |
| c. | Other back window(s). . . | 1 | 2 | 9 |

---

| *If none of above, go to Q. 125.* |
|---|

---

b. *How far is the next residence behind this dwelling?*

| _____ *Driveway widths* | ___ ___ |
|---|---|
| No residence (Go to Q. 125) . . . . . . | 00 |
| INAP. . . . . . . . . . . . . . . . . | 99 |

c. *Does the dwelling behind this residence have surveillance*
*points with respect to this dwelling? (i.e. bedroom, hall*
*windows, etc.)*

| | |
|---|---|
| Yes . . . . . . . . . . . . . . . . | 1 |
| No (Go to Q. 125) . . . . . . . . . | 2 |
| D.K. . . . . . . . . . . . . . . . . | 8 |
| INAP. . . . . . . . . . . . . . . . . | 9 |

| *(Code all that apply)* | *Slight Obstruction* | *Fairly large Obstruction* | *Total Obstruction* | *INAP* |
|---|---|---|---|---|
| a. *Wall* . . . . . . . . . . . | 1 | 2 | 3 | 9 |
| b. *Fence* . . . . . . . . . . | 1 | 2 | 3 | 9 |
| c. *Hedge* . . . . . . . . . . | 1 | 2 | 3 | 9 |
| d. *Bushes, trees* . . . . . . | 1 | 2 | 3 | 9 |
| e. *Garage or other building* . | 1 | 2 | 3 | 9 |
| f. *Landscaping* . . . . . . . | 1 | 2 | 3 | 9 |
| g. *Hidden recesses* . . . . . | 1 | 2 | 3 | 9 |
| h. *Other (specify)_____* | 1 | 2 | 3 | 9 |

124d. *Describe surveillability:*

No residence behind dwelling . . . . 1
Excellent . . . . . . . . . . . . . . 2
Slight obstruction(s) . . . . . . . . 3
Fairly large obstruction(s) . . . . . 4
Total obstruction(s), no
surveillance opportunity at all . . . 5
Other (specify) _____ . . 6
D.K. . . . . . . . . . . . . . . . . . 8
INAP. . . . . . . . . . . . . . . . . 9

125. *Are there any of the following behind this residence?*

|  | YES | NO | D.K. | INAP |
|---|---|---|---|---|
| . . . laneway or alley | 1 | 2 | 8 | 9 |
| . . . ravine | 1 | 2 | 8 | 9 |
| . . . park | 1 | 2 | 8 | 9 |
| . . . school | 1 | 2 | 8 | 9 |
| . . . factory or other industry. | 1 | 2 | 8 | 9 |

| Go to page 58, Q. 127a |

*If Apartment:*

126a. *On which floor is that apartment contained?*
*(If basement, record basement)* _____   ____ ____

INAP . . . 99

b. *How many floors in this building?* _____   ____ ____

INAP . . . 99

c. *How many dwelling units sharing a corridor:*

Under 5 . . . . . . . . . . . . . . . 1
6 - 10 . . . . . . . . . . . . . . . . 2
Over 10 . . . . . . . . . . . . . . . 3
D.K. . . . . . . . . . . . . . . . . . 8
INAP. . . . . . . . . . . . . . . . . 9

d. *Are there any stores, or offices, beauty parlors, tuck shops, etc.*
*in this building?*

Yes - Stores, or offices in the complex . 1
Yes - Stores used by residents only . . . 2
Yes - Other (specify) _____ . . . . 3
No . . . . . . . . . . . . . . . . . . . . 4
D.K. . . . . . . . . . . . . . . . . . . . 8
INAP. . . . . . . . . . . . . . . . . . . 9

126e. *Are the corridors in this building mainly . . .*

. . . *double-loaded (apartments on <u>both</u>
sides of a common corridor* . . . . . *1*
. . . *single-loaded (apartments on <u>one</u>
side only) and <u>with</u> windows on one
side* . . . . . . . . . . . . . . . . *2*
. . . *single-loaded (apartments on <u>one</u>
side only) and <u>without</u> windows on
one side* . . . . . . . . . . . . . *3*

*INAP* . . . . . . . . . . . . . . . *9*

f. *Is this apartment next to or opposite an elevator
or staircase?*

*Next to or opposite elevator only.* . *1*
*Next to or opposite staircase only* . *2*
*Next to or opposite both* . . . . . . *3*
*None of these.* . . . . . . . . . . *4*
*INAP* . . . . . . . . . . . . . . . *9*

g. *Is there a doorman?*

*Yes.* . . . . . . . . . . . . . . . *1*
*No* . . . . . . . . . . . . . . . . *2*
*D.K.* . . . . . . . . . . . . . . . *8*
*INAP* . . . . . . . . . . . . . . . *9*

h. *Is there a working intercom system?*

*Yes.* . . . . . . . . . . . . . . . *1*
*No* . . . . . . . . . . . . . . . . *2*
*D.K.* . . . . . . . . . . . . . . . *8*
*INAP* . . . . . . . . . . . . . . . *9*

i. *Is the corridor in which the apartment is located
used as a play area for children or for any other
reason other than to convey residents to and from
their dwelling?*

*Play area.* . . . . . . . . . . . . . *1*
*Loitering area for children and
adults* . . . . . . . . . . . . . . *2*
*Corridor used to dry shoes, boots.* . *3*
*Other (specify)* _____ . *4*
*No* . . . . . . . . . . . . . . . . *5*
*INAP* . . . . . . . . . . . . . . . *9*

j. *Are apartment doors leading to the corridors open (even slightly)
or closed? Are they. . .*

. . .*all closed* . . . . . . . . . . . . *1*
. . .*one or two open.* . . . . . . . . . *2*
. . .*several open* . . . . . . . . . . . *3*
. . .*about half and half.* . . . . . . . *4*
. . .*most open.* . . . . . . . . . . . . *5*
. . .*all open* . . . . . . . . . . . . . *6*
*INAP* . . . . . . . . . . . . . . . *9*

---

ASK EVERYONE:

---

127a. *Are any of the residences on this block . . .*
   *(Block is defined to include houses and structures on*
   *both sides of the street to the corner and including*
   *corner structures)*

|  | YES | NO | D.K. |
|---|---|---|---|
| 1. . . . detached or single houses | 1 | 2 | 8 |
| 2. . . . attached houses (to non-residential structures) | 1 | 2 | 8 |
| 3. . . . semi-detached or double houses | 1 | 2 | 8 |
| 4. . . . row houses | 1 | 2 | 8 |
| 5. . . . duplexes | 1 | 2 | 8 |
| 6. . . . apartments, triplexes, multi-dwellings | 1 | 2 | 8 |
| 7. . . . mobile homes | 1 | 2 | 8 |

b. *Rank the two major types of residences listed above.*
   *(Code 9 for INAP)*

   Mostly _____   _____

   Next _____   _____

c. *Are there any of the following on this block?*

|  | YES | NO | D.K. |
|---|---|---|---|
| Commercial structures (stores, shops, etc.) | 1 | 2 | 8 |
| Industrial structures (factories, plants, etc.) | 1 | 2 | 8 |
| Park(s) | 1 | 2 | 8 |
| School(s) | 1 | 2 | 8 |
| Church(es) | 1 | 2 | 8 |

d. *Is this residence on a . . .*

   . . . Major artery . . . . . . . . . . . . 1
   . . . Sidestreet . . . . . . . . . . . . . 2
   . . . Deadend street . . . . . . . . . . 3
   . . . Open country . . . . . . . . . . . 4
   Other . . . . . . . . . . . . . . 5

END   OF   INTERVIEW

THANK YOU VERY MUCH FOR YOUR CO-OPERATION !

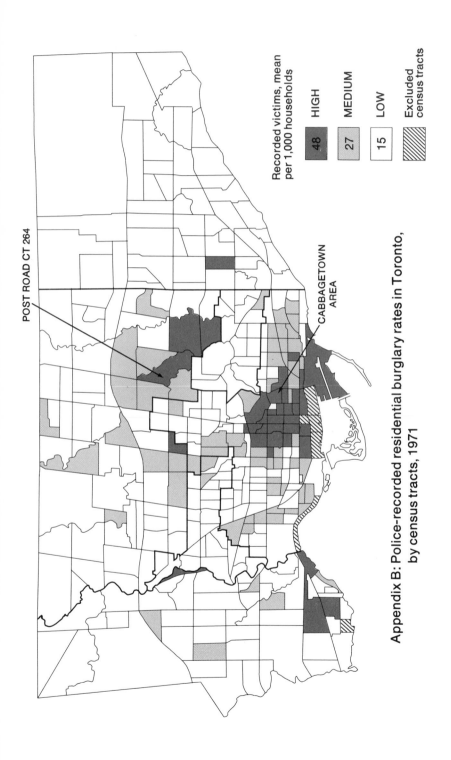

POST ROAD CT 264

CABBAGETOWN AREA

Recorded victims, mean per 1,000 households

HIGH 48

MEDIUM 27

LOW 15

Excluded census tracts

Appendix B: Police-recorded residential burglary rates in Toronto, by census tracts, 1971

# Bibliography

Akman, D., and A. Normandeau 1966 *A Manual for Constructing a Crime and Delinquency Index in Canada* (Montreal: Department of Criminology, University of Montreal)

Anttila, I. 1974 'Victimology – a new territory in criminology' *Scandinavian Studies in Criminology* 5:7-10

Ardrey, R. 1966 *The Territorial Imperative* (New York: Dell Publishing)

Argana, M. 1973 'The measurement of crime through victimization surveys: The Census Bureau experience,' paper prepared for presentation at the American Statistical Association Meeting, New York, December

Aromaa, K. 1973 'Victimization to violence: a gallup survey,' based on a paper distributed at the First International Symposium on Victimology, Jerusalem, September

– 1974a 'Our violence' *Scandinavian Studies in Criminology* 5:35-46

– 1974b *The Replication of a Survey on Victimization to Violence* (Helsinki: Institute of Criminology)

Ash, M. 1972 'On witnesses: a radical critique of criminal court procedures' *Notre Dame Lawyer* 48:386

Bailey, W. 1973 'Comments on the papers in seminar,' pp. 39-62 in *The Economics of Crime and Punishment* edited by S. Rotenberg (Washington, DC: American Enterprise Institute for Public Policy Research)

Beattie, R. 1960 'Criminal statistics in the United States – 1960' *Journal of Criminal Law, Criminology and Police Science* 51:49-65

– 1971 'Problems of criminal statistics in the United States' *Journal of Criminal Law, Criminology and Police Science* 46:178-86

Belson, W. 1968 *The Extent of Stealing by London Boys and Some of its Causes* (London: Survey Research Centre, London School of Economics)

Beran, N., and E. Allen 1973 'Criminal victimization in small town U.S.A.,' paper presented at the First International Symposium on Victimology, Jerusalem, September

Berg, D. 1972 *A Study of Citizens' Reaction to Crime in the District of Columbia and Adjacent Suburbs* (District of Columbia: Office of Criminal Justice Planning and Analysis)

Berton, P. 1972 *Klondike: The Last Great Gold Rush* (Toronto
  McClelland and Stewart)
Biderman, A. 1966 'Social indicators,' pp. 111-19 in *Social Indicators,*
  edited by R.A. Bauer (Cambridge, Mass.: The MIT Press)
−  and A. Reiss 1967 'On exploring the "dark figure" of crime' *The Annals
  of the American Academy of Political and Social Science* 374:1-15
−  1967a *Report on a Pilot Study in the District of Columbia on Victimization and Attitudes Toward Law Enforcement* (Washington, DC: Bureau of
  Social Science Research [US President's Commission on Law Enforcement
  and Administration of Justice, Field Surveys, no. 1])
−  1976b 'Surveys of population samples for estimating crime incidence'
  *The Annals of the American Academy of Political and Social Science*
  374:16-33
−  1972 *An Inventory of Surveys of the Public on Crime, Justice and
  Related Topics* (Washington, DC: US Department of Justice, National
  Institute of Law Enforcement and Criminal Justice)
Black, D. 1968 *Police Encounters and Social Organization: An Observation
  Study*, PH D Thesis, University of Michigan (Ann Arbor: University
  Microfilms)
−  1970 'Production of crime rates' *American Sociological Review* 35:733-48
Black, S. 1970 'A reporter at large, burglary-1,' pp. 329-57 in *Crime in
  America: Perspectives on Criminal and Delinquent Behaviour*, edited by
  B.J. Cohen (Itasca, Ill.: F.E. Peacock)
Blackburn, A., and T. Repetto 1973 'Residential burglary as an operation,'
  paper presented at the 44th National ORSA Meeting, San Diego, November
Block, M. 1972 'Theft: an econometric study,' paper presented at the
  Second Inter-American Congress of Criminology, Caracas, Venezuela,
  November
Block, R. 1971 'Fear of crime and fear of the police' *Social Problems*
  19:91-101
Boggs, S. 1967 'Urban crime patterns' *American Sociological Review*
  30:899-908
Brill, W. 1972 'Innovation in design and management of public housing: a
  case study of applied research,' pp. 17-1-1 − 17-1-8 in *Environmental
  Design: Research and Practice: Proceedings of the Environmental Design
  Research Conference,* edited by W. Mitchell (Los Angeles: University of
  California)
California Legislative Assembly, Interim Committee on Criminal Procedure
  1968 *Deterrent Effects of Criminal Sanctions* (Sacramento)
Canada, Bureau of Statistics *Crime Statistics, 1962-71* cat. 85-205 (Ottawa:
  Information Canada)
Canada, Canadian Committee on Corrections 1969 *Toward Unity: Criminal
  Justice and Corrections; Report* Chairman: Roger Ouimet (Ottawa:
  Queen's Printer)
Canada, Ministry of the Solicitor General 1973 *The Criminal in Canadian
  Society: A Perspective on Corrections* (Ottawa: Information Canada)
Canada, Statistics Canada *Census of Canada: 1971 Citizenship and Immigra-
  tion* Cat. 92-728 (Ottawa: Information Canada)

Cedar Rapids, Iowa, Police Department 1971 *Installation, Test and Evaluation of a Large-Scale Burglar Alarm System for a Municipal Police Department; Interim Report* (Washington, DC: National Institute of Law Enforcement and Criminal Justice)

Chappell, D. 1965 'The development and administration of the English criminal law relating to offences of breaking and entering, PH D Thesis, University of Cambridge

– 1972a *No Questions Asked: A Consideration of the Crime of Criminal Receiving* (Albany, NY: State University of New York)

– 1972b *Receiving Stolen Property: The Need for Systematic Inquiry into the Fencing Process* (Albany, NY: State University of New York)

Chimbos, P. 1973 'A study of breaking and entering offenses in Northern City, Ontario' *Canadian Journal of Criminology and Corrections* 15:316-25

Clinard, M. 1963 *Sociology of Deviant Behaviour* (New York: Holt, Rinehart and Winston)

Cloward, R.A., and L.E. Ohlin 1960 *Delinquency and Opportunity; A Theory of Delinquent Gangs* (Glencoe, Ill.: Free Press)

Cobb, W. 1973 'Theft and the two hypotheses,' pp. 19-20 in *The Economics of Crime and Punishment*, edited by S. Rotenberg (Washington, DC: American Institute for Public Policy Research)

Cohen, B. 1970 *Crime in America: Perspectives on Criminal and Delinquent Behaviour* (Itasca, Ill.: F.E. Peacock)

Conklin, J. 1971 'Criminal environment and support for the law' *Law and Society Review* 6:248-65

– 1971 'Dimensions of community response to crime problems' *Social Problems* 18:373-85

– and E. Smigel 1972 'Norms and attitudes toward business related crimes,' paper for Symposium on Studies of Public Experience, Knowledge and Opinion of Crime and Justice (Washington, DC: Bureau of Social Science Research)

– 1972 *Robbery and the Criminal Justice System* (Philadelphia: J.B. Lippincott)

– and E. Bittner 1973 'Burglary in a Suburb' *Criminology* 11:206-31

– 1975 *The Impact of Crime* (New York: Macmillan)

Courtis, M. 1970 *Attitudes to Crime and the Police in Toronto: A Report on Some Survey Findings* (Toronto: Centre of Criminology, University of Toronto)

Criminal Code 1974 *Martin's Annual Criminal Code* (Agincourt, Ontario: Canada Law Book)

Crosby, R., and D. Snyder 1969 *Crime Victimization in the Black Community: Results of the Black Buyer Survey* (Bethesda, Md.: Resource Management Corporation)

– 1970 *Crime Victimization in the Black Community: Results of the Black Buyer II Survey* (Bethesda, Md.: Resource Management Corporation)

Curtis, B. 1971 *Security Control: External Theft* (New York: Chain Store Age Books)

David, D., and P. Kleinman 1973 'Factors influencing protection against crime in a ghetto community,' paper presented at the meeting of the American Society of Criminology, New York, November

Davies, C. 1970 'Four hundred burglary suspects' *Abstracts on Criminology and Penology* 10:470

Davis, F. 1952 'Crime news in Colorado newspapers' *American Journal of Sociology* 57:325-30

Dodge, R., and A. Turner 1971 'Methodological foundations for establishing a national survey of victimization,' paper presented at the American Statistical Association Meetings, Fort Collins, Colorado

Doleschal, E. 1970 'Hidden crime' *Crime and Delinquency Literature* 2:546-72

Drapkin, I., and E. Viano 1974 *Victimology* (Lexington, Mass: Lexington Books)

Einstadter, W. 1972 'Contingencies and risk in criminalization: on becoming a systematic robber,' paper presented at the Second Inter-American Congress of Criminology, Caracas, Venezuela, November

Ennis, P. 1967 *Criminal Victimization in the United States: A Report of a National Survey* (Chicago: National Opinion Research Center, University of Chicago, Field Surveys, 2)

Evans, R. 1973 *Developing Policies for Public Security and Criminal Justice* (Ottawa: Economic Council of Canada, Special Study, no. 23)

Fairly, W., and M. Liechenstein 1971 *Improving Public Safety in Urban Apartment Dwellings: Security Concepts and Experimental Design for New York City Housing Authority Buildings* (New York: Rand Corporation)

Falk, G. 1952 'The influence of the seasons on the crime rate' *The Journal of Criminal Law, Criminology and Police Science* 43:199-213

Fattah, E. 1971 *La Vicime est-elle coupable?* (Montreal: les Presses de l'université de Montréal)

– 1972 'A study of the deterrent effect of capital punishment with special reference to the Canadian situation,' paper presented at the Second Inter-American Congress of Criminology, Caracas, Venezuela, November

– 1975 'The Canadian public and the death penalty: a study of a social attitude' (Ottawa: Ministry of the Solicitor General)

Feagin, J. 1970 'Home Defense and the Police (Black and White Perspectives)' *American Behavioural Scientist* 13:797-814

Ferdinand, T. 1969 'The criminal patterns of Boston since 1849' *The American Journal of Sociology* 73:84-99

Ferracuti, F. and M. Wolfgang 1962 'A study of police errors in crime classification' *Journal of Criminal Law, Criminology and Police Science* 53:113-19

Fooner, M. 1966 'Victim-induced criminality' *Science* 153:1080-3

– 1967 'Adventitious criminality: a crime pattern in an affluent society' *International Criminal Police Review* 22:246-50

– 1969 'Some economic factors in crime and delinquency' *New York Law Journal*, 7 March

– 1971a *8,000,000 Victims: A Study of Personal Cash Loss in the United States*, based on a survey conducted by Response Analysis Corporation, Princeton, New Jersey, for American Express Company (New York)

- 1971b 'Money and economic factors in crime and delinquency' *Criminology* 8:311-32
- 1972 'Crime prevention through environmental defenses,' paper presented at the Second Inter-American Congress of Criminology, Caracas, Venezuela, November

Furstenberg, F. 1971 'Public reaction to crime in the streets' *American Scholar* 40:601-10
- 1972 *Fear of Crime and Its Effects on Citizen Behaviour* (Washington, DC: Bureau of Social Science Research)

Gallup 1969 'Gallup Poll sees concern on crime: survey finds public favours "hard fines" by courts' *New York Times,* 16 February
- 1974 'Public Attitudes of Severity of Punishment' (Toronto: Canadian Institute of Public Opinion)

Garner, H. 1968 *Cabbagetown: a Novel* (Toronto: Ryerson)

Gibbons, D. 1968 *Society, Crime and Criminal Careers* (Englewood Cliffs, NJ: Prentice-Hall)
- 1969 'Crime and punishment: a study in social attitudes' *Social Forces* 47:391-7

Gilbert, G. 1958 'Crime and punishment' *Mental Hygiene* 42:550-7

Girard, P. 1960 'Burglary trends and protection' *Journal of Criminal Law, Criminology and Police Science* 50:511-18

Goodman, L. 1968 *A Study of the Deterrent Value of Crime Prevention Measures as Perceived by Criminal Offenders* (Washington, DC: Bureau of Social Science Research)

Greenhalgh, W. 1964 *A Town's Rate of Serious Crime Against Property and Its Association with some Broad Social Factors* (London: Home Office, Scientific Advisor's Branch)

Grupp, S. 1971 *Theories of Punishment* (Bloomington: Indiana University Press)

Gunning, J. 1973 'How profitable is burglary?' pp. 35-8 in *The Economics of Crime and Punishment,* edited by S. Rotenberg (Washington, DC: American Enterprise Institute for Public Policy Research)

Hall, J. 1952 *Theft, Law and Society* (Indianapolis: Bobbs-Merrill)

Hann, R.G.W. 1973 *Decision-Making in the Canadian Criminal Court System: A Systems Analysis* (Toronto: Centre of Criminology, University of Toronto)

Harries, K.D. 1973 *The Geography of Crime and Justice* (New York: McGraw-Hill)

Harris, Louis and Associates 1968 *The Public Looks at Crime and Corrections: Report of a Survey* (Washington, DC: Joint Commission on Correctional Manpower and Training)

Hauge, R., and P. Wolf 'Criminal violence in three Scandinavian countries' *Scandinavian Studies in Criminology* 5:25-33

Hawkins, R.O. 1970 *Determinants of Sanctioning Initiations for Criminal Victimization,* PH D Thesis, University of Washington (Ann Arbor: University Microfilms 1972)
- 1973 'Who called the cops? decisions to report criminal victimization' *Law and Society Review* 7:527-44

-  and P.E. Smith 1973 'Victimization: types of citizen-police contracts and
   attitudes towards the police' *Law and Society Review* 8:135-52
Healy, R. 1968 *Design for Security* (New York: John Wiley and Sons)
Heinzeleman, F. 1974 *Community Crime Prevention* (Washington, DC:
   National Institute of Law Enforcement and Criminal Justice)
Henley, A. 1971 'Muggers of the mind' *Todays Health* 49:39-41
Hentig, Hans von 1947 *Crime: Causes and Conditions* (New York and
   London: McGraw-Hill)
High Impact Anti-Crime Program 1972 *The Cleveland High Impact Anti-
   Crime Program Plan* (Cleveland, Ohio: The Mayor's Office)
-  1972 *The Denver High Impact Anti-Crime Program: 1972 Crime Reduc-
   tion Evaluation Plan* (Denver, Co.)
-  1972 *The High Impact Anti-Crime Program* (Washington, DC: National
   Institute of Law Enforcement and Criminal Justice)
-  1972 *High Impact Anti-Crime Program Evaluation* (Washington, DC:
   National Institute of Law Enforcement and Criminal Justice)
-  1972 *Robbery and Burglary: A Study* (Portland, Oregon: Urban Studies
   Center, Portland State University)
-  1972 *The St. Louis High Impact Anti-Crime Program Plan* (St. Louis, Mo.:
   Commission on Crime and Law Enforcement)
Hindelang, M. 1974a 'Decisions of shoplifting victims to invoke the criminal
   justice process' *Social Problems* 21:580-
-  1974b 'Preliminary report of the impact cities victim survey results'
   (Albany, NY: School of Criminal Justice, State University of New York)
Hirschi, T. 1969 *Causes of Delinquency* (Berkeley: University of California
   Press)
Hogarth, J. 1971 *Sentencing as a Human Process* (Toronto: University of
   Toronto Press)
Hood, R. and R. Sparks 1970 *Key Issues in Criminology* (Toronto:
   McGraw-Hill)
Hunter, G. 1967 *How to Defend Yourself, Your Family and Your Home*
   (New York: David McKay)
Insurance Bureau of Canada 1972 *Home Insurance Explained* (Toronto)
-  1972 'Facts of the General Insurance Industry in Canada,' 1st Annual
   Edition (Toronto)
Irwin, J. 1970 *The Felon* (Englewood Cliffs, NJ: Prentice-Hall)
Jacobs, J. 1961 *Death and Life of a Great American City* (New York:
   Random House)
Jeffery, C. 1971 *Crime Prevention Through Environmental Design* (London:
   Russell-Sage Publications)
-  1972 'Environmental design and the prevention of behavioural disorders
   and criminality,' paper prepared for the Second Inter-American Congress
   of Criminology, Caracas, Venezuela, November
Kelling, G.L. 1974 *The Kansas City Preventive Patrol Experiment: A
   Summary Report* (Washington, DC: Police Foundation)
Klein, J. 1974 'Professional theft: the utility of a concept' *Canadian Journal
   of Criminology and Corrections* 16:133-44

Kleinman, P., and D. David 1973 'Victimization and perception of crime in a ghetto community' *Criminology* 11:307-43

Klockars, C. 1972 'The fence: caveat emptor, caveat vendor,' paper presented at the Second Inter-American Congress of Criminology, Caracas, Venezuela, November

Klotter, J.C. 1968 *Burglary Prevention, Investigation and Prosecution* (Louisville, Ky.: The Southern Police Institute, University of Louisville)

Knudten, M.S., R.D. Knudten, and A.C. Meade 1974 'Crime victims and witnesses as victims of the administration of justice,' paper presented at the American Society of Criminology Meetings, Chicago, November

Kobrin, S. 1972 *Deterrent Effectiveness of Criminal Justice Sanction Strategies: Summary Report* (Washington, DC: US Government Printing Office)

Kolodney, S. 1970 *A Study of the Characteristics and Recidivism Experience of California Prisoners. Volume 1 – Summary Report* (San Jose, California: Public Systems Incorporated)

Krohm, G. 1973 'The pecuniary incentives of property crime,' pp. 31-4 in *The Economics of Crime and Punishment*, edited by S. Rotenberg (Washington, DC: American Enterprise Institute for Public Policy Research)

Kutchinsky, B. 1968 'Knowledge and attitudes regarding legal phenomena in Denmark' *Scandinavian Studies in Criminology* 2:125-59

Lauzon, D. 1971 'Burglary in Montreal,' M SC Thesis, University of Montreal

Law Reform Commission of Canada 1974 *The Principles of Sentencing and Dispositions* (Ottawa: Information Canada)

– 1976 *Studies on Imprisonment* (Ottawa: Information Canada)

Lentz, W. 1966 'Punishment vs. rehabilitation: social status and attitudes toward social control *Journal of Research in Crime and Delinquency* 3:147-54

Letkemann, P. 1971 'Modus Operandi – Crime as Work,' PH D Thesis, University of British Columbia

– 1973 *Crime as Work* (Englewood Cliffs, NJ: Prentice-Hall)

Lipset, S. 1971 'Why cops hate liberals – and vice versa,' pp. 23-39 in *The Police Rebellion: A Quest for Blue Power*, edited by W. Bopp (Springfield, Ill.: Charles C. Thomas)

Lorenz, K. 1966 *On Aggression* (London: Methuen)

Luedtke, G. 1970 *Crime and the Physical City* (Detroit, Mich.: National Institute of Law Enforcement and Criminal Justice)

Maltz, M. 1972 *Evaluation of Crime Control Programs* (Washington, DC: National Institute of Law Enforcement and Criminal Justice)

Martinson, R. 1974 'What works? – questions and answers about prison reform' *Public Interest* 35:22-54

Mayhew, P., et al. 1976 *Crime as Opportunity*, Home Office Research Report, no. 34 (London: H.M. Stationery Office)

McClintock, F.H., et al. 1968 *Crime in England and Wales* (London, Eng.: Heinemann Educational Books)

Metropolitan Toronto Police Dept. *Annual Statistical Report* 1971-73 (Toronto)

Mitchell, W. 1972 *Environmental Design Research Conference* (Los Angeles: University of California at Los Angeles)

Mohr, J.W. 1965 'Towards phenomenological models of criminal transactions: actus reus reconsidered,' paper presented at the 5th International Criminological Congress, Montreal, August

Morris, D. 1969 *The Human Zoo* (London: Cape)

Mulvihill, D.J. 1970 *Crimes of Violence*, a staff report submitted to the National Commission on the Causes and Prevention of Violence (Washington, DC: US Government Printing Office)

Nader, L. 1971 *Protecting Your Business Against Employee Thefts, Shoplifters and Other Hazards* (New York: Pilot Industries Inc.)

National Crime Panel 1974a *Crime in Eight American Cities: Advance Report* (Washington, DC: National Criminal Justice Information and Statistics Service)

- 1974b *Crime in the Nation's Five Largest Cities: Advance Report* (Washington, DC: National Criminal Justice Information and Statistics Service)

National Institute of Law Enforcement and Criminal Justice 1973a *Urban Design, Security and Crime*, proceedings of a seminar (Washington, DC)

- 1973b *Residential Security* (Washington, DC)

Newman D.J. 1957 'Public attitudes toward a form of white collar crime' *Social Problems* 4:228-32

Newman, O. 1972 *Defensible Space* (New York: Macmillan)

- 1973a *Architectural Design for Crime Prevention* (Washington, DC: National Institute of Law Enforcement and Criminal Justice)

- 1973b *Deterrence of Crime in and Around Residences* (Washington, DC: National Institute of Law Enforcement and Criminal Justice)

- 1975 *Design Guidelines for Creating Defensible Space* (Washington, DC: National Institute of Law Enforcement and Criminal Justice)

'NYC wants to help black groups fight crime.' 1973 *Criminal Justice Newsletter* 4:27, 30

Nye, F.I., and J.F. Short 1957 'Scaling delinquent behaviour' *American Sociological Review* 22:326-32

Ohlin, L. 1968 'The effect of social change on crime and law enforcement' *Notre Dame Lawyer* 43:834-46

Oliver, E. 1969 *A Future for Correctional Rehabilitation* (Olympia, Wash.: Division of Vocational Rehabilitation)

Parkinson, J. 1973 'Who is responsible for stopping crime?' *Police Chief* 40(4):18

Pennsylvania Board of Parole 1965 *Characteristics of Persons Arrested for Burglary* (Harrisburg, Pa.)

Pennsylvania University Center of Criminological Research 1963 *Constructing an Index of Delinquency* (Philadelphia)

Post, R. 1972 *Combating Crime Against Small Business* (Springfield, Ill.: Charles C. Thomas)

Quinney, R. 1970 *The Social Reality of Crime* (Boston: Little and Brown)

Radzinowicz, L., and M.E. Wolfgang 1971 *Crime and Justice* (New York: Basic Books)

Ravetz, A. 1973 'What is vandalism?' *Royal Institute of British Architects Journal* 80:620-8

Reiss, A. and D. Black 1967a 'Career orientations, job satisfaction, and the assessment of law enforcement problems by police officers,' in *Studies in Crime and Law Enforcement in Major Metropolitan Areas* V.2 (Washington, DC: US Government Printing Office)

– 1967b 'Patterns of behaviour in police and citizen transactions,' in *Studies in Crime and Law Enforcement in Major Metropolitan Areas* V.2 (Washington, DC: US Government Printing Office)

Reppetto, T. 1972 'Age, race and drug use as determinants in criminal behaviour among burglary offenders,' paper delivered at the Second Inter-American Congress of Criminology, Caracas, Venezuela, November

– 1974 *Residential Crime* (Cambridge, Mass.: Ballinger)

– 1976 'Crime prevention and the displacement phenomenon' *Crime and Delinquency* 22:166-77

Rettig, S., and B. Pasamanick 1959 'Changes in moral values over three decades, 1929-1958,' *Social Problems* 6:320-8

Reynolds, P. 1973 *Victimization in a Metropolitan Region: Comparison of a Central City Area and a Suburban Community* (Minneapolis: Department of Sociology, University of Minnesota)

Richardson, R. 1972 *Perspectives on the Legal Justice System: Public Attitudes and Criminal Victimization* (Chapel Hill, NC: Institute for Research in Social Science, University of North Carolina)

Roberts, C. 1974 'Responses to victimization,' paper, University of Kentucky

Robison, J., and G. Smith 1971 'The effectiveness of correctional programs,' *Crime and Delinquency* 17:67-80

Rose, A. 1955 'Does the punishment fit the crime?: a study of social valuation' *The American Journal of Sociology* 61:247-59

Rosenberg, M. 1968 *The Logic of Survey Analysis* (New York: Basic Books)

Rosenthal, J. 1969 'The cage of fear in cities beset by crime' *Life Magazine* 11 July: 18-21

Sagalyn, A. 1971 *The Crime of Robbery in the United States* (Washington DC: US Government Printing Office

*San José Methods Test of Known Crime Victims* 1972 (Washington, DC: National Institute of Law Enforcement and Criminal Justice, Statistics Division, Statistics Technical Report, no. 1)

Scarr, H. 1972a 'On cyclical behaviour – especially cyclical criminal behaviour,' paper presented at the Second Inter-American Congress of Criminology, Caracas, Venezuela, November

– 1972b *Patterns of Burglary* (Washington, DC: National Institute of Law Enforcement and Criminal Justice)

– 1973 *Patterns of Burglary*, 2nd ed. (Washington, DC: National Institute of Law Enforcement and Criminal Justice)

Schmidt, C. 1960a 'Urban crime areas: part I' *American Sociological Review* 25:527-42

– 1960b 'Urban crime areas: part II *American Sociological Review* 25:655-78

Schwartz, R. 1970 'On legal sanctions,' pp. 533-47 in *Society and the Legal Order*, edited by R. Schwartz and J. Skolnick (New York: Basic Books)

Sellin, T., and M. Wolfgang 1964 *The Measurement of Delinquency* (New York: John Wiley)

Shearing, C.D. 1973 'Dial-a-cop: a study of police mobilization,' (Centre of Criminology, University of Toronto)

Short, J. 1965 *Group Process and Gang Delinquency* (Chicago: The University of Chicago Press)

Shover, N. 1971 *Burglary as an Occupation*, PH D Thesis, University of Illinois (Ann Arbor, Mich.: University Microfilms, 1975)

– 1972 'Structures and careers in burglary' *Journal of Criminal Law, Criminology and Police Science* 63:540-9

– 1973 'The social organization of burglary' *Social Problems* 20:499-514

Silverman, R. 1973 'Victim precipitation: an examination of the concept, presented to the First International Symposium on Victimology, Jerusalem, September

Sjoquist, D. 1970 *Property Crime as an Economic Phenomenon*. Washington, DC: National Institute of Law Enforcement and Criminal Justice

Skogan, W.G. 1975 'Measurement problems in official and survey crime rates' *Journal of Criminal Justice* 3:17-32

Skolnick, J. 1966 *Justice Without Trial: Law Enforcement in Democratic Society* (New York: John Wiley)

Smigel, E. 1956 'Public attitudes toward stealing as related to the size of the victim organization' *American Sociological Review* 21:320-7

– 1970 *Crimes Against Bureaucracy* (New York: Van Nostrand Reinhold Company)

Smith, J.C. 1968 'Burglary under the theft bill' *Criminal Law Review* 297-309, 367-74

Sommer, R. 1969 *Personal Space: The Behavioral Basis of Design* (Englewood Cliffs, NJ: Prentice-Hall)

Sparks, R. 1972 'The perception of violence' *Medicine, Science and the Law* 12:244-8

Sparks, R.F. H. Genn, and D. Dodd. 1977 *Surveying Victims* (London: Wiley)

Spelt, J. 1973 *Toronto* (Toronto: Collier-Macmillan)

Stanciu, V. 1968 *Criminalité à Paris* (Paris: Centre Nationale de Recherche Statistique)

Stinchombe, A. 1963 'Institutions of privacy in the determination of police administrative practice' *The American Journal of Sociology* 69:150-60

Susini, J. 1957 'Vols dans les demeures historiques ou cambriolages des chateaux' *Revue de Science Criminelle et de Droit Penal Comparé* 12:210-13

Sutherland, E., and D. Cressey 1970 *Criminology*, 8th ed. (New York: J.B. Lippincott Company)

Sutherland, E. 1937 *The Professional Thief* (Chicago: The University of Chicago Press)

Thornberry, T., and R. Figlio 1972 'Victimization and criminal behaviour in a birth cohort,' paper presented at the Second Inter-American Congress of Criminology, Caracas, Venezuela, November

Toronto, Canada. 1970 *Toronto Star* 1 January
- 1972 *Toronto Star* 22 January
Turner, A. 1972 *Victimization Surveying – Its History, Uses and Limitations,* prepared for the National Advisory Commission on Criminal Justice Standards and Goals (Washington, DC: National Criminal Justice Information and Statistics Service)
- 1973 *Classification and Counting Rules Employed for Personal Crimes* (Washington, DC: National Criminal Justice Information and Statistics Service)
Unkovic, C. 1970 'Cops and robbers look at thievery' *American Journal of Corrections* 32(1):6-13
USA Congress, Senate, Committee on Small Business 1969 *Crimes Against Small Business: A Report* (Washington, DC: US Government Printing Office)
- 1972 *An Analysis of Criminal Redistribution Systems and their Economic Impact on Small Business; Staff Report.* (Washington, DC: US Government Printing Office)
USA Federal Bureau of Investigation. 1966 'Burglary – its drain on the public' *F.B.I. Law Enforcement Bulletin* 35(1):16-21
- 1971 *Uniform Crime Reports for the United States.* (Washington, DC: US Government Printing Office)
USA President's Commission on Crime in the District of Columbia. 1966 *Report* (Washington, DC: US Government Printing Office)
USA President's Commission on Law Enforcement and Administration of Justice. 1967a *The Challenge of Crime in a Free Society* (Washington, DC: US Government Printing Office)
- 1967b *Crime and Its Impact: Task Force Report* (Washington, DC: US Government Printing Office)
- 1967c *Narcotics and Drug Abuse: Task Force Report* (Washington, DC: US Government Printing Office)
- 1967d *The Police: Task Force Report* (Washington, DC: US Government Printing Office)
- 1967e *Science and Technology: Task Force Report.* (Washington, DC: US Government Printing Office)
Vidmar, N. 1974 'Retributive and utilitarian motives and other correlates of Canadian attitudes toward the death penalty' *The Canadian Psychologist* 15(4):337-56
Waller, J.I. 1974 *Men Released from Prison* (Toronto: University of Toronto Press)
Wallerstein, J.S., and C.J. Wyle 1954 'Our law abiding law-breakers' *Probation* 25:107-12
Walsh, W. 1973 'Good locks, the first line of burglary defence' *Canadian Consumer* 3(4):20-2
Weis, K., and E. Milakovich 1974 'Political misuses of crime rates' *Society* 11:27-33
Weldon, J. 1967 'High-rise policing techniques,' pp. 755-61 in *Law Enforcement Science and Technology.* V.I., edited by S.A. Yefsky (Chicago: I.D.T. Research Institute)

Wels, B. 1971 *Fire and Theft Security Systems*, 1st ed. (Blue Ridge Summit, Pa.: G/L Tab Books)

West, D. 1969 *Present Conduct and Future Delinquency* (London: Heinemann Educational Books)

West, W.G. 1974 *Serious Thieves*, PH D Thesis, Northwestern University

Wilks, J.A. 1967 'Ecological correlates of crime and delinquency,' pp. 138-56 in *Task Force Report: Crime and Its Impact − An Assessment*, Appendix A, US President's Commission on Law Enforcement and Administration of Justice (Washington, DC: US Government Printing Office)

Willcock, H.D. and J. Stokes 1963 *Deterrents and Incentives to Crime Among Youths Aged 15 to 21*, Part II, Government Social Survey no. 352 (London: H.M. Stationery Office)

Wolfgang, M. 1958 *Patterns in Criminal Homicide* (Philadelphia: University of Pennsylvania Press)

−  1962 *Sociology of Crime and Delinquency* (New York: John Wiley and Sons)

−  1972 *Delinquency in a Birth Cohort* (Chicago: University of Chicago Press)

Wood, E. 1967 *Social Aspects of Housing and Urban Development* (New York: United Nations)

Wormeli, P. 1972 'The crime-specific model: a new criminal justice perspective' *Journal of Research in Crime and Delinquency* 9:54-65

Yancey, W. 1972 'Architecture, interaction and social control: the case of a large scale housing project,' pp. 126-36 *Environment and the Social Sciences: Perspectives and Applications*, edited by J.F. Wohlwill and D.H. Carson (Washington, DC: American Psychological Association)

Zimring, F., and G. Hawkins 1973 *Deterrence: The Legal Threat in Crime Control* (Chicago: University of Chicago Press)

# Index